ANGELS
AT THE CROSSROADS

ANGELS

AT THE CROSSROADS

Jerry Shepherd's Story of Redemption and Love

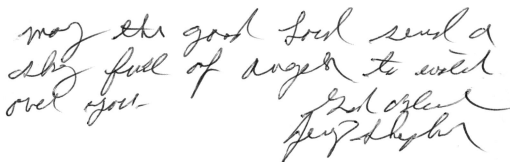

May the good Lord send a sky full of angels to watch over you.

God Bless
Jerry Shepherd

ANN H. GABHART

May angels guard your pathways!

Ann H. Gabhart

Psalm 91: 11-12

iUniverse, Inc.

New York   Lincoln   Shanghai

Angels at the Crossroads
Jerry Shepherd's story of redemption and love

iUniverse books may be ordered through booksellers or by contacting:

iUniverse
2021 Pine Lake Road, Suite 100
Lincoln, NE 68512
www.iuniverse.com
1-800-Authors (1-800-288-4677)

ISBN-13: 978-0-595-38707-6 (pbk)
ISBN-13: 978-0-595-83089-3 (ebk)
ISBN-10: 0-595-38707-1 (pbk)
ISBN-10: 0-595-83089-7 (ebk)

Printed in the United States of America

To Connie, Shayne, Christy and Tab who taught me how to love and be loved.
—Jerry Shepherd

To my husband, Darrell, and all his fellow gospel singers who stay on the road uplifting the name of Christ and spreading the gospel through song.
—Ann H. Gabhart

A PERSONAL NOTE FROM JERRY SHEPHERD

For many years while telling my life story after I was released from prison, people would come up to me and tell me that I needed to have my story put into a book. I thought about it every now and then over the years, but then I would back off when I saw everything involved in getting a book together and getting it published. Well, it was too much for this old county farm boy to deal with, so things would cool off real fast and the thought of a book, let's just say, would be put on the back burner. I would give God another one of my excuses and leave it at that.

After I had been singing with the Patriot Quartet for four years, I came to another one of those crossroads that always seem to pop up in my life. With many hours and many miles on my body starting to take a toll on my health, I had to make a decision about continuing with the quartet or going into solo ministry to once again tell my story. Then along came Ann who is married to Darrell Gabhart, the bass singer in the Patriot Quartet. Ann is a writer and she had heard me tell parts of my story. She took an interest. We got together and all of a sudden the *big* word, *book* popped up.

God never ceases to amaze me. God always has a plan. God always brings the plan together in His own time. Thanks, Ann, for letting God inspire you to pick up pen and paper and write about my life. I pray this book will touch and bless someone at a crossroad in his or her life.

CHAPTER 1

The chase was over. Jerry's car was almost out of gas. He'd outrun them when they had first pulled in behind him with their lights flashing as he headed home down U.S. 60. He'd floored the gas pedal, speeding well over a hundred, dodging other cars that spun off the road away from him and the police cars chasing him, and he'd lost them. He might even have gotten away, found a place to fill up and gone on to Louisville and who knew where after that. Maybe California. He'd run there once. He could do it again. But he'd wanted to see his mom and dad one last time before he ran again or the police caught him.

With an eye on his rear-view mirror, he'd cut through the country roads to get back to his farm. He knew the roads. He could have made it if only his gas needle hadn't been sitting on empty. A car's wheels stopped rolling without gas.

He had one last chance. He turned down a gravel lane he remembered from his school days where couples parked to make out. It was daytime. Nobody was there. He pulled down among the trees and hoped they'd give up the chase. He didn't pray. He didn't figure there was any use of that since he'd long since gone beyond the mercy of prayer. He just hunkered down behind the wheel and tried to be invisible.

But they found him. The car that pulled up behind him didn't have bubble lights on top, but its long antennas whipped in the wind. Without a doubt, police. They'd tracked him down and now it was time to pay for what he'd done.

Jerry kept his eyes on the car in his rearview mirror. They had been bound to catch him sooner or later, but he couldn't keep from wishing it had been later. He wanted, no needed to tell his parents goodbye, to see them one more time while he was still free. He'd been on the run for weeks. It was April 1969. Jerry was nineteen.

He'd thought about turning himself in. He'd done the crime. He was ready to pay for it, but he hadn't been able to decide how to do it. Even now he wasn't sure what to do as he pulled the mirrors down so he could better see the men climbing out of the police car. One of them walked slowly toward Jerry's car. At least his car now. Never really his car.

Jerry didn't have a gun, but he could make them think he did. Or he could just jump out of the car and take off running across the fields. They'd shoot. They'd shout at him to stop and then when he didn't, they'd shoot. He stared into the mirror at the man approaching his car and tried to decide if he looked like a man who could shoot. If Jerry ran, he'd want the man to be a good shot.

As his fingers touched the door handle to pull it up, he shifted in his seat and felt the Bible in his back pants pocket. Instead of opening the door, he reached around to take hold of the small serviceman's Bible the Gideons had given him what seemed like a lifetime ago while he was in basic training. He'd kept it with him through everything. He wasn't sure why. Courage maybe. Strength. Comfort. Definitely comfort. Now he knew he didn't want anybody else to get hurt because of him. Not even his parents, but it was way too late to be wishing that.

He didn't take the Bible out of his pocket, just curled his fingers around it. He watched the man in the suit and tie moving closer. The other man stayed at the car. He could feel the men's eyes watching for him to make some kind of move. Jerry's feet felt itchy and thoughts were exploding in his brain like a string of firecrackers all lit at once.

Then a calm voice bubbled up in his mind overpowering all the other thoughts. *Peace be still. Peace be still.* He gripped the Bible tighter and waited, hardly daring to breath.

The officer leaned down to Jerry's open window and asked, "Are you Jerry Shepherd?" The man looked older than his father and had gray hair and wary eyes.

"Yes, I am." It felt strangely good to admit that was his name after using another man's name these past weeks. A man who was dead because of Jerry.

The officer's eyes swept over him and the front seat of the car. "Are you carrying any weapons of any kind?"

"No, sir," Jerry said.

"Let me see your hands and step out of the car, please." The officer kept his hand near his coat. Jerry could almost smell the gun that was surely strapped to the policeman's chest. The other officer cautiously moved closer to them. His hand was already inside his coat.

Jerry turned loose of his Bible, held up his hands, and got out of the car. The top of the car was warm when he laid his hands there while the man searched him. The other man read him his rights and told him they were arresting him for attempting to elude a police officer, for grand larceny, and for murder in the first degree. Jerry didn't argue. He just did as they said and put his hands behind his back. The handcuffs they clasped around his wrists were cold.

They opened the back door of the police car and pushed his head down to be sure he didn't bump it as they put him in the car. Jerry wasn't very big. Five foot ten, but every inch muscle. He'd won all the performance prizes in basic training last fall. Running and pushups were easy. It was living he was having trouble with.

He shifted to get more comfortable with his hands pinned behind his back. He could still touch the Bible in his back pocket. The peace stayed with him, but at the same time he couldn't imagine what his mother would say. And how in the world would he be able to bear his father seeing him in handcuffs? He wanted to disappear, just vanish into thin air before he had to see his parents again.

It wasn't the first time he'd felt that way. He'd even managed to make it happen a few times. The disappearing. And there had been plenty of times he'd thought his mother would be happy if he did disappear forever. Ugly memories of times he'd failed to be the son she'd wanted poked at him from all sides. He shut his eyes and tried to make his mind go blank, but one of the long ago memories slithered out into the open where he couldn't keep from thinking about it.

"Gerald Warren Shepherd, you're worthless. You can't do anything right. You can't even get up to go to the toilet." His mother had shouted at him as she yanked back the covers on his bed. The smell of urine was strong. "Six years old and still needing diapers."

"I'm sorry, Mama. I won't do it again," Jerry had whimpered. He'd have given every toy he'd ever had to stop wetting the bed, but no matter how hard he'd tried not to, it just happened. And he had felt worthless. And bad. But mostly he had felt lost.

Everything at the new farm they'd just moved to was so different. He'd missed the tree he could climb at the old house. He'd missed Ginger, his cat they'd left at the old barn. His father had said Ginger would be happier there. Jerry had wanted to be at the old farm with Ginger. He'd been happier there, too. Every time he got used to a place, every time he got used to people, somebody kept coming along and changing everything. He didn't have a place to belong. People were always disappearing out of his life.

"I'm sorry." He'd despised the whine in his voice as he'd begged for his mother's forgiveness. It never did any good anyway. He couldn't even do that right.

She'd slapped a diaper against his chest. "Here, put this on. If you're going to act like a baby, you'll have to dress like a baby."

He'd blinked hard to keep from crying as he'd taken off his wet pajama bottoms, put the folded diaper between his legs, and let her pin it on him. He'd wanted to crawl under his bed and just hide there in the dark corners. He hadn't wanted anybody to see him in the diaper, especially not his father. Jerry had tried to remember if his father was at home that day or out driving his Greyhound bus route. He was probably gone. He was nearly always gone. Jerry had wished he was on the bus with him, sitting in the first seat right behind him, staring at his ramrod straight back and riding his route with him. He hadn't wanted to hear what his mother would say five hundred times all day. "Look at the big baby."

Now sitting in the back of the police car, Jerry shook his head to rid himself of the memory. But dozens more were there ready to pop up in its place. He'd never been able to do anything to suit his mother. Not when he was six. Not when he was sixteen. Not even when he was singing songs in church and leading the music at revivals. Certainly not now, arrested and on his way to jail. That would have to be the ultimate shame for her.

Maybe she would wash her hands of him and be done with him. It was obvious now that he would never be her perfect child, and she might have to admit to her sisters that she wasn't the perfect parent. Nobody in his family, nobody he knew, had ever gotten so messed up that they'd been arrested. And nobody had ever tried to just disappear forever.

But Jerry had. When he was seventeen. The year he was a senior in high school.

CHAPTER 2

Everybody was always saying your senior year in high school should be the best year of your life. It was a given. Finally you got to reap the rewards of all those long years of homework and teachers and tests and studying. Senior year. Homecoming games and dances. Proms. Graduation. That's what Jerry was looking forward to in 1967 as he finished up his junior year at Oldham County High School. A whole year of fun with long time friends before they had to step out into the real world of decisions about college or jobs, before the boys had to face the prospect of being drafted and shipped out to shoot or be shot at by some faceless enemy in the jungles of Vietnam.

And then his parents dropped the bombshell on him. They just up and told him one day that they'd be moving that summer. His father had sold their farm in Oldham County as if it didn't make the least bit of difference where they lived. His father said it wasn't like they were leaving the country of anything. They were just moving over the county line to a farm in Shelby County.

For a few foolish moments, Jerry had hope. He could drive back to Oldham County High to go to school and be with his friends. August would be the start of a new semester. He'd get the A's and B's his mother was always after him to get, so he wouldn't be grounded the way he'd been most of his junior year because of bad grades. He told his father that. "I'll keep up with my homework and get the grades. All A's. Even in math. Just let me go back to Oldham County High. You said yourself it isn't that far."

His father frowned. "I might need my truck, son."

"I can work hard this summer and buy my own car or I could even ride my bike. I can ride that far if I have to," Jerry pleaded. "Remember how in the seventh grade I used to bike to baseball practice. That was fourteen miles round trip. It wasn't so hard. No problem at all."

"You can't be riding a bicycle that far on those roads. It wouldn't be safe." His mother spoke up and Jerry's hopes withered inside him. "And the weather. Try to think straight for once in your life, Jerry. You couldn't be riding that old bicycle in the rain and cold."

"You could take me when the weather was bad." Jerry knew it was hopeless even before he said it. She'd never been willing to drive him to anything, not even to Louisville to be part of the Lawrence Welk show the year before. He could have been on television, but his parents had said the only place he needed to be was helping them on the farm or singing at the church. Still he had to ask. He didn't want to go to school in Shelby County. He wanted to go to school with his friends. When his mother's eyes flashed at him, he cringed and waited for the verbal bashing.

"You never think about anybody but yourself, Gerald Warren Shepherd. It's always what you want. You're the most selfish child I've ever had the misfortune to be around, never grateful for anything your father and I have done for you, the sacrifices we've made for you. You should get down and kiss your daddy's feet for the way he's provided for us and always kept a roof over our heads."

Jerry switched off his ears. He heard her talking, but he wouldn't let the words come into his head. Enough of her hurtful words were already floating around in there poking him at unexpected times, making him want to run off to the woods with a tube of glue or a can of gasoline to sniff so he could get a buzz and escape the sound of her voice at least for a few minutes.

He started listening again when he heard his father's voice. "Shelby County High is just as good a school as Oldham County. You'll do fine there."

"My friends won't be there," Jerry protested.

"We're moving and that's it." His father didn't say much about what Jerry should do or not do. He left most of that up to Jerry's mother, but when he did say something, there was no room for argument. That was it.

Still Jerry tried one more time. "I could live with Billy's family. They wouldn't mind. I could help them do chores and stuff and still help you on the weekends."

His father's frown grew deeper, and it was all Jerry could do not to put his hands over his ears to shut out the words when he started talking. "That's not going to happen," he said. "You're our son and you can't live with anybody else. You're just going to have to go to Shelby County." His father's face softened the barest bit. "You'll do fine, son, once you get started there."

For a minute Jerry thought his father might reach out and touch his shoulder, show him he knew it wasn't going to be all that easy for Jerry. But he didn't. His dad wasn't much for hugging or showing affection. There were days Jerry wasn't even sure he knew how to smile, but then his dad was always working so hard. And he'd seen some bad times. Times that might make anybody forget how to smile.

His father had flown bombers in the South Seas during World War II when he wasn't much older than Jerry was now. He didn't talk about it much, but he'd been through a lot getting his planes shot up, landing with some of his crew dead in the plane, and facing death himself every time his plane was slingshot off the carrier.

And that wasn't the only time he'd faced death. He'd been nearly killed in a barn construction accident when Jerry was thirteen. The thought of it still made Jerry's heart squeeze tight in terror. His father had been standing about one hundred feet to the side watching some men remodel a barn when a nail ricocheted off a piece of metal and split his eye wide open. If the nail hadn't bounced off his nose, his father would have died right there, killed by a nail out of a barn builder's nail gun after surviving all those Japanese bullets.

Jerry had come home from school that day to find the house empty. He had looked on the table but there hadn't been a note, just no one there. It had felt funny. While he was never sure what his mother might say to him when he got home from school or whether he'd be able to do enough of the right things to keep her from yelling at him, he still expected her to be there.

Later when his mother had finally called and told him what had happened, he'd barely made it out to the porch to throw up. He'd been that worried. He'd felt even worse after he went to see his father lying in the hospital bed bandaged up, looking half dead already. It hadn't appeared as if it would take much more to push him on into eternity. Even his mother's face had been tight with worry, but at least she hadn't found a way to blame Jerry for the accident. He'd been safely away from the scene at school.

Of course if his father had died and left him alone with his mother, he wasn't sure what he might have done. Jerry had lain awake nights while his father was in the hospital and worried about that. He had kept the chores up on the farm, kept going to school, had prayed desperately for his father to recover, but underneath everything was a terrible dread of being left alone with his mother. There was no way he could stand that.

He had tried explaining that to the Lord in his prayers, and then when the Lord hadn't given him a clear feeling that he was going to let his father live, Jerry had stepped closer to pure panic at the thought of not having his father at least there in the background while his mother tore him apart for whatever he'd done wrong lately. His father might not say anything, but he was there.

What would he do without his father? Late at night, in his darkest moments, Jerry had decided if the worst did happen, if his father did die, he would simply have to kill his mother. It was that simple. That would be the only way he could survive.

It had been a great relief when his father finally came home from the hospital, but with one eye blinded, his Greyhound bus driving days were over. That made farming that much more important for him, and one of the ways his father and mother made money was by buying farms, cleaning them up, and then selling them. Jerry didn't mind moving as long as they stayed in Oldham County the way they had when they'd moved the last time. He thought his parents liked it in Oldham County. They knew Jerry did. They knew Jerry wanted to graduate with his friends at Oldham County High or they should have. They could have waited a year to buy another farm. Just one more year. That's all Jerry asked. After that he wouldn't care.

But somebody had offered his father a good price for the farm where they were living. There was another farm for a good buying price in Shelby County. His father said it didn't matter where they lived. They were a family and God was everywhere. He understood Jerry had friends in Oldham County, but Jerry could make new friends. His father wouldn't even try to understand, and his mother just thought Jerry was being silly, immature, and difficult as usual.

From the day they told him, Jerry began planning. He was seventeen. He wasn't a kid anymore. He could go wherever he wanted to go. They couldn't make him go to high school at Shelby County. But first he needed money and a car. He couldn't exactly just take off in his dad's new truck.

School ended in May and they moved to the new farm. It wasn't a terrible place even though they had to live in a trailer while they were fixing up the old house. There was plenty of work to do on the farm and plenty of other farmers in the area and back in Oldham County who needed Jerry's help in their hayfields and tobacco patches. He liked farm work, liked the plowing and planting and seeing the crops grow in the sunshine and rain.

He even liked putting in hay, rising to the challenge of keeping up as the hay bales fell off the conveyer belt in the dusty haylofts. He made every move count as he lifted and stacked the bales while hayseeds stuck to his sweaty arms and neck. It was something he could do right. He liked the way the farmers bragged about how many bales he could stack.

And on the weekends and sometimes during the week, churches called him to lead the music at their revivals. He sang specials, directed the choirs at the churches, did whatever they asked. Sometimes they paid him.

So he worked on the farms during the week and sat on this or that pew listening to a preacher or an evangelist exhorting the people to turn away from their sins and live for Christ on the weekends and at night. Everybody thought that was what Jerry had done when he was thirteen. He'd walked the aisle, professed Jesus as his Savior, done what everybody expected him to do. But it hadn't been right. He'd done it to please his parents and Mrs. March, his Sunday school teacher and Br. Williams, the preacher. It was what he was supposed to do. Be saved. Join the church. Be baptized.

He had done it all, but it hadn't meant anything to him. He was pretty sure the Lord was up there in his heaven somewhere, but Jerry didn't think much about what the Lord wanted with him. Jerry was singing and directing the choirs and going to church and reading the Bible, but he hadn't really surrendered anything. He was just doing what he'd always done while thinking about doing some new things that didn't have all that much to do with what the Lord might want him to do.

Besides his mother was always telling him how he couldn't do any of it right anyway. If he couldn't please his own mother, how in the world could he expect to please the Lord? Not while he was sniffing glue with his friends, and for years he hadn't been able to stop doing that. Not until he had started passing out all the time and gotten scared his mother might find out.

He saw people get saved at the revivals. He shook their hands and welcomed them into the family of God, but it was a family he didn't really feel part of himself. It didn't bother him. He prayed, read the Bible, went to Sunday school, sang his specials, but the day he joined the church was the day he began walking away from God.

He didn't think about what the words of the songs he sang in the churches were saying. He thought about how he sounded, how he could make his voice go up and reach the high notes, how he could make the people out in the church pews get teary-eyed just by the way he sang a few words, and how they'd give him money for doing something so easy. It didn't matter that later on the way home his mother would tell him what he could have said or done better. He didn't care about anything except the money he was adding to his stash in his sock drawer.

In June his father unknowingly gave his escape plan a big boost when he told Jerry about the 1964 Dodge Dart on a car lot in Louisville. It was perfect. Only sixteen thousand miles. Good gas mileage. The car dealer might have even been telling the truth when he said the car had been owned by a little old lady who only drove it to the grocery store and church.

Jerry polished it until its baby blue top and sides glimmered in the sun and thought about how that was going to change. This car was going places.

CHAPTER 3

When the first day of school rolled around the end of August, Jerry drove his Dodge Dart to Shelby County High and gave the school a chance. Maybe his parents were right. Maybe he would make friends. Besides he needed a little more time to make money before he left. It was tobacco harvest time. He could make a lot of cash in the tobacco fields after school, and revival season wasn't really over till the end of September.

The seniors at Shelby County were all buddied up in groups and Jerry couldn't spot any openings. Everybody talked around him, but not to him. If anybody did notice him it was to point a finger and laugh. He hated every minute he was in the school building. He wanted to be at Oldham County hanging with his friends, flirting with his old girlfriends or thinking about asking out one of the girls who'd suddenly gotten prettier over the summer.

At Shelby County he kept to himself. He went to class, listened to the teachers, but didn't care what they said about homework. Doing homework didn't add to his pile of money, and he didn't plan to be around long enough to get a report card. Chorus class wasn't too bad, but the teacher wasn't like Mrs. Owens at Oldham County. Nothing was like it had been at Oldham County. He had friends there he could talk to, who helped him get through things. Like the time he wrecked his father's new truck last spring.

Somehow Jerry's dad had talked his mother into letting Jerry start driving the truck even though he hadn't gotten the grades she insisted he had to get. Jerry had tried. All spring he'd done his best to pull up his grades to prove he could be the kind of son his parents wanted. But he'd blown a couple of tests and no matter how much he studied, he just couldn't keep that math stuff in his head. He had to keep a copy of the multiplication table in the top of his notebook all the time so he could look at it whenever he needed to know what eight times six or whatever was.

Numbers and formulas just would not stick in his head. He could remember the words to hundreds of songs. He could give a speech that would knock a person's socks off, had even won speech competitions, but those math rules and formulas just slid right out of his head without leaving a trace. And then the teachers would give a test and Jerry would end up staring at the paper without the first idea what to do.

His mother was good at remembering. She could remember everything he'd ever done wrong, every bad grade he'd made, every note he'd sung wrong. He hadn't even wanted to think about having to take home his next report card. His teachers expected too much. Everybody expected too much. He just couldn't do it. He'd even messed up at chorus practice after school, forgetting the words of his solo. He had hated that. It made him mad. Mad at everybody. Mad at himself. He was always letting people down, not doing things right.

The madder he got, the harder he had pressed on the gas pedal. Then the truck tires had begun slipping as he went into a curve. It had seemed like a sign.

"Why don't you just get it over with and end it all?" he'd asked himself. "That way you won't be a bother to anybody any more."

Jerry had turned the steering wheel until he was heading straight for a tree and mashed the gas pedal all the way to the floor. The truck had hit a bank, slid to the side and hit the tree at an angle. He had been slung against the door and banged his head, but he hadn't really gotten hurt. He couldn't say the same for the truck. It had been pretty smashed. He'd felt bad about that. He hadn't even thought about how the truck might get banged up. He hadn't planned to be around to hear his folks fuss about it.

They hadn't understood. They'd thought he'd wrecked the truck on purpose so they'd have to let him drive the family car to date his girlfriend, but they just hadn't understood. He hadn't intended to hurt the truck, just himself. He had loved that truck.

His friends hadn't understood either. At least not what he had really been trying to do, but they'd rallied around, done stuff to cheer him up, had given him rides to chorus practice when he got grounded again. Now here in Shelby County, he didn't have any friends. They were all miles away at Oldham County High. They'd probably forgotten all about him anyway.

None of that mattered. He was going to be away from it all soon. He just needed a little more money.

Then one day he got up, pulled the covers up on his bed, and knew he wouldn't be pulling them down to sleep there that night. It was a Saturday. The same as always, he went to the field to work with his parents. They were putting in hay and only had one load to go when he told his dad some story about going to the house for water or something.

It felt funny stepping through the door into the kitchen and knowing he was leaving. It was an old house. The people who sold it to Jerry's dad said President

Truman's great great grandparents had gotten married in the house. Jerry wondered how many other people had packed up their things and left this house forever.

He stuffed his roll of money deep in his pocket and jammed all his underwear in a paper sack. He swept the clothes out of his closet still on hangers and threw everything in the trunk of his car. He took one last look around his room to make sure he'd gotten everything he needed. He grabbed the pillow and a blanket off his bed and stuck his Bible up under his arm. In the kitchen he took a jar of peanut butter and a loaf of bread and fixed a jug of water. He could live on that a while. He didn't plan to spend his money on anything but gas to get him as far away from here as he could get.

He looked at the table where sometimes his mother left notes for him. He thought about writing a note, but what would he write? *So long. See you later. I'm out of here. You won't have to be bothered with me any more.* None of that seemed exactly right, so he just turned around and went out the door. When he shut it behind him, all he felt was relief. This part of his life was over. He was going west, maybe all the way to California. His spirits lifted. He couldn't wait.

He didn't worry too much about his parents. He'd always been more of a bother to them than anything else anyway. Except of course when they needed help on the farm. That didn't really upset him. He liked working on the farm, but they could hire somebody to do that for them. They'd probably be happier now that he was gone. He'd always sort of felt as if they weren't really his parents anyway, just these two people he lived with and had to try to please. And he'd been nothing but a failure at doing that. This would be better for everybody.

He was sure of it as he drove away from the farm in the direction opposite the way his parents would come if they decided to check on what was taking him so long at the house. He didn't drive too fast. He didn't want to get stopped for speeding even though he was anxious to get out of the county. He pulled out on the interstate going west. His heart beat faster. He'd thought about this moment for weeks. He was free. On his own. Nobody would yell at him. Nobody would even know which direction to yell.

He sang along with his radio and wondered how long it would be before they realized he was gone. Really gone. They might not even look in his room till tomorrow. They might think he'd gone to see a friend, not something he did that often, but they'd think that before they'd think he'd gone to California. The thought made Jerry smile. His little blue car was purring along. He had a full tank of gas. He had money in his pocket. He had peanut butter if he got hungry.

He wondered if it would be hot in California when he got there. He wondered how long it would take him. There wasn't all that much rush. Maybe he'd do some sightseeing on the way. The Grand Canyon was between here and there. He had the rest of his life. California wasn't going anywhere. He was the one going somewhere.

He glanced up in his rearview mirror and saw a truck coming up behind him. Not his dad. This truck was tan, an old Chevy. His heart didn't even start beating harder. His dad wouldn't come after him anyway. At least not right away. He'd tell his mother not to worry, that Jerry would come home. He'd tell her there wasn't any need running all over the country hunting the boy. Where could he go anyhow?

Jerry smiled as he thought about them talking about where he'd go. They'd think he'd gone to Billy's house. Or maybe to Carrie's. They'd wait till dark to start calling people. And then they'd go look in his room, but he'd shut the door to his closet. They wouldn't have any reason to look in there and see all his clothes gone. The way he had it figured he had at least three days before they came looking and by then he'd be so far west they'd never find him.

The wheels on the car kept spinning, eating up the miles. He thought about making a sign and putting it in his back window. "Go west, young man. Go west." He'd heard that all his life and it seemed like a good enough plan to him.

He turned the music on his radio down and began singing one of his favorite songs. "The Impossible Dream." That's what he was going to start living this minute.

CHAPTER 4

The first time Jerry stopped to fuel up and take a whiz, he thought people were eyeing him as if wondering what a kid from Shelby County, Kentucky was doing so far from home. But he just looked straight back at them and paid for his gas as if he were just on his way to choir practice in Arkansas or somewhere. He bit into his peanut butter sandwich as he drove on down the road. Maybe at the next stop he'd buy some jelly. That wouldn't take much of his money.

He kept counting his money in his head and trying to figure how far it would take him, but thinking about it made his head hurt. He just wasn't good with numbers. Not like his mother and father who didn't have to think five seconds before they could come out with how much to pay a farmhand for a day's labor in the tobacco field or what this or that cost and how much it was a pound or a gallon or whatever. Gas was thirty-two cents so that meant he could get around three gallons for a dollar and if he got twenty-three miles to the gallon that much gas would go how many miles? Maybe not enough. It was a lot of miles to California. All the way across country. It was going to take a lot of gas.

By the time he stopped the second time to fill up close to Memphis, he was already worrying a little. The roll of bills in his pocket was still nice and thick, but each time he peeled one off, it was gone with no way to replace it.

It was late and he was beginning to nod a little behind the wheel when he saw the sign for the rest area. As he turned off the road, a Greyhound bus zoomed past him. All those people in the bus were going somewhere just like he was. His dad used to talk about the people who rode his buses when he was driving. Some of them would be going a long way and some just to the next town. As Jerry got his pillow and blanket and made himself a bed in the back seat of the car he thought about the empty seat. He had room for passengers. He could be a bus for a couple of people if they were going his way. If they were going west.

When the sun came up the next morning, he was at the Greyhound Bus Station watching people line up to buy tickets. He took his time looking people over, and finally settled on a couple, not too old, not too young. The man was jingling the change in his pocket, looking a little worried. The woman's eyes were droopy and she was yawning. Maybe she'd want to sleep and not talk the whole way if they did decide to ride with him.

Jerry had changed his shirt, combed his hair and washed his face in the bus station restroom. He wanted to look clean cut, trustworthy, safe. He'd even practiced a smile in the restroom mirror. Not too big. Not too small. Kind of the smile he used when he was meeting a preacher for the first time before he sang a special at the preacher's church.

It must have worked. They didn't look a bit worried when he walked up to them and said, "How you doing, folks? I'm Jerry Shepherd and I'm on my way out west. Do you happen to be going that direction, too?"

The man smiled back at him. "As a matter of fact, we are. Headed to Arkadelphia just the other side of Little Rock."

"You know I'm heading right for Little Rock. I never heard of this Arka whatever but I'd be glad to take you for half whatever your bus ticket would cost. That sure would help me on my own gas money, you know." He stretched his smile a little wider without looking too eager.

The deal was a lot easier to make than Jerry had expected. Even the woman was smiling at him. Of course a lot of the women he met at churches thought he was cute. It was the girls his own age and his mother who kept knocking him off his pedestal. Jerry gave his head a mental shake. That was all in the past. This was the now. This was on the way west.

The couple didn't have much luggage. Jerry just piled it in the front passenger seat and let the couple climb in the back together. The man talked to him. Jerry didn't mind. It helped him stay awake when the heat climbing off the road threatened to send him into a trance. They were going to see the man's grandmother who'd been sick, and the man had heard about a chance for a job out in that area. He wasn't happy working where he was. Jerry let the man's words slide around him while he nodded every once in a while to let the man know he was listening. He even answered a few questions about what he was doing out on the road by himself. Of course he didn't tell the truth, but he didn't exactly lie. He'd never been very good at lying straight out.

"I got out of school last year and decided to take off and see the country. So I worked all summer on the farms out my way to save up a little money. I figure I'll have to get a steady job and stuff soon enough. Probably even get drafted." Jerry glanced up at them in the rear view mirror and asked, "You know any neat places to visit in Arkansas?"

The woman spoke up for the first time since she'd gotten in the car. "'Bout the most interesting thing you're going to see in Arkansas is a dead armadillo on the side of the road."

The man laughed and said his wife was from the east and she'd wanted to go back that direction instead of toward Arkansas.

"West sounds better to me," Jerry said. "And I've never seen an armadillo. Might be interesting."

As soon as he dropped them off, he went straight to the next closest bus station and picked out another couple. He liked the short trippers best because they didn't have time to get too curious about him and he could get them where they were going without having to drive all night. Every time he added another bill to his roll of money he felt better. He didn't even go in and eat at the restaurants when they stopped. He just ate his peanut butter and bread, turning down the riders when they offered to buy him something.

He didn't know why his mother had always made such a fuss about eating vegetables anyway. Something about needing roughage to keep a person's system working right, but his system seemed to be working just fine. So what if he was a little constipated? That was heaps better than being the other way when a fellow was on the road.

Things couldn't have been going better. His car was running like a top. His tires still had plenty of tread. It was hot, but with all the windows down letting the air blow in on his sweaty skin, it wasn't too bad. He'd seen the dead armadillo in Arkansas. He'd seen mile after mile of flat open spaces in Oklahoma. He'd driven through Oklahoma City where nearly everybody in Oklahoma must live.

As he drove across the Texas panhandle Jerry told the guy riding with him he didn't see how a cow could find enough to eat to stay alive out there, but the man said folks farmed there, or rather ranched. But they had to have big ranches. Maybe ten acres to a cow. Jerry figured it would wear the poor old cow's legs out to have to walk that far to find a sprig or two of grass.

Then just when he thought the landscape couldn't get any more different, he drove into the canyon lands. He imagined cowboys and Indians up the gullies and crawling across the dry plains needing water. He sang along with the Beatles and Elvis when he could pick up a radio station. He was alone now. He'd dropped his last couple off just west of Albuquerque and hadn't picked up anybody else. Being out here felt a little like being on the moon and it wasn't every day he was on the moon. He wanted to look around a little.

Besides it was hot, really hot in Arizona, and folks might rather pay double to get where they were going if the Greyhounds had air conditioning. Not to mention it felt good not to have to make conversation for a while. Plus it might help the no vegetable problem if he got out and walked around some. He wasn't all that far from the Grand Canyon. He'd just read in Psalms a couple of nights ago before he settled down in the back seat to sleep about God making the mountains and the valleys. It would be almost sinful to pass by one of the Lord's most amazing creations without taking a look.

It was calm out here away from the cities where everything seemed to move in slow motion. It gave him time to think about the big things—the world and God. When he slept out in the car at night, the stars practically dropped down to shine right in his car windows. And the silence was deep and unbroken except by a bird now and again or a coyote. No motors. No tractors. No trains. Just quiet. Nothing but the natural sounds of the country.

Things were going good, better than he'd ever imagined even before he'd left. He could handle things. He had a direction. He had gas in his car and there wasn't a soul but him on the road. He pushed the speedometer up to seventy-five. The speed limit was seventy but the roads were so straight and flat he could probably go ninety without the first problem as long as a cop wasn't around.

The thought had no more than crossed Jerry's mind when he spotted a car in the distance coming toward him, moving fast. He had a bad feeling about it as if he'd conjured up a policeman just by thinking about one. The other car was still a good distance away when he made out the bubble lights.

Jerry groaned. "I'm in trouble now." He backed his speed down to sixty-five just in case his speedometer was off a few miles. He kept his eyes on the road and pretended he wasn't the least bit concerned about the state trooper, but the trooper slowed down anyway when he went past Jerry. He stared straight over at Jerry.

Jerry was almost afraid to breathe. He'd seen some troopers on the interstates, but there they'd had lots of cars to pick from. Here he was the only car for miles, and he stuck out like a sore thumb with his Kentucky license plate. His parents probably had some kind of warrant out on him. His goose was cooked.

The trooper went on past. Jerry kept his speed steady as he watched the taillights of the trooper in his mirror. He was beginning to be able to breathe again. Another minute and the trooper's car would be out of sight. Then all at once the trooper's taillights went red as he put on his brakes and did a U-turn.

"Oh, no," Jerry said out loud as his heart sank. "This is it. They've got me and I didn't even get to see the Grand Canyon. Looks like I could have made it to the Grand Canyon."

The trooper came up behind him fast, then slowed down and followed him. He didn't turn on his lights or siren. Jerry thought he'd been sweating buckets because of the heat before the trooper had come on the scene, but now his t-shirt and the waistband on his pants were soaked. The cop followed him for about a mile before he switched on his lights and siren. Jerry was almost relieved. He pulled over to the side of the road.

The trooper pulled over behind him and got out of his car. He came up to Jerry's window and asked for his driver's license and registration. The policeman studied them for a moment before he asked, "What are you doing out here, kid?"

Jerry said the first thing that came to mind. "I thought I'd do some sightseeing. See the Grand Canyon and stuff, you know."

"This says you're seventeen. Don't you go to school?"

"Not now. I quit."

The trooper frowned a little. "That's a bad thing to do, young man."

"I know." Jerry started to smile then thought better off it as he rubbed the sweat off his forehead with the back of his hand.

"Where you headed?"

"California. Well, after I go check out the Grand Canyon."

"California, huh," the trooper said. "What are you planning to do out there in the big state of California?"

"Just see the sights and sounds." It seemed as good an answer as any.

The trooper looked him straight in the eyes. "Do your parents know you're out here?"

"No, sir." Jerry groaned inwardly. What an idiot! He should have told the man that sure, his parents had let him come, that they thought it was a great idea him seeing the country while he was young. Before he had to go to the army and maybe Vietnam. That he was going back home as soon as he saw some things. But no, he was stupid and told the truth.

"Are you on the run?" the policeman asked.

"No, sir. I'm driving." Now he'd been a double idiot. Saying a smart aleck thing like that. He half expected the cop to grab him by the ear and haul him straight off to jail.

The trooper twisted his lips to the side. Jerry wasn't sure if it was to keep from smiling or because he was mad. The man said, "Would you step out of the car, please?"

"Sure." Jerry opened the door and got out. He felt like a limp rag.

"Would you unlock your trunk for me so I can check it out?"

Jerry didn't ask what he was checking for. He just opened up the trunk. There were all his clothes in a jumble and the peanut butter jar and a new loaf of bread he'd bought that morning. The ice had long since melted out of his jug of water from the service station fifty miles back.

"It looks like you might have loaded things kind of fast."

"Yes sir," Jerry said.

"So you didn't tell your parents you were taking off across country?"

It didn't seem like the time to start lying, so Jerry just said, "No sir."

"Are you going to call them?"

"Eventually," Jerry said.

The trooper stared at him a minute before he asked, "You do anything wrong?"

"No sir, not except running away from home." He figured he would just keep telling this guy the truth. He was busted already anyhow.

The trooper nodded a little. "I'm going to call and check you out. You just wait here a minute or two."

Jerry leaned on the car and let the hot Arizona sun bake the sweat out of his t-shirt. It was a different hot out here than at home. Lots of things were different out here, but he wasn't sure the policeman would be different. He'd take him to his station and make him call his parents. Jerry had no idea what he'd say.

He was feeling a little sick by the time the patrolman got out of his car and came back toward him. He was almost afraid to look at him, but he'd always looked people in the eye so he looked straight at the trooper. The trooper smiled the barest bit and said, "Well, everything's clear. You're not wanted for anything, but I advise you to get to the nearest phone and call your parents and let them know you're all right."

Relief flooded through Jerry, but he didn't let himself smile. He kept his face straight and serious as he said, "Yes sir. I'll do that, sir. Just as soon as I get to a phone."

Late that afternoon he sat on the lip of the Grand Canyon and ate his peanut butter sandwich while he watched the sun go down. Then he kept sitting there until all the other people had gone back to their cars. When he was alone, he sang "For the Beauty of the Earth." He'd led that song in churches dozens of times, but he'd never sung it the way he sang it this night with the Grand Canyon spilling away from him. What other wonders was he going to see? Briefly he thought of his promise to the state trooper, but he wasn't anywhere near a phone. And eventually hadn't gotten here yet.

CHAPTER 5

He crossed into California in the middle of the day. He'd made it. There was the "Welcome to California" sign. Finally, at last! It wasn't exactly what he'd been expecting. It didn't look that much different than Nevada here where he was, but still it was California, the place he'd been aiming his car toward for days. Kentucky seemed like it was in another universe as he kept driving toward the Pacific Ocean.

But what now? He was in California. What was he going to do next? It had been days since he'd had any paying riders, and his money wasn't gone but it was going. San Francisco. He saw the name on a sign and turned that way. It was several hundred miles away. Far enough that maybe he'd have time to think of what to do before he got there. And he had plenty enough gas money to get that far at least.

He didn't know why he stopped when he saw the man with his thumb up on the side of the road. He hadn't picked up a hitchhiker all the way across country, hadn't even thought about it when he saw them along the road. Hitchhikers could be trouble, maybe psychos like in the movies. Still something made him put on the brakes and pull over. It wasn't that the man was young, his age. He looked almost as old as his father, but nothing like his father who was always military neat. This guy needed a haircut and a bath, but then so did Jerry.

"Hey, fellow, you want a ride?" Jerry yelled out the window at him.

"You bet." The man threw his duffel bag in the back seat and wasted no time climbing in the car. "Where you headed, kid?"

"Nowhere special. Just going wherever the road takes me."

"Did I see right on your license plate? Kentucky?"

"Yeah, you saw right, but I'm in California now."

"You're a long way from home, kid."

"Just about long enough," Jerry said before he asked the man. "Where are you going?"

"Now don't laugh, but fact is, I'm headed home to New Jersey."

"New Jersey?"

"Yeah." The man looked at him without saying anything for a couple of minutes. "You ever been to Jersey?"

"Nope."

"That's not too surprising. It's not exactly a vacation hot spot or anything. But you know what? There isn't all that much out here in California a kid like you needs to get mixed up in. Tell you what, if you take me back to Jersey, I'll pay half the gas and food and once we get there you can stay with me at my mother's house until you get on your feet. I'll even help you get a job."

"You look like you could use a job yourself," Jerry said while he thought about New Jersey. New Jersey? He'd never once thought about going to New Jersey, but now it was sounding like as good a place as any. He'd been asking what he was going to do in California. Maybe this was another sign.

"Guess that's the truth, but I don't have any trouble finding a job. It's keeping them that gives me fits. I may look old to a wet behind the ears kid like you, but I've never felt old enough to settle down."

"What's your mama think about that?"

"She gave up on me a long while back, kid. So what you say? You game to drive back across the country? It's not like you don't know the way. You just head east instead of west."

East? Why not? Here he was west, but he didn't have any reason in particular to stay. This was a reason to go. So he pulled back out on the interstate watching for the signs that said east now instead of west. The man told him his name was Pete Harmon and that he'd just been bumming around. Now he was ready to go home and see his folks again. He might even settle down this time if he found a job that didn't drive him totally crazy.

They took turns driving and sleeping and made good time. On the second or third day when they were back in the flat hot section of the country where Jerry sometimes wondered if they were moving at all with the way the cornfields alongside the road looked the same all day long, Pete noticed Jerry's Bible on the dashboard. "What you doing with this?" he asked as he picked it up.

"I don't know." Jerry looked over at him then back at the road. "I read it some just to pass the time at night or whatever."

Pete opened it up and read, "Presented to Gerald Warren Shepherd by Hazel and Dewey Shepherd. Your folks, I guess."

"That's right." Jerry thought about reaching over and grabbing the Bible and stuffing it under the seat, but he didn't want to make Pete mad or anything. So far they'd been pretty good traveling companions.

Pete leafed through a few more pages. "Your parents religious? Churchgoers?"

"Every time the doors are open," Jerry said. "As long as the ox isn't in the ditch."

"Oh, yeah. You said they were farmers." Pete turned a few more pages in the Bible. "Here's one of my favorite stories about Joseph going off a slave and ending up the main cheese of everybody."

"You go to church?"

"When I'm at home. It makes my mother happy."

"You have a hard time doing that?" Jerry asked. "Making her happy?"

"Well, I guess she'd probably be a lot happier if I'd settle down and raise a family instead of knocking about all over the country, but she doesn't give me too hard a time. She just welcomes me back whenever I show up at the door."

"You think she likes you?"

"Well, yeah. She's my mother."

"I've never been all that sure my mother liked me. I don't hardly ever do anything to make her happy."

"Is that why you ran away?" Pete asked, still leafing through the Bible.

"I didn't say I ran away."

"But you did, didn't you?" Pete didn't wait for an answer. "It's okay if you did. I've been running away all my life."

"Well, I left. I didn't like school."

"Me neither. I went. Got my high school diploma. Even went a little to college, but I didn't like going to class. So I flunked out."

"Was your mother mad?"

"Not too bad. She never thought I was the nose in a book kind of guy anyway, least ways no studying type books. She said I'd find my way someday. I guess someday hasn't gotten here yet."

"She sounds neat. What are you going to tell her about me when we get there?"

Pete laughed at little. "I don't know. That I brought home a stray, I guess. She's always had a soft heart for strays. She'll probably especially like one that carries a Bible with him."

And she did. Mrs. Harmon took one look at him and said he could stay as long as he wanted to. Then she cooked him up some meat loaf, apples, and green beans and told him to leave his peanut butter in the car for the time being and eat some real food. When she talked about getting his system back in order, it didn't sound as bad as when his mother talked about it.

It was different in New Jersey. The weather was cool already and there were people all around them. No wide-open spaces to take a walk or sit and watch the sun go down. No tractors in the fields. Pete got him a job at a factory. The work was boring but not too hard. And even it had been, Jerry had never been afraid of working. He even missed working on the farm.

He sometimes thought about what his father would be doing. He'd probably already sown the cover crops and put in the last cutting of hay. If the weather had cooperated, he might be stripping the tobacco and getting it ready for market. With winter coming on, he'd need to start feeding the cows and checking for new calves.

Sometimes at night when Jerry was settling down in the Harmon's spare bedroom, he'd think about his father. He'd wonder if he was missing him. He figured his mother was relieved he wasn't there to be such a bother anymore, but his father might miss his help on the farm. Then he'd throw a little prayer up for them before he went to sleep. "Bless Mom and Dad."

CHAPTER 6

It drove Mama Harmon crazy—the fact that his folks didn't know where he was. She had taken Jerry under her wing and treated him like he'd been born into her family. She liked him. She introduced him at church as Pete's friend and everybody made him feel like he belonged. He liked belonging. He liked going days without anybody telling him how he was doing everything wrong. He was glad he'd picked up Pete and driven all the way back to New Jersey.

Still Mama Harmon wanted him to call his folks. He'd told her the truth about how he'd run away without leaving a note or calling or anything. Mama Harmon was easy to talk to. Even when she was telling him he should call his parents, she did it like she really cared about him.

"I'll call them eventually," he told her. He heard the echo of his promise to the patrolman in Arizona in his head, but he just wasn't quite ready yet. He looked at Mama Harmon. "You have to promise me you won't call them or write them yourself."

"I won't, honey," Mama Harmon promised him. "But I just can't keep from thinking how worried your poor mama is bound to be, you so young and all, and her not having the first idea where you are. It just tears me up inside knowing how she must be feeling."

"You don't know my mama," Jerry told her.

"I know she must be worried, and I've been praying for her every night and for your daddy, too."

It took her a while, but finally because he liked her so much he told Mama Harmon he'd call home. He didn't practice what he was going to say. He just dialed the number and said a little prayer that his father would answer instead of his mother. He wasn't sure he'd be able to talk if his mother answered. He might have to just hang up without even saying hello.

Jerry had to swallow a couple of times before he could say anything after his father answered the phone. Finally he forced out, "Hey, Dad, it's me. I've got a job." He mashed the receiver up against his head so hard it bruised his ear.

His father started talking too fast as if afraid the connection would be broken off before he found out what he needed to know. "Jerry. Are you okay, son?"

"I'm fine, Dad. Doing really good and stuff."

"Where are you?"

"I can't tell you that right now, but I just wanted you to know that I'm safe. In good hands. I've got a roof over my head and a job."

"But can't you tell us where? We've been worried sick about you."

"I know, Dad, but I'm not coming home. Things are going good here. How's things on the farm?"

His dad told him about Jerry's cows, which ones had new calves, which calves he'd sold. "I'm saving the money for you. I could send it to you if you tell me where to send it."

"No, I don't need it now. I told you I had a job."

A little silence stretched between them. Finally his father said, "Your mother's missing you, son. We've been praying every day that you'd call."

"I've been praying for you, too," Jerry said. "I'll call you again." And then he hung up before his father could hand the phone to his mother.

Mama Harmon was so proud of him that she baked his favorite chocolate cake. After that it didn't seem so hard to call. The next time he called he even talked to his mother, and she didn't sound mad or anything, just worried about whether he was okay. So when she asked him for the address for the tenth time, he gave it to her. She promised they wouldn't come after him, that they'd let him decide when it was time for him to come home.

Jerry wasn't sure he ever wanted to go home. He liked it there in Jersey. Mama Harmon was always hugging him, bragging on him for doing the littlest things like helping her clear off the table and wash the dishes or sweeping the snow off the steps. When she heard him singing in his room a couple of times, she got him to sing some of the old hymns for her. Her favorite, "Amazing Grace," wasn't all that hard to sing without music. At night she'd sit at the kitchen table before she went to bed and read her Bible. Sometimes Jerry would go in and sit with her, and they'd talk.

"I know you've got a job and all, Jerry, but that's not what you want to do the rest of your life. The Lord has something special in mind for you. I just know it," she said one night.

"My mama used to always tell me the same thing, but if he has, the Lord hasn't let me in on the plan," Jerry said.

"He will, honey, when the time's right, but before then, you need to be doing all you can to be ready. You need to finish high school. Nobody gets very far without finishing high school. Even Pete got his diploma years ago. Hasn't done him a lot of good since he never could figure out what he wanted to do with it, but you're not like that. You can make something out of your life. But you need to finish high school first."

"Have you been talking to my mother?"

"Not today, but I have talked to her and I know your mama and daddy care about you and they want you to come home."

"But I like it here. Don't you want me to stay?" he asked. The kindness radiating off Mama Harmon's face made tears come to Jerry's eyes. She was like a special grandmother who was going to love him no matter what he did, but he didn't want to disappoint her.

Mama Harmon reached over and laid her hand on his cheek. Her blue gray eyes were sad. "You know I love you and I'd give anything if you could just stay with us forever, but that wouldn't be right. I've prayed about it and that's not what the Lord wants. He wants you to give your mama and daddy another chance. He wants you to go home and finish school."

"I'm not sure I can. You just don't know how my mother is. I can't do anything right when I'm there."

"She may be different now. She loves you. I can tell she does by the way she calls and writes. So just think about it for me. That's all I'm asking. Just think about it."

The very next day Jerry got a package in the mail from his parents. There was a batch of chocolate fudge, some new white socks and underwear, a pair of leather gloves, a jar of his favorite dill pickles, and an envelope with a twenty-dollar bill stuffed in it.

He cried the day he packed up his stuff to go home. He looked around the little room that didn't have anything of his in it but his Bible and his clothes, but it felt like home. Mama Harmon had made it feel like home, and now he was going to leave her behind. He hugged her and told her he'd write as soon as he got home, but she shook her head.

"I don't think that would be a good idea, honey. This is killing me to see you leave, but you need to go on home and get on with your life there. You can't be thinking about us up here. You need to put all your thoughts on doing what you need to do there. Going to school and patching things up with your parents."

She stood on the front walk and waved at him until he was out of sight. He wanted to turn around and go back, but he kept driving. Soon he crossed the New Jersey state line and then he was crossing into Ohio and heading west again. He drove straight through. He'd told his parents he was coming. He couldn't turn back. He thought about just heading back out toward California again, but he'd promised Mama Harmon. And maybe she was right. Maybe it would be better now. It would be Christmas soon. A person ought to be at home with his family at Christmas.

He wished he'd gotten Mama Harmon something for Christmas before he left. He couldn't get her anything now. She'd told him not to write to her or send her anything. But she'd be praying for him. She'd promised him that, and he could pray for her.

It felt funny driving back down the old familiar roads toward Shelbyville. He'd still rather be going back to the old farm in Oldham County, but he shook that thought away. That farm was gone. It felt different driving here now after he'd been all the way to California and back to New Jersey. He looked down at the speedometer on his car. He'd added thousands of miles to it. He wasn't the same boy who'd driven away from here. Things would have to be different because he was different.

And then he was driving up his driveway and his dad was running across the yard to meet him without even taking time to put on a coat. He had a smile all the way across his face. His mother was standing in the doorway waiting. Jerry couldn't see if she was smiling or not.

CHAPTER 7

Maybe he wasn't different enough. Things were just the way they'd always been. At least some things were. His dad was happy to have him home. He talked non-stop about the farm and all the things Jerry had missed while he was gone. He wanted to hear about what Jerry had seen and done while he was away, but he didn't push Jerry to talk if he didn't want to.

But things weren't all that different with his mother. He still couldn't do anything right and running away had simply proven that. "A person has problems, he tries to fix them," his mother told him. "You don't just up and run clear across country while your parents go crazy with worry. You've got to learn to think, Jerry, or you're going to be the death of your father and me."

Even when she didn't say anything, Jerry felt her disapproval heavy and black hanging over his head. If he was ever going to get her forgiveness for what he'd put her through the last few months, he was going to have to earn it, and his first task was catching up on his schoolwork.

Somehow his mother had talked the principal into letting Jerry come back to school and just pick up where he'd left off to finish his senior year. He had a big stack of make up work, but once he did that, they would overlook the weeks he'd missed school.

Jerry looked at all the books and papers and thought about New Jersey and how much easier it might have been to just stay up there working at the factory, but he was home now. And he'd promised Mama Harmon he'd give it a try. She'd convinced him he needed his diploma. She was praying for him. She thought he could do it. So he dived into the work and forced himself to read the boring textbooks and do the worksheets. His mother spent a lot of time looking over his shoulder to make sure he was doing everything right.

Christmas morning came, and they got up, fed the pigs and cows, and opened presents the same as any other year. His father pulled him aside out at the barn and told him having him home was the best present he could have gotten, that it would have just been too hard on all of them if Jerry hadn't come home before Christmas. Jerry went back to church and everybody acted as if he'd just been away to camp or something. He even sang "O Holy Night" at the Christmas service. Nearly everybody there told him nobody could sing that song like he could and how glad they all were that he was back to sing for the church again.

School wasn't much better than before he ran away, but this time because he was determined to stick it out and get that all important piece of paper, he started talking to some people in the halls and made a few friends. They weren't like his friends at Oldham County. They didn't worry about the rules and doing what they were supposed to do. They were always looking for a party, but they didn't mind Jerry tagging along. Still Jerry stayed away from the booze that was always at the parties. He had to keep his grades up.

He put in time studying, but some of the teachers kept giving him bad grades. Nothing he did suited them. He thought they wanted him to fail because they were mad he'd been allowed to come back to school after missing so many days. Mr. Chester, his choir teacher, was okay with it. He was glad to have Jerry's voice in the a cappella choir. They were winning awards at the state competitions and Jerry stayed after school two days a week to work one on one with the teacher on his singing. Mr. Chester kept telling Jerry that his voice was a gift and he shouldn't waste it.

Janice thought he'd make the big time someday, too. Janice was in his English class and she was always ready to help him when he hadn't gotten around to doing his homework. They started dating right after Christmas on and off. They'd go on a few dates, break up over something silly for a few days and then get back together. She kept saying if he really cared about her he'd let her wear his class ring, and one night he slipped it off his finger and put it in her hand. Janice kissed him till he was dizzy, but the next morning when his mother asked him where his ring was, she threw a fit.

"You did what?" she asked. She slammed his plate of eggs and bacon down in front of him and then leaned over to stare in his face.

Jerry looked around for a way to escape.

"Look at me when I'm talking to you," she yelled.

"Yes ma'am," Jerry said. He shrank back in his chair and got as small as he could. He kept his eyes on her face but inside his mind he pulled down a black shade to block her out.

Still the words came through. "You and that girl are way too young to even think about getting so serious. You weren't thinking again, Jerry. You've got to start thinking. Your father didn't pay his hard earned money for that ring so you could throw it away on some girl. It's a good thing he's not here to hear how ungrateful you are. Giving your ring to that girl. Janice Crossfield of all people."

"I'll get it back."

"Today," his mother ordered.

So Jerry got his ring back and broke it off for good even though Janice didn't think he really meant it. Not for good.

He was hoping breaking up with Janice would mollify his mother. He needed to get her off his back about something, because his grades were doing a downward spiral. When the last grading period started in the spring, he was so sure he was going to flunk out that he just quit studying. If he was going to fail, he might as well fail with flying colors. If that was possible.

Then Mr. Chester told him about the senior play. *The Crucible* by Arthur Miller was a serious drama, not a musical, but Mr. Chester said Jerry had great presentation with his songs and that was part acting and he'd won speech contests in the Future Farmers of America Club. He thought Jerry should audition for one of the parts.

Nobody was any more surprised than Jerry when he got the part of John Proctor. He'd never done any acting before and now here he was in a starring role. He might still be failing some of his other classes, but acting was exciting. It wasn't hard to remember the lines, not like it was remembering math formulas, and the director, Mr. Riddle, had a way of getting them all to forget they were just high school kids while helping them to become whatever part they'd won. Jerry knew about pretending anyway. He'd been doing it for years. But this was more fun.

The play was set back in the 1690's during the Salem witch hunts. It sounded crazy people blaming their babies dying and their crops failing on witches, but then there had been times when Jerry hadn't been all that sure he didn't have a curse on him when everything kept going wrong.

If his parents ever heard him say a thing like that, they'd jump all over him. They'd tell him the only curse he had on him was the one of not trying hard enough, not studying, not doing his homework, not paying attention, not listening, not being what he could be. Not making the grade.

Every time he thought about report card time, his throat got so tight he could hardly swallow. What if he didn't graduate? His mother would die of shame. Especially after she'd gone to all that trouble talking the principal into letting him back into school after his "little trip across country." And Mama Harmon would be disappointed, too. Jerry didn't see how she could know about it, but if she did somehow find out, she'd be disappointed in him. He was just a let down to everybody.

Then that afternoon at play practice, he'd flubbed his lines, totally forgotten a few of them. Nobody had yelled at him or anything, but he shouldn't have forgotten. Sometimes he just felt like bashing his head against a wall. He'd wanted to bash something earlier that day when Mrs. Smithers had talked to him about his Government Studies grade. She hated him. She was happy he was failing. She wanted to grind him into the ground and never let him up. She expected too much. Just like his mother.

Jerry's wheels squealed as he went around a curve. He was going too fast. Then instead of slowing down, he pushed the gas pedal all the way to the floor. He didn't want to make the curve up ahead. He'd thought about that curve before. He'd kept it in his head as the most likely place to end it all. There were big trees there. He'd hit one of them. He'd die. That would be better than failing.

He went into the curve and started sliding. All at once one of the scenes from the play was in his head. They were going to put it on in a week. He had to stay alive for that. He yanked the steering wheel hard to the left to get back on the road, but it was too late. He kept sliding. The car banged into a tree on the passenger side.

Metal crunched around him, the windows shattered and showered glass on the seat beside him. And then it was quiet again. So quiet it hurt his ears. Stunned, he sat there still gripping the steering wheel for a long moment. He took a deep breath. He was alive. He lifted his hands off the steering wheel and opened and closed his fingers. He felt his head, wiggled his toes in his shoes. He wasn't even hurt. He was sitting there in a cocoon of safety and he was going to have to go home and tell his parents he'd had another wreck. They'd punish him, take his driving privileges away. They'd say he couldn't do anything right. And they'd be right. He couldn't even kill himself.

He slung open the door of the Dodge Dart and jumped out. He grabbed a limb about the size of his leg and began slamming it into the car. He couldn't even kill himself. Any idiot ought to be able to kill himself. He banged the limb on the roof of the car and yelled when it caved in. He pounded on the car until he couldn't lift his arms.

And then he sat down beside the car, leaned up against the wheel, and cried. He'd gone all the way to California in this car and now he'd ruined it. He always ruined everything.

His parents took away his driving privileges. Of course, he didn't tell them the truth about the wreck. He just said he'd been driving too fast and slid off the road and bounced off a few trees. They told him he could fix his car when he earned enough money to pay for it, but until it was fixed, it would be up to him to get where he wanted to go however whether walking or riding the school bus or whatever. They weren't going to be hauling him around. There was too much work to be done on the farm for that. If he couldn't find a ride to play practice, then he'd just have to drop out of the play.

He found rides. His friends came through so he could be in the play. That was all that held him together as the school year wound down to a close. He took tests, even passed some of them without studying. He was going to fail Government Studies for sure. He wasn't as sure about the other classes, but he was on the edge of disaster in everything except A Capella Choir and Advanced P.E. He could sing and he could run and do pushups.

And he could act. Everybody said so. They came up to him after the first performance and loaded him down with compliments. Mr. Riddle told him he should give serious thought to acting as a career, told him that he'd been a better John Proctor than some professional actors he'd seen perform the part.

Jerry replayed all their words over and over in his head. Maybe he'd found what he could do with his life. Maybe he should have stayed in California and gone to Hollywood. When his parents saw what he could do, they'd be proud of him at last. They hadn't seen the play yet. They were waiting for the last performance when Jerry's aunt and uncle could come with them.

That last night, the curtains pulled back the same as the other nights, but things started going wrong from Scene I. It was as if his mother was jinxing his performance just by sitting out in the audience. He flubbed his lines and missed a couple of cues. The crowd just sat there and stared at them, and everybody up on the stage quit acting. They were just walking through their scenes, saying words, not living them the way they had the night before.

After the final scene and they'd done curtain calls to polite applause from the audience, Jerry's parents and aunt and uncle told him they had enjoyed the play. Jerry wanted to scream at them that they weren't supposed to enjoy the play. They were supposed to be moved by it, bothered by the fact that he as John Proctor had been hung as an innocent man. Instead he smiled and let them talk.

Before the cast left, Mr. Riddle gathered them together for a parting word. "You all did a fantastic acting job. This was a serious play, not some piece of fluff everybody would forget before ten o'clock tonight. You've done something real and professional and your performances will have people in Shelby County thinking for weeks to come."

As Jerry was picking up his duffel bag to leave, Mr. Riddle pulled him aside to say, "You were a great John Proctor, Jerry. One of the best I've ever seen."

"I flubbed my lines," Jerry said.

"Don't worry about that. You can't have perfect performances every night. Really, you ought to think about acting in your future. You have a gift. Of course, it's hard to get started, but you never know. Everybody was an unknown at one time."

"I'm about as unknown as they come," Jerry said.

"Well, you don't have to head to Hollywood today. In fact maybe considering your history, I should tell you definitely not to head to Hollywood today." Mr. Riddle laughed. "Now get out of here and go and enjoy. Half the fun is celebrating once the play closes down and it's always more fun when it's a successful run. You wait until you read the paper next week. You'll see that they thought you were great."

"Come on, Jerry. Let's go," Jacob yelled at him from in front of the stage. Jacob had helped with the lights and had been one of the guys who had ferried Jerry back and forth to practices after his wreck. "Everybody's waiting for us."

Jerry jumped down off the stage and Jacob threw his arm around his shoulders. "Waiting? What for?" Jerry asked.

"So we can party. You close down a show, you party. It's tradition. Even Mr. Riddle says so."

"Where? Here?"

"Nah, not here. You can't have fun at school," Jacob said. "And we intend to have some fun tonight."

"I'm in," Jerry said. "Lead the way."

"It would be an honor to lead such a renowned actor to my car. I mean you just walked off to be hung. This is your second chance at life."

Jerry followed Jacob out of the gymnasium. He'd run around with the guys, but he'd always turned down the beer they pushed at him. Tonight he wouldn't turn anything away. Maybe if he swallowed enough of something, he could forget that look in his mother's eyes when she'd asked him if he'd forgotten his lines. The look that said he might as well forget trying to do anything right. Ever.

The beer tasted better than he'd thought it would. He drank three bottles straight before he came up for air. By then he was beginning to feel fine.

CHAPTER 8

He didn't know why it had taken him so long to discover beer. His friends had been right. It did solve a lot of problems and if the problems got a little bigger, he just popped a pill or two to go along with the booze. His head hurt some in the mornings and he couldn't even think about breakfast after a night out with the guys, but it wasn't anything he couldn't hide from his parents. He'd never been extra cheery in the mornings before school anyway. And he sweated out most of the alcohol in P.E.

His English and Anatomy teachers both told him he still had a chance to pass if he'd study a little for his semester exam. Jerry would look at his books, but then he'd go out with the guys. The hardest thing about the beer was getting it, but then he got a job pulling tobacco plants on Mr. Abram's farm one Saturday and got to talking to Harvey Smith, a full time farm hand in the community.

"Getting beer ain't no problem," Harvey said as he stuck a nail through the gunny sack they'd just filled with tobacco plants to pin the ends together.

"Not for you maybe," Jerry said. "Not now. But how did you get it when you were in school?"

"Everybody always knows somebody who's twenty-one."

"Yeah, you're twenty-one, aren't you?"

"And some." Harvey grinned at him across the tobacco bed. "You give me the money and I'll get you all you want. You're eighteen, ain't you? Had to sign up for the draft already, I reckon. If you're old enough to get drafted and sent off to be shot at in 'Nam, you're old enough to drink a little beer."

"Gee, that'd be great, Harvey." Jerry pulled a couple of fives out of his pocket on the spot.

Harvey folded the money and stuck it in pocket. "Just don't tell your folks. If your mama found out I was buying you beer she'd come after me with a hoe."

Jerry's stock rose with his friends overnight. Now they had a reliable source for their beer, and so when Senior Day arrived, their one day reward of getting to skip school after going faithfully for twelve years, they were ready with plenty of booze thanks to Jerry and an empty house thanks to Bennie's parents both being at work.

They didn't plan for things to get out of hand the way they did. They didn't plan for so many people to show up. It was just supposed to be a little party with some drinking. It wasn't supposed to turn into a riot scene with everybody so drunk they were either passed out or punching holes in the wall just because they could. The neighbors must have called Bennie's father because he came home early before they had time to clear out. Bennie was passed out on the floor, so his dad lit in on the rest of them.

Jerry didn't remember much about it except Bennie's father had a really loud voice, and he didn't want to listen when Jerry tried to tell him they would clean things up. Jacob grabbed Jerry's arm and pulled him out the door. Jacob jumped in his car and barely waited till Jerry was in the passenger seat before he hit the gas. The back of the car fishtailed and almost hit a mailbox. Jacob didn't slow down. He pressed down the accelerator and left black marks on the road as sirens began wailing in the distance.

Jerry spent the night with Jacob. Jacob's parents tended to look the other way when Jacob came dragging home late after a party. His father could put away the booze himself, and he didn't seem all that upset to see Jacob following in his footsteps. Not like Jerry's mom and dad would have been if he'd gone home. He'd have had to sleep out in the barn with the pigs once they got through yelling at him.

The next day back at school, his buddies ratted on him. All of them pointed their finger at Jerry, as if everything that had happened at Bennie's house was his fault. He didn't know why. He hadn't punched the first hole in a wall. But he had brought the beer. And lots of it.

Graduation was just one day away, but Jerry figured it might as well be twenty years when he was called into the principal's office. He stood in front of Mr. Harrison's desk for what seemed like an hour before the principal looked up from the papers he was working on to skewer Jerry with his eyes.

"Jerry Shepherd, I'm disappointed in you. You have let down your parents, your school, your teachers, and your friends. And me. You've let me down. All the good you've done over twelve years in school undone in one day. And for what?"

Jerry started to say something in his own defense, but the principal raised his hand to stop him. "I don't want to hear any stories you've made up about what you did or didn't do. I know what you did. I've talked to Bennie's parents. You're lucky you aren't behind bars."

He finally let Jerry speak. "Things just got out of hand," Jerry said, looking down at his feet.

"That has to be the understatement of the year." Mr. Harrison leaned back in his chair and tapped his pen on the desk.

Another uncomfortable minute went by. Over the tapping of Mr. Harrison's pen, Jerry heard his classmates out in the hallway going to the gym for graduation practice. "What are you going to do?" Jerry finally asked when he couldn't stand the principal's silence any longer. He looked the man in the face. "You going to tell my folks?"

"Your folks. Do you know how hard your mother worked to get you back in school after that stunt you pulled last fall? She practically camped on my doorstep until I promised her I'd give you another chance. But how many chances do you deserve, Jerry Shepherd?"

"I don't know, sir. One more, I hope."

The principal shook his head. "I can't imagine what your mother is going to say. And your father. He's a good man, an asset to our community."

"I promise I won't do it again. I didn't think things would go so crazy."

"That's the trouble, Jerry. You didn't think. When you get to be a senior in high school, you're supposed to think about the consequences of your actions. You're not a child any longer. You can't just think about yourself. You have responsibilities to your parents and your school."

"Yes sir." Jerry hung his head again and stared at the scuffed toes of his shoes. "Am I going to graduate?" He peeked up at Mr. Harrison.

"I don't know. I should just kick you out of school and be done with it, but your mother would take to her bed." A strange look crossed Mr. Harrison's face as if he were thinking about the calls Jerry's mother would be making to him when she found out Jerry wasn't going to graduate. After a minute he cleared his throat and said, "I just don't know. When you get your diploma, you'll just have to open it up and see if it's signed. Now get out of here. I'm tired of looking at you."

"Yes sir," Jerry said.

Jerry's stomach was in knots at graduation the next night. He'd put on the cap and gown. He'd walked in with the rest of his classmates. Some of them wouldn't meet his eyes. He figured they were the ones who'd put all the blame on him for the party, as if they hadn't popped the tops of the beer bottles themselves.

They always gave out all the awards first, so he'd have a long wait to find out if Mr. Harrison had decided to sign his diploma. He didn't even want to think about what he'd tell his mother if he unrolled it and there wasn't a signature. Maybe he could fake the principal's signature. He'd tried to fake a few grades on report cards more than once. Of course he'd always gotten caught and ended up in worse trouble than ever.

He wasn't half paying attention as the principal droned on about the awards. Joseph Phillips got the math award. Everybody knew he would. Everybody knew who would get all the awards. That was practically decided by the time you hit your sophomore year. If he'd gotten to stay at Oldham County he might have gotten some kind of award. If he'd stayed at Oldham County a lot of things might have been different.

People were clapping as Rebecca Jackson climbed up on the stage to get the English award. No surprise there. She was always carrying around some book by an author with a name nobody could pronounce.

He was all primed to hear them announce Marianne Matthews as the National Choral Award winner. He was rolling his neck to get the kinks out of it when his own name slammed into his ears. "Jerry Shepherd, National Choral Award."

He just sat there for a second. He couldn't believe it. He must have heard wrong. April Sanders, who was sitting next to him, poked him with her elbow and whispered, "You have to go up and get it."

He stood up and his feet worked. Mr. Harrison almost smiled at him when he handed him the award. Jerry looked over at his parents as he went back toward his seat. He'd barely sat down when Mr. Harrison announced that Jerry had won the Drama Award. As he headed back off the stage to his chair, Mr. Harrison told him to wait that he'd also won the Best Actor Award. Jerry couldn't quit smiling. He didn't even worry about whether his diploma would be signed until they started calling out the names to go up and receive their diplomas from Mr. Whitson, the superintendent.

They filed up in alphabetical order with cheers and raucous cries greeting some of the names as if their family and friends never thought they'd actually make it through school. Jerry could hardly swallow by the time his name was called and he took the rolled up diploma from Mr. Whitson who shook his hand and congratulated him. He had to wait until he got back to his seat. He couldn't unroll it while he was walking. While they called out the W names, he peeked inside his diploma. He'd never been so glad to see William Harrison's name in his life.

"Thank you, Lord," he whispered, putting his hands together in prayer. "And thank you, Mama." Sometimes having a mother who was hard to get along with paid off. Even Mr. Harrison hadn't wanted to deal with her again.

By the time the principal presented the class of '68 to the world, Jerry was almost laughing he was so happy. He yanked off his cap and slung it so high it hit one of the gym lights. He'd done it. He'd graduated.

CHAPTER 9

"So what are you planning to do now that you're out of high school, Jerry?"

It was an innocent enough question. The people at church and in town who kept asking him about his plans for the future had no idea what a firestorm it kept setting off inside Jerry. He wanted to go somewhere to study music or drama. That's what he was good at. Everybody told him he was. The Lawrence Welk people who'd wanted him to sing on their television program, his chorus teachers, everybody. But his parents told him he couldn't make a living with that. Music was fine for a sideline but not for a career.

He might have just stayed on the farm, but the war was still going on in Vietnam. He'd be drafted if he didn't go to school somewhere. So he signed up with the Spencerian Business School in Louisville. The aptitude tests Jerry had taken last year at school showed he might do well in business classes. He could learn to type, organize offices, run a business.

It was the best he could come up with since his parents wouldn't pay the first bit of attention to what he really wanted and he didn't have the money to go to school without their help. He needed the money he was making at revivals and hiring out to farmers to fix his car. Thank goodness, his dad was letting him drive the truck until he got enough saved up.

His mother mostly stayed off his back. He'd graduated. He didn't have a serious girlfriend, and he had a plan for school. She had gone to business school herself out of high school. She'd spent years working as a secretary for Greyhound before she'd married his father. She said the business field was a good one to get into. That he'd be able to get a job just about anywhere. His father didn't look as sure, but he didn't say much about it as they worked on the farm through the summer.

On Sundays Jerry sang in the churches and on Friday and Saturday nights, he went out with his buddies. As Jacob was always saying, if God hadn't intended for man to drink beer, he wouldn't have made it taste so good. Jerry wasn't real sure where God was that summer anyway. Sometimes in church when he was singing one of the old hymns, he'd almost feel something, but then the church service would be over and all he'd feel was empty inside. He kept trying to fill up that emptiness with beer and pills.

And it took a lot of beer to do it. Even Jacob got on his case a couple of times when Jerry drank so much he passed out. "Slow down, man," Jacob told him when Jerry came to at his house the next morning. "You don't want to kill yourself. You just want to get drunk."

That was all Jacob knew about it. Jerry didn't just want to get drunk. He wanted to go to some place where he didn't have to think, where he didn't have to worry about what he was going to do with his life now that he'd graduated, where he didn't have to hear his mother telling him he was doing it all wrong. He already knew he was doing it wrong. He didn't need her to tell him that.

With September getting closer, Jerry's feeling that it was all wrong just got stronger. The only time he didn't feel the nervous little ants crawling around inside his skin was when he was smashed. One night he was supposed to get with the guys, but he started drinking early. Maybe Jacob was right and he could drink enough that he would just pass out and never wake up. That would be an easy enough way to go. Or another wreck. Wasn't there a saying that third time was charm?

He chugged down a whole case of beer, but it wasn't enough to make him pass out. So he kept driving. His wheels kept slipping off the road on first this side and then the other, but he wasn't all that worried about staying on the road. He just wanted to find the right curve, the right tree this time. He felt a little guilty since he was in his father's truck, but his father could get it fixed. Once Jerry was gone, his father wouldn't have to pay for this crazy business school idea. He could use that money to fix the truck.

Jerry didn't really know what happened. One minute he was driving fast, weaving back and forth, waiting for the curve that was going to get him. The next minute the truck was crashing into a tree. He was thrown clear, out in the middle of a field. He hit hard, but he didn't feel any pain. He tried to stand up, but his head kept spinning and his muscles felt like wet noodles. He tried to push himself up off the ground again and sat his hand down on a piece of glass. He picked the glass up and looked at it. A broken beer bottle. He tilted it up and held it over his mouth in case it still had a drop or two inside it.

Somebody must have called his father, because he was there before the police. But Jerry heard the sirens. They were on the way.

"What in the world, son?" his father said as soon as he saw Jerry wasn't bleeding or anything. "The whole field smells like a brewery."

Jerry held up the broken beer bottle, sniffed, and then laughed. "It does, doesn't it?" His tongue felt thick, but he thought the words came out okay.

"How much beer did you have in the truck?"

"I don't know," Jerry said, suddenly near tears now. "Are all the bottles broken, sir?"

"I hope so," his father said. "How much have you drunk tonight?"

Jerry tried to stand up, but fell back. "Not so much, sir. Just a case."

"A case? Twenty-four beers?" His father looked over at the sheriff's deputy who'd made his way from the road through the field to them. "You'd better call an ambulance, Harold."

"Is he hurt, Dewey?" the deputy asked as he flashed his light on Jerry's face.

Jerry groaned and threw his arm up to keep the light out of his eyes.

"Not that I can tell, but he's got way too much alcohol in his system," his father said.

"This isn't the first time your boy's been out drinking. You know that, don't you, Dewey? We done caught him with some of his buddies and warned them all a couple of times."

"He's just a boy, Harold. You remember how it was when you were a boy."

"Yeah, I know, Dewey, but I'm going to have to write him up. I can't just look the other way this time," the deputy said.

"Do whatever you have to, but call the ambulance. The boy's going to be sick."

The deputy flashed his light around them. "Well, if the alcohol don't get him, the poison ivy might. Did you ever see such a healthy stand of the stuff?"

Jerry ended up in the hospital for a week. Once they decided he wasn't going to die from the alcohol overdose, he broke out in poison ivy. He thought he might die from that. His eyes swelled shut and they had to tie his hands down to keep him from digging at his arms and legs. His mother said it served him right. That he was nothing but a drunk.

The word pierced through him. He wasn't a drunk. He'd been drinking, but he wasn't a drunk. After that, September and the start of school couldn't come fast enough. He wanted to be out of his mother's sight. But at the same time he didn't want to go to the school. He wanted to stay in the fields working with his father. His father knew the drinking was just a mistake he'd made, just like the time when he was fourteen and his father had caught him inhaling gasoline fumes out in the tobacco patch. And Jerry could quit. He'd quit the glue as soon as he started passing out when he sniffed it. He'd quit the gasoline fume sniffing. He could quit the beer and pills if he wanted to. His dad didn't call him a drunk. He just told him to work harder on the farm.

And Jerry was good at farm work. Hadn't he kept this whole farm rolling last spring and summer? He couldn't imagine being good at business. Didn't a person have to know math for that?

He kept on a brave face as his mother shopped for him and helped him pack up. They took him to Louisville and unloaded his stuff into the room they'd rented for him at the YMCA. They'd paid for a week. After that they'd send him more money. They thought he was going to do well. Business school would be a good beginning. It would even help if he stayed working with them on the farm. And he wouldn't be drafted. The last wasn't said, but it was in all their minds.

He went to classes the first day. He knew just looking at the teachers that it wasn't going to work. They were going to expect too much out of him. He'd just end up failing again. It seemed sort of stupid to sit through a bunch of dull classes just to fail again.

He didn't go back to class the next day. He stayed in his room and slept through the daylight hours. He wandered around some at night. He didn't know anybody. He stayed the full week in the room since it was already paid for, but he didn't go back to classes. At the end of the week, he had to move out, but he couldn't go home. Still he had to go somewhere.

He clicked the back of his class ring on the telephone receiver as he tried to think of somebody to call. The ring made him think of Janice, his old girlfriend last year at school. He had the feeling she still liked him. She'd be a senior this year. Older, cuter maybe. Her parents had always been nice enough. Maybe if he came up with a good enough story, they'd come get him and let him stay there a few days till he decided what to do. If Janice asked them to.

Janice sounded excited when he talked to her on the phone. He told her maybe they could go steady again, but that his folks were mad at him for quitting school and he needed a place to stay till they got over it. He was just bending the truth a little. His parents were going to be mad at him when they found out he'd quit. They just didn't know yet. They thought he was in Louisville, sitting in class, learning to be who knew what. Certainly nothing he could be.

Janice talked her dad into coming down and picking Jerry up at the school. It worked out for a week. He gave Janice his class ring. He thought it was the least he could do. Her mother was okay with him being there, and her father was ready to tolerate it until he caught them necking out on the back porch. Janice cried and said she loved Jerry, but that just made her father's face turn even redder.

Mr. Crossfield took a deep breath and ordered her to go inside so he and Jerry could have a man-to-man talk. When the door slammed behind her, he said, "This isn't going to work out, Jerry. You need to go home."

"But, sir, we weren't doing anything wrong. Just kissing a little," Jerry pleaded his case with no effect.

"That may be true, but I was young once. Things like this can get out of hand in a heartbeat. I'm not saying you and Janice can't date, but it's a sure thing the two of you are way too young to be living under the same roof. I understand you have some problems with your parents, but they're good people. You go home and work things out with them, and after that, then you can give Janice a call."

"Yes sir," Jerry said.

"Get your things together and I'll take you home."

They dropped him off at the end of the driveway. Janice was still crying when she waved goodbye to him. He watched their car drive out of sight. He wished he'd gotten his class ring back, but it hadn't seemed the best time to ask for it.

He looked up toward the house. It looked the same as always. Old but sturdy. A safe harbor for families for generations. He didn't want to go up the driveway to the house. Nobody was outside. Nobody saw him to come meet him. He made himself start walking up the driveway. With every step he felt a little sicker. It felt like miles. He should have called them and warned them he was coming.

Maybe they wouldn't be home. Maybe he could just go inside and up to his room and hide out there for a few days without them even knowing he was there. Sometimes he felt as if they lived in separate rooms anyway. That they never actually lived together. That he was in his own little room and they were in theirs.

But of course they were there, sitting in the kitchen, just finishing up supper. They'd done the evening chores. They were planning the next day the way they did every night. He could see them in the light through the window before he opened the door. His stomach felt like he'd swallowed twenty-five bumblebees. It was all he could do to push open the door, set his suitcase down and say, "I'm home."

They both looked at him as if they were seeing some kind of apparition. Finally his father said, "Well, where have you been?"

"I've been here and I've been there." Jerry tried a grin but it sort of died on his face.

"I don't think that answer is good enough, son," his father said.

"Why aren't you at school? That's where you're supposed to be," his mother said.

"School didn't work out," Jerry said. "I couldn't do it, so I left."

"You can't just keep running away from things," his mother said. "You'll never amount to anything if you don't start facing whatever problems and challenges come your way."

Jerry's dad held up his hand to stop his mother's tirade. "Where have you been, son? Out on the road again?"

"Janice and her folks came and got me. I've been over at their house a few days. They just dropped me off."

"At Janice Crossfield's house?!" His mother's voice went up a few decibels. She sounded ready to explode. She kept talking, but Jerry quit listening. He'd learned to do that a long time ago when she got this mad. He didn't know how long it lasted before his father spoke up again.

"Just go on to bed, son. We'll figure out what to do after we get the hay in this week," he said.

The next morning Jerry got up and went down to breakfast like always. His mother had quit yelling, but she hadn't quit frowning or fussing. She just couldn't understand why he'd thought it necessary to go to his girlfriend's house instead of coming straight home and somebody was going to explain why no one had called to tell her where he was. Jerry was glad when he and his father left for the hayfield. It was easy out there. Just load up the bales and carry them to the barn and stack them up in the loft. It was a good place to be with the hay bales closing in on him on all sides, promising the cows wouldn't get hungry when the snow started to fly. And his mother never worked in the loft. She always drove the tractor when the wagons were being loaded, so he didn't have to hear her.

That night when he came in from the barn, his mother had been in his room. She'd found everything he'd kept that had anything to do with Janice and had taken it and stuffed it in Janice's mailbox. Jerry didn't understand why she was so mad at Janice. Janice hadn't done anything. He was the one who had quit school. He was the one who couldn't do anything right.

After they got the hay in, Jerry went down to the recruiting office and joined the army. His father said that was the only thing to do. His parents were scared to death he'd be shipped right out to Vietnam if he was drafted, but if he volunteered he could go to some kind of training school and maybe stay out of the fighting.

His daddy knew what it was like being shot at from serving in World War II, and he told Jerry he wasn't anxious to see him follow in those particular footsteps.

CHAPTER 10

He had to report to Fort Knox for basic training right away. His father said October would be a good time of the year to do basic. The weather wouldn't be too hot the way it would have been if he'd signed up in July. His dad was just trying to bolster him up. His mother didn't say much. Jerry figured she didn't think he could make the grade.

All his buddies and friends warned him basic training would be awful, but it wasn't all that bad. Jerry had been working on the farm all summer. He was used to getting up at sunrise and working hard every day. He had no problem doing the running and other training exercises. His body got even tougher and stronger as the weeks went past, and he won every award they gave away in basic including an Expert in Marksmanship. Targets were easier to hit than the squirrels and rabbits he used to hunt out on the farm. He even got Colonel's Orderly. He was proud of himself for the first time in he didn't know how long. Even his mother sounded pleased in her letters to him.

His leave time couldn't have worked out better. He finished up basic late in December, and they let him go home for Christmas before being shipped out to his assignment. He wasn't too sure about that, but they'd tested him and decided he was qualified to be an electronic instrument repairman, something the army had a big need for right then.

"I don't want to be an electronic repairman, sir," Jerry had told his training officer when he got notice of his assignment. "I don't know whose tests you've been looking at, but it couldn't have been mine."

"The Army doesn't make those kind of mistakes, Private," the officer had said.

"But I won't be good at electronic anything. My math is bad, and I'm pretty sure you have to know math to do electronics," Jerry had said. "Can't you assign me to something else? Anything else. There's an M.P. school down there, too, isn't there?" He thought he might do okay in M.P. school. He could shoot and he was strong and quick on his feet.

But the officer had just looked at Jerry as if he hadn't said the first word. "You're in the army now, soldier. You'll go where you're assigned when you're assigned and that's all there is to it."

So Jerry had that hanging over him all through Christmas. When he told his father he wished he could just stay in basic, his father said, "Don't worry about it, son. You need to give the school a chance and if it doesn't work out, they'll assign you to something else. Just enjoy your time off. It's Christmas and you've made me and your mother both proud the way you were an honor student in basic and everything. We always knew you could do it."

The training school wasn't ready when his leave was over, so he went back to Ft. Knox for a few weeks until they shipped him out to the Ft. Gordon Electronics School in Georgia. He tried telling them again that he wouldn't make it in the electronics school. He even told them they could test him again to see what he might be able to do but that he still had the feeling he'd make a good M.P. They heard him out but told him the army needed electronic repairmen and he'd have to stay with his assignment.

The first week wasn't bad. He went to the classes and some of what the teachers said even made sense, but then they started expecting him to put wires together, to make things work. The other soldiers around him could do it, but he just looked at those wires and cords and had no idea what they wanted him to do. It was as if they were speaking Japanese. For another week he twisted wires and poked them here and there and tried to look as if he understood Japanese.

Thank goodness somebody always had plenty of beer and pills for the weekends. Some of the guys took the uppers, but he stuck with downers. They went with the booze better.

He didn't know when he decided to walk away from it all. Maybe when he found out he'd get grades in the school. He'd just thought he'd learn a job, then do it, and if he couldn't do that job, they'd let him do something else. But they wouldn't. They kept saying he had to be an electronics repairman. Even the sound of the words made him sick at his stomach.

It wasn't that he didn't try. He tried his best just the way his dad had told him to. He did whatever any of his superior officers said. He didn't speak the first word of disrespect or dissent to Lieutenant Roberts or anybody else. He jumped to do whatever they told him to do, but when he saw that forty-five on his grade sheet, he knew it was hopeless. He told Lt. Roberts that and begged him to let him go somewhere else, even to Vietnam. At least if he died over there it would be for his country and for a cause. But Lt. Roberts told him he couldn't transfer. He had to stay in the electronics school until he learned the job.

Jerry had stood up straighter and said, yes sir. He'd gone back to his barracks, gone back to class, but he knew his next grade wasn't going to be any better. This time he'd not only let down his parents, he'd let down Lt. Roberts and his other commanding officers, his unit, the whole army. He was going to be booted out of the service, sent home in disgrace. All his achievements in basic would be for naught. They didn't care that he could run and shoot. They wanted him to stick wires together.

He tried to talk to the chaplain about it. That's what his parents had told him to do. If he had a problem he should pray about it and ask the chaplain for help. He didn't know he had to go through special channels to see the chaplain. They'd probably told him, but there had been so much to remember that first week. Sergeant Harrod had really let him have it for that. Made him do extra duty. Made him do pushups. Made him polish everybody's shoes. Called him a shirker, a liar, and worse.

And not just the sergeant. The guys in his unit were on him, too. "Aw, Shepherd needs to pray about his grades. Shepherd can't tell a red wire from a white one. Shepherd's a wash out."

One day he just walked off the base. It was either that or punch them in the face until they couldn't talk anymore. He didn't know what he was going to do, but he wasn't going to class again. He didn't have much money and nothing but the clothes on his back. Thank goodness he had his coat. He tried to pray as he walked away from the base, to see if the Lord would point him in some direction, but he just felt blank inside.

He used up most of his money on beer and pills that first week. He hardly knew where he was most of the time, but then the money ran out and he woke up in a junky old Mercury on the back of a car lot. He was hungry. He fingered the change left in his pocket. Some quarters and a few nickels. He could try to get a job, but he was still too close to Ft. Gordon. They'd catch him for sure.

He remembered the story about the prodigal son in the Bible. His daddy was like that father. He had hired hands. Jerry could go home and work for him till they decided what to do. His mother would feed him. She might yell at him but she'd feed him. He went back out on the road and hitched a ride with a guy in a pickup truck and rode as far north as he was going. He told the man he was on leave, going home to see his folks. It was mostly true.

It was raining a little and cold when an old guy in a Chevy dropped him off just across the border into Tennessee. He wanted to ask if he could go home with the old man and warm up, but he didn't. He just said thanks, got out of the car, and started walking.

It was a long time before a salesman picked him up. He had a whole rack of clothes hanging across his back seat. "Poor kid. You look about froze," the man said when Jerry got in. "Where you going?"

"To Kentucky to see my folks."

"Well, how about that? I'm headed to Kentucky, too. I've got a client in Louisville." The man shifted his car into gear and pulled back out on the road.

"That sounds about perfect," Jerry said. Maybe the Lord was watching over him a little after all, because Jerry wasn't sure how much longer he could have made it before he fell in front of a truck. He had no idea how long he'd been on the road. More than a week, he was pretty sure. He was ready to be home.

"Are you in the service? On leave?"

"Yeah, on leave," Jerry said. "Hitching home. You care if I go to sleep?"

"Nope. Go right ahead. You look like you could use the rest. I'll put the heater on high to warm you up." The man flicked a knob and the heater fan roared louder.

"Thanks. That's feels great." Jerry was already half asleep. "Are you an angel?"

The man laughed. "That's the first time anybody's accused me of that since I was a little squirt on my grandma's lap. She thought I was the greatest thing since sliced bread."

It wasn't much trouble getting the rest of the way to the farm after he got to Louisville. Nobody yelled at him when he got home or if they did, he didn't hear them. He hardly knew where he was. If was as if the world was blowing up around him, and he was just standing there letting the debris fly past him. He wasn't even sure he was really standing there in the kitchen.

The next morning things were clearer. After he ate breakfast, his mother went out to feed the animals and left him alone with his dad so they could talk. Jerry told his dad what had happened, how Sergeant Harrod had called him a liar. He'd never been a liar. He was a failure, maybe, no use to anybody for sure, but he wasn't a liar.

"It's okay, son," his dad said. "I know you're not a liar, and he shouldn't have said you were, but army sergeants aren't known for their sweet tempers. They like to bash you over the head just to be bashing something sometimes."

"I told them I couldn't do math, Dad. Why didn't they listen?"

"I don't know, son." His father put his hand on Jerry's arm. They were quiet for a few minutes before his father said, "What are we going to do now?"

"I want to go back, do my duty. I never aimed to run away from my responsibilities, but I just can't do that school. Can you talk to them, Dad?"

"I've been talking to the lieutenant down there ever since you went off the base."

"What did he say? Will they put me in the stockade?"

"No, I don't think so. He said it was a minor disciplinary problem, but if you went on back, they'd work it out with you."

"You never had this kind of trouble when you were in the service, did you, sir?"

"No, but that was different. They let me do something I wanted to do."

"Do you think I could fly bomber planes?"

"Not in the army. Maybe we should have tried for the Air Force or Navy, but I didn't think your grades were good enough for that."

"I like the army okay. Do you think they'd let me go to Vietnam?"

"Let's not look that direction just yet, son. You don't want to go over there if you can keep from it."

"It'd be better than the electronics school." Jerry felt the sick feeling in his stomach just saying the name of the school. "So they said I could just come back?"

"Lieutenant Roberts told us to send you back as soon as you got home and he'd take care of everything. Are you sure that's what you want to do, Jerry?"

"Yes sir. They'll have to transfer me somewhere else now, don't you think?"

"I don't know, son, but you talk to them when you get back and I'll talk to them, too. I think you might need some extra medical help, maybe some counseling. They are supposed to have good counselors there at Ft. Gordon."

His father put him on a plane to Atlanta. He'd called the base and asked if they'd pick Jerry up, but they said getting back was Jerry's problem. He'd have to get back to Ft. Gordon however he could. Nobody would come pick him up. Jerry told his dad it would be okay. He'd take a bus or hitchhike if he couldn't find the right bus. It wasn't that far. Even if he had to walk, he'd get there. He told his father not to worry.

But neither of them had counted on the military police at the Atlanta airport.

CHAPTER 11

The guy grabbed him before he could get out of the airport to go look for a bus. He said he was military police.

"You look like a soldier who's going where he ain't supposed to be going," the man said as he put his hand on Jerry's shoulder. One of the man's arms could have made two of Jerry's, and he looked ready to crush Jerry with one blow. His face was cold and hard as his nearly black eyes bored into Jerry.

"Hey, let go of me." Jerry tried to jerk free of the man's hold, but it was like trying to push a five hundred pound boulder off him. "I've been on leave and I'm headed back to my base."

"Yeah, kid, and I'm on the next rocket to the moon," the guy said as he clapped a pair of handcuffs on Jerry's wrists.

"You can't do that."

"Yeah, I just did. Now shut up and don't give me no problems. A few days in the cage will get you in a more truthful frame of mind."

"Call them at Ft. Gordon. They'll tell you I'm on the way back there."

"We'll check it out," the man said. "When we get the time. No sense getting in no big hurry. There's other deserters just like you out here begging us to catch them."

"I'm not a deserter," Jerry said, but the man didn't even glance around at him.

They put him in a cage, a freestanding cell made of metal bars. There wasn't even a bed. Another guy, in a similar cage on the other side of the room, kept his eyes fixed on the floor as if he was afraid the big man might take notice of him there. After the man went out of the room, the other prisoner looked up warily and said his name was Paul and that he'd been there two days. He said things weren't going to get any better for Jerry.

"I wouldn't treat a dog like this," the guy said.

"Are they really MP's?" Jerry asked.

"Who knows what they are." Paul looked even younger than Jerry. His face was pale under the faint shadow of a two-day growth of beard. He sneaked a peek at the door and added, "Other than scary."

"Shut up in there," somebody yelled from the next room.

"Hey, I've got to go take a leak," Jerry yelled back.

"Well, you should've thought about that before you got yourself all locked up," the man in the next room yelled back.

"If you keep hollering long enough, they'll finally let you go," the guy named Paul said after a minute. "But you have to get hoarse first."

"They have to let us call somebody. They can't just stick us in here and not let us call somebody."

"They haven't let me call nobody yet. I'd even call my sergeant who hates my guts and let him make me do pushups till I puked to get out of here." Paul kept his voice low "I may just go clean off my rocker if I have to sit here much longer."

"How about food?"

"They pitched me a couple of hotdogs yesterday. Not cooked, but they weren't bad. Better than the stale crackers and cheese the day before."

"This can't be happening. Not in America." Jerry stared over at Paul who just looked back at him. "Can it?"

"We ain't both in the same nightmare. Then again maybe we are. A wide awake nightmare."

The nightmare went on and on. Jerry jumped up and down and shouted and yelled, but it was still two hours before they let him out to go to the john. After that he sat down on the floor in the corner and wrapped his hands around his knees. He wouldn't let them break him. They'd have to let him call somebody sooner or later. Till then somehow he'd have to keep his mind on something else to keep from going crazy. He tried to remember every Bible verse he'd ever learned in Bible School. And then he sang songs in his head until he fell asleep sitting up.

The days and nights ran together. More men were shoved with them into the cages. They talked a little, but not much. There wasn't much to talk about. They took the first guy, Paul, out first. Then they came for Jerry on the third or fourth day. He wasn't sure. He'd lost track of the days and nights.

They put him in an MP van and drove him back to Ft. Gordon. Jerry was almost glad to see the place, to see any place besides where he'd been for the last few days. He was hungry. He hoped they'd let him eat before they disciplined him.

Lt. Roberts met with him when he got to the school. He said he was giving Jerry another chance, to go back to his barracks, and clean up. He didn't want to hear about where Jerry had been or what had happened to him in Atlanta. He didn't want to hear about Jerry wanting another assignment. He didn't want to hear that Jerry would like to talk to the chaplain. All he wanted to hear was yes sir. So that's what Jerry said.

When the sergeant and the other guys in the barracks got through making fun of him that night, Jerry wrote his parents after lights out by the moonlight filtering through the window. He told them about what had happened in Atlanta. He told them the lieutenant wouldn't listen. He told them he couldn't go back to the school. He told them he loved his country, but he couldn't do what his officers wanted him to do. He told them he'd rather die than go back to school. He told them he thought dying sounded like the best plan he'd made for days. Then he signed it "your loving son."

He folded the letter, put it in an envelope, and stuck it in the mail slot the next morning. He ate breakfast at the mess hall. Then he walked off the base instead of going to class. Maybe the MP would find him again and this time Jerry would fight him and maybe the big guy would just mash him into nothing.

He headed home, hitchhiking again. He needed to be at home. He'd be safe there. His father would help him. He was hungry, half out of his head. He had a few cold medicine pills in his pocket and he took them just to keep his feet moving up the road. He tried to sing some songs he'd sung a hundred times, but the words kept slipping away from him. He got some rides but he didn't remember much about any of them.

Then he found himself in a town that looked almost familiar, and he pulled himself out of his fog long enough to recognize where he was. He used to visit his grandparents here. They were dead now, but his Uncle Silas and Aunt Betty still lived there. It was late. He didn't have a ride. He didn't even see a concrete bridge he could bed down under. It was spitting snow and he was cold. He found the house. It wasn't any trouble getting in the basement. They never kept their doors locked. He'd just camp out there until morning. They'd never even have to know he was there.

He thought the house was empty the next morning when he woke up. He was still hungry. His Aunt Betty wouldn't miss a little food, so he crept up the steps to go see what she might have in the refrigerator. Or maybe he could swipe a jar of peanut butter. He could almost smell the peanuts. He wouldn't bother hunting crackers or bread. He'd just dig the peanut butter out with his fingers and lick it off.

He was in the living room when he heard Aunt Betty humming in the kitchen. He ducked down behind the couch in the living room. He wasn't sure why except he didn't want her to see him like this—dirty, needing a shave, so hungry he was ready to steal. He pulled the collar of his coat up high over part of his face. He'd just lie there quiet as a mouse on the floor until she went out or down to the basement or somewhere. Then he'd slip away. He thought regretfully of the peanut butter jar that was sure to be there in her cabinet, but he couldn't just stand up now and say hello, Aunt Betty. It would scare her, him being right there in the middle of the living room.

He had a bad feeling when he heard her get out the sweeper, but maybe she'd just hit the high spots. He should have known better. Not his Aunt Betty. She had to poke the sweeper everywhere. She screamed when she saw him just the way he'd known she would. He jumped up and kept his coat collar up around his face while he said, "Don't. Don't scream!"

In two minutes he was out the door. She never even knew it was him. It was better that way. She thought he was a good boy, doing whatever he was supposed to be doing, not running away from his duty with the army. But they shouldn't have made him do the electronics stuff. He could have scrubbed toilets, anything, as long as it didn't take math.

He let his mind just go into idle as he walked away from Aunt Betty's neighborhood through backyards and across fences. Dogs barked at him, but he hardly noticed. He just wanted to get far away in case Aunt Betty had called the police. It felt almost like being home when he got back out on the highway. And he got a ride right away. The guy even let Jerry have a handful of the chips he was eating before Jerry nodded off.

It took him three days to get home, the same amount of time Jesus was in the tomb. Jerry felt sort of like he was in a tomb and hadn't come out. He didn't think he could come out.

It was snowing and cold and the middle of the night. He stood in the driveway and stared at the dark house until his coat sleeves and hat had a thick layer of snow on them. Then he went to the barn and started the old farm truck. Maybe the barn would be tight enough to keep the fumes in. He'd heard carbon monoxide poisoning wasn't a bad way to die. You just went to sleep and didn't wake up. He didn't want to wake up. There was no reason for him to wake up.

But he did. The truck ran out of gas. The cold crept back and shook him awake. It was still dark, hours before daylight. Jerry climbed through a window into the garage and found an old heater. He wanted to be warm. More than he wanted to eat. More than he wanted to sleep somewhere soft. More than he wanted to breathe almost.

The next morning when his father went out to feed, he spotted Jerry's footprints in the snow. He found him in the garage before Jerry woke up. His father didn't fuss at him. He didn't even look mad as he put his arms around Jerry and pulled him into the warmth of the kitchen. His mother didn't yell at him either. She just looked at him while tears rolled down her cheeks. He wanted to tell her things weren't that bad, that she didn't have to cry. He opened his mouth, but no words would come out of the empty dead place he was in.

He ate and he slept. His parents talked to him. He wasn't sure what they said, not in words, but they wanted him to go back. They said he couldn't stay AWOL. So he told them he wanted to go back. Didn't he always do what people wanted him to do? He was an obedient son. A soldier ready to do his duty. He didn't lie. He knew the Ten Commandments. Honor your father and mother. Stop failing at everything you do. Be tough. Stick it out in the army.

Sunday morning, his parents skipped church to drive him back to Ft. Gordon. They talked about the farm, about how Jerry could partner with him after he got out of the service. They talked about what they thought Jerry might do well in the army. They didn't talk about him going back into the electronics school. It was as if that couldn't happen.

The army didn't agree. His father waited out in the hall while Jerry reported back to Sergeant Harrod on Monday morning, March 3. Jerry tried to explain. "Sir, I've just been mixed up in my mind, but I went home and talked to my parents and they've helped me see things straight now. I enlisted. I want to serve my country. But I just can't stay in the school. I don't know how to do what they want me to do, sir. So I'm respectfully requesting a transfer. I'll serve anywhere else. Do anything else. Go anywhere. Even Vietnam."

"Vietnam?! A lily livered sorry excuse for a soldier like you wouldn't last two days in Nam and while that might be a favor to the army and the country in general, you're so pathetically inept, you'd take half your unit down with you."

"No sir, I wouldn't do that. I could handle it, sir."

The sergeant let out a long line of curses. Jerry tried to shut his ears, but the words barked through until he wanted to curl up in the floor and put his arms over his head. Instead he stood ramrod straight. His father was out in the hall. His father had been a soldier. His father had said to just do whatever they told him to do and he'd get by. The sergeant paused in his rampage and Jerry shouted, "Yes sir."

"And not only that, you're a liar, Shepherd. You can do the work at this school. Your tests show you can. You just aren't giving it the effort the army demands. So stop lying and running away and do your duty."

"Yes sir," Jerry shouted again.

"Now get your contemptible sorry face out of my office, go draw your billet supplies and get an assignment to a billet in the quarters. And don't let me ever catch you trying to run away from your duty again."

"Yes sir," Jerry said again. He did what the sergeant said. He told his father goodbye and did what the sergeant said.

Everybody was on him. The ridicule circled him like buzzards circling a dead possum. Even after the mouths of the men around him quit moving and they all went to sleep, the horrible things they said echoed in his ears all night.

In the morning he wrote something upbeat on the birthday card he had for his father and stuck it in the mail slot before he went to buy some cold pills. The clerk looked at the three packages of pills and then Jerry. "Expecting an epidemic, soldier?"

Jerry managed a smile before he wiped his nose on the back of his hand. "Just getting extra for some of my buddies. A bad cold's going around our barracks."

The barracks was empty when he went back to his bunk. Everybody was at the school learning to twist wires. It took Jerry a long time to push all thirty of the cold pills out of their foil squares. He'd push out five and swallow them and then push out five more. And then he said a prayer for his mother and father and lay back down on his bunk. It felt good to go to sleep.

CHAPTER 12

Letters from home:

March 6, 1969
Dear Jerry,

As usual our regular guests (the Bertrams!) were here so I couldn't get a letter mailed. We also had to go to Shelbyville to finish setting up the loan for the dairy. The cistern is almost finished. They won't work tomorrow because it's snowing hard now.

Monday, we got to Mary's at 7 p.m. She wanted us to stay over Tuesday so we left there Wed. morning and got home about 7 p.m. I saw nothing in the Carolinas that I want, but Virginia is O.K. and some of Georgia. Dewey says your Base is beautiful.

Jerry, I hope your card to your Dad means what he thinks it does, that things are working out good, that you got your February pay.

We told you exactly how things were, Jerry. Dewey fought hard to see that you had a good home and love. We both deeply regret that we didn't realize long ago that we were making a mistake by not telling you. None of the things that happened before Dewey and I met was yours or Dewey's fault. You have nothing to regret or be ashamed of. We are proud of you, Jerry.

And we are not mistaken! You do have a good mind and ability. Talk to your Sergeant or Lt. If you stay in school, give it all you've got. If you & the Army decide on something else, put the past behind you—forget it. Look ahead.

Can't write another page. It won't go in the envelope. Call once a week, Jerry. And write when you can. Remember—we never have nor ever will, turn our back on you. Take care of yourself.

Love always, Mom

Dear Jerry,

Your birthday card and money came in the mail today. Do you think I should spend all the money on our special gal, or keep it and spend it on a big milk cow? Son, I hope you're back on regular status by now. We got home at 7:00 p.m. Wed. We had a nice trip. Everything here was just like we left it except the snow was gone. Yesterday and today were pretty days, but the snow is falling out there right now. We went into Shelbyville today and left your car at Mr. Shaddocks so he could sell it for you. So, I hope it will sell right away so you will have a little money for your bank account.

The pigs insulted me this morning, from the way they acted, they didn't even miss me. I believe they liked Harvey just as well. Everything is just set and ready to build the milking parlor when the weather lets up.

Jerry, we miss you around here very much and we are looking forward to the day you can be back and try your hand at milking cows. Your ma will have plenty of good old cold milk to make homemade ice cream.

Son, we love you with everything we have got and we hope that with your help and God's help we have been able to explain enough about your life as a child, that you can overcome this empty feeling you have had so long. Son, I hope you will be able to get things straight in the army. Please don't let things get you down in the dumps. When you are in the dumps your pa is in the dumps and I don't like it in the dumps.

Jerry, I know this sounds crazy, but we are very close to each other. The distance we are apart in miles don't mean a thing as far as the way we feel about you. We are where we will be waiting for you when your Army enlistment is over. Jerry, you are just as much a part of our lives as any son could be, you being in the Army and away from home don't have anything to do with the way we feel about you, or effect the place you fill in our home, yours, your ma's and mine.

Right now our greatest hope is for you to be satisfied and happy in the Army for the duration of your enlistment. Son, I am looking forward to hearing from you soon.

Love, your Dad

Letters returned to sender due to soldier going A.W.O.L.

CHAPTER 13

He didn't die. Suicide must have something to do with math. That's why he could never do it right.

He woke up in the infirmary. They pumped his stomach and said he was okay to go. Back to duties. Back to school. He didn't report back anywhere.

He went straight to the chapel. His head was spinning. He felt sick. It was all he could do to lift one foot in front of the other. He wished the pills had worked. He wished he was still asleep. He wished he were dead.

The chapel was dim and quiet. No one was there, not even the chaplain. Jerry held his head and tried to think. He wasn't supposed to just try to see the chaplain on his own. He was supposed to ask somebody, but he couldn't remember who.

He decided to sit down in the back of the chapel and see if his head would clear a little. He softly sang the Lord's Prayer. He hadn't forgotten everything.

He liked it in the chapel. It was peaceful. The Lord was there and hadn't a Sunday school teacher somewhere told him once that Jesus loved him no matter what he did? Jerry needed somebody to love him, but he doubted right then that even Jesus could. He'd done everything anybody could do wrong.

It was probably even wrong to fall asleep in the chapel, but that's what he did. He lay on the very back pew and went to sleep. The sound of a door opening somewhere woke him up. Without thinking why, Jerry rolled off the pew and silently hit the floor. The feet moved past him toward the front of the church. They looked like regular army issue shoes. Jerry didn't know if chaplains wore special shoes or not. Then the man was kneeling at the front, saying a prayer.

Jerry crawled under the pews and slipped out into the side rooms.

"Is somebody there?" a voice called from the chapel.

Jerry slid into a supply closet. He sat down in the corner between some brooms to wait till the chapel was empty again. He didn't actually decide consciously to stay in the chapel. He just did. Nobody ever saw him. They'd come in and out, but nobody ever looked under the pews. The hours passed.

At first he was too sick to even think about food, but after a while—he had no idea how long—his stomach began demanding food. It was dark when he sneaked out of the chapel and went looking for food. He found the telephone first. He ignored it, but then he saw another phone and another until it seemed like a sign. He dialed his parents' number. When his mother said hello, he tried to sound normal as if everything was going almost all right.

"I've been sick. I had a fainting spell and the doctors wanted to check me out to be sure I hadn't had a stroke or something." He didn't know where the bit about the stroke came from. Old people had strokes. People his age didn't have strokes except maybe heat strokes. And it was winter now. He wondered if the doctors had told him something about a stroke or if that had just floated up from nowhere. He wished some food would float up from nowhere.

His mother was asking questions. He answered her, but he had no idea whether he was making sense or not. He didn't know much about what happened to somebody when they had a stroke. There was something about being paralyzed. He felt half paralyzed now, so that's what he told his mother. That he'd been a little paralyzed, but he was okay now. Saying he felt paralyzed wasn't as much of a lie as saying he was okay now. They talked for a few minutes. He had no idea what else he said. Words were coming out of his mouth, but it was empty noise. Noise with no meaning.

He wandered around the base for half the night, staying away from lights and people. Toward morning, he spotted some workers going into the PX. They didn't lock the doors behind them. He waited a few minutes and slipped inside. The only food that he didn't have to venture too far out into the light to swipe was the candy on the counter by the door. Gingerly he picked up two chocolate bars. Then he was back out the door and five minutes later back in the chapel. Somebody had left a candle burning. Jerry stood by it and looked at the candy bars. He'd never stolen anything before. Ever.

Thou shalt not steal. It was in the Bible. Maybe the Lord would strike him down for eating stolen candy bars in the chapel. Jerry pulled back the wrappers and ate the candy bars one after the other. Nothing happened. He went into the rest room and drank out of the sink.

The sun came up and went down. People came in and out of the chapel. He stayed out of sight. He stole more candy bars. He slept. When he woke up, he lay still as a stone and stared up at the bottoms of the pews. Some of them had chewing gum stuck on them. He didn't try to peel it off. He didn't want to move. He thought about the chaplain finding his bones under the pews five years from now.

He didn't think about what he should do. He couldn't think. Everything was too confusing. Everything was in a fog over to the side. He tried to reach into the fog and come up with a plan but then his hand just got lost, too. A few times he came to himself enough to wish he was at home working on the farm with his father and eating whatever his mother had cooked that day, but he couldn't go home. They would just tell him to come back, to do what the army said he had to do even if he couldn't.

He started out keeping count of the times the sun came up and went down, but after a while he quit noticing the sun. He was just drifting in a timeless void. And then the hunger became a mighty roar inside him. He couldn't ignore it. He had to get something to eat no matter what he had to do to get it. He cleaned up as best he could in the rest room and went to the mess hall. He still had his meal ticket. He could get breakfast.

He had never seen anything that looked as good as those eggs and bacon strips. He ate one of the biscuits on the way to a table back in the corner. He should have just stuffed the food in his pockets and walked on out the door. He hadn't even finished the eggs before Sergeant Harrod and another sergeant nabbed him. Jerry shoveled in a few more bites as fast as he could before they made him stand up and leave the food.

They took him out of the dining room to another area and assigned another soldier to watch him. The specialist looked kind so Jerry asked him if he could have another glass of milk. When the man told Jerry to go get it himself, Jerry just walked on out the back door. It was that easy. He didn't stop walking until he was off the base. He hid out for a while in some trees till it was almost dark. Then he started walking again.

He needed a car. The first place he passed was a dry cleaning store with a garage beside it. It was closed down for the day. He went around to the back, found a jack handle on the ground, and broke out a window in the door. After that it was easy to get in. He fished a few coins out of a jar there before he tried to break through the door into the garage. He pushed his shoulder into it, but it didn't budge. He jumped at it with his feet, but it held tight.

He couldn't open the door. He should have been able to knock open the door. He couldn't do anything right. In a rage, he grabbed what looked like a piece of a broomstick off the floor and began beating everything in sight. Things crashed off the shelves and broke. Racks of clothes in plastic bags tumbled to the floor. He kept swinging the stick until there wasn't anything left to break. Then he went outside, found the jack piece he'd used to break the window in the door and beat on the garage door till it finally broke in half.

The keys were in the 1963 Chevy inside the garage. It started, but ran rough. Still the fuel gauge showed it had almost a full tank of gas. If he could keep it running, it would get him on down the road. Where he didn't know. Anywhere away from the base.

He hadn't gotten far when he spotted a hitchhiker. He slammed on the brakes before he thought about what he was doing. The guy looked rough, but he was glad enough for the ride.

"Where you going?" the hitchhiker asked him as he got in.

"Just traveling," Jerry said. "How about you?"

"Yeah, me too. Just going on down the road."

They rode a ways before the guy said he was thirsty and that if Jerry would stop, he'd buy them both some beer. Jerry hadn't eaten hardly anything for a couple of weeks so the alcohol exploded in his system. He couldn't see straight, much less drive straight. He told the hitchhiker he was going to have to stop, grab a few zzz's, and let his head clear. The guy pointed out a motel up ahead where they could park awhile. He said they might even find somebody to help them out if they knew how to take advantage of whatever came along.

The hitchhiker didn't tell Jerry his name. Said to just call him Butch and he'd call Jerry Buddy. He said sometimes names could get a man into trouble and that Jerry looked as if he had enough trouble already without piling on a useless name.

Jerry didn't care. He didn't need a name. He needed a plan. A what to do next idea. Something besides heading home again. He wasn't some kind of homing pigeon. Hadn't he run off to California and disappeared in New Jersey for weeks?

Jerry pulled the car into the motel parking lot. He barely got it between the white lines before the motor wheezed and stopped. Just for the heck of it, Jerry tried to start it again, but the old Chevy had had enough.

"Piece of junk," Jerry muttered. He wished he'd left off some of the beers because his head was too addled to figure out how to get the car running again. Of course it was almost out of gas anyway and Jerry didn't have any money for gas. Butch probably didn't either, now that they'd spent his money on booze.

"Don't worry about it, Buddy." The hitchhiker was peering out the window as if looking for something or somebody as he kept talking, "We'll find another car. Cars are everywhere. The parking lot is full of them."

Jerry was half dozing when the hitchhiker poked him in the shoulder. "Come on, let's go over there where that old guy is carrying in his bags. I need to use the john."

The man with the bags propped open his motel door and headed back to his car. Jerry followed the hitchhiker into the room. While the hitchhiker kept watch, Jerry stumbled back to the bathroom, used the john, and splashed some water on his face. He couldn't get his head straight. Black balls kept popping up in front of his eyes.

When Jerry opened the bathroom door he heard a bunch of screaming and hollering. His heart began pounding hard. He didn't know what was going on. All he knew was that he had to get out of the room. He tried to run for the door, but some old guy stepped in front of him and started screaming in his face. His spit sprayed Jerry's nose.

"Please just move so I can get out of here," Jerry begged. "I don't want to hurt you. Please."

But the man kept screaming in his face. Jerry's heart was crashing madly back and forth in his chest and he couldn't get enough air. He was going to die if he didn't get to the door. He had to get out. He started swinging. His fist made contact with somebody, but Jerry wasn't sure who. Maybe the old man. Maybe somebody else. Somebody who was in Jerry's way. Somebody who was keeping him from getting out of the room. Somebody who kept screaming at him.

And then the face in front of him changed, shifted, became his mother's face. Jerry kept swinging, kept pounding his fists into whoever was between him and the door. His fists beat into the flesh over and over.

CHAPTER 14

When Jerry came to himself, he was lying on the floor beside the body of a man he'd never seen before. It wasn't the hitchhiker. He'd been young. This guy was old. And dead. No doubt and absolutely positively dead.

Nobody else was in the room. The hitchhiker was gone. The door was closed. Jerry had blood on his hands.

He looked at the man on the floor and tried to will him to breathe. When the man's chest stayed still, Jerry closed his eyes and tried to wish himself somewhere else. Back in the chapel hiding under the pews just dreaming all this. At home in his bedroom waiting for the sun to come up so he could go work out in the fields. Out on the road running three miles. Anywhere but here. He eased his eyes open. The man was still there. Still not breathing.

Jerry didn't ask the Lord for forgiveness. How could the Lord forgive this? *Thou shalt not kill.* But he did whisper the 23rd Psalm as he pulled the bedspread off the bed to cover the man's body. That made things easier. It was like he'd made the man disappear. He hoped the poor man's family wouldn't grieve for him too much. He was old. And alone. Maybe nobody would miss him that much.

Jerry went to the bathroom and threw up in the commode. Then he washed his hands until he almost scrubbed the skin off them. He rubbed off his shoes with one of the towels and then went back out into the motel room. The body was still there under the cover.

Jerry sat down on the bed and tried to think. He didn't know what to do. The black balls came in front of his eyes again and he thought he was going to faint. He breathed in and out slowly until the room came into focus again. A car started up outside. That's what he needed. A car. He had to get away.

The man's wallet, keys, and a few quarters and pennies were on the table beside the bed. Jerry picked up the wallet and opened it to look at the man's driver's license. Edward Baylor from New York. He was seventy-three. That might be easy enough to change to twenty-three. He checked for money but the back pocket of the wallet was empty. The vinyl picture pockets were filled up with credit cards instead of pictures. Jerry was glad. He didn't want to see any pictures of a smiling wife or kids.

He stuck the wallet in his pocket along with the man's keys. He picked up the closed suitcase off the luggage rack. The man was bigger than Jerry, but some of his clothes might fit well enough. He started to go through the man's clothes right then and there. Change out of the ones he had on, but he had to get out of there. Get away from the body under the bedspread.

He lifted up the edge of the heavy curtain on the window and peeked out. The parking lot was empty. No sign of the hitchhiker. No sign of anyone. It was late. Everybody was asleep.

Jerry opened the door inch by inch in case somebody was waiting on the other side of the door to get the drop on him, but nobody was there in the shadows. He put the "Do not disturb" sign on the outside doorknob and pulled the door shut. Then he went to the man's car, a gray 1969 Grand Prix. The man must have been well off.

Jerry glanced around again before he bent down and fumbled with the keys until he found the right one to fit the door lock. He felt safer once inside the car. He started it up and backed out of the parking space. He didn't turn on the headlights until he was pulling out of the motel parking lot.

He kept waiting to hear sirens racing up behind him, but the night was quiet. Almost too quiet. He breathed easier when he pulled back out onto the interstate headed south. He wondered again what had happened to Butch, the hitchhiker. Maybe there had never even been a hitchhiker. Maybe there hadn't been a dead man in the motel room. But then where did he get the car? The thing that was hardest to think on was his mother's face in the dark and the way he'd kept beating the man, feeling his fists slam into the man's body but seeing his mother's face.

It was too hard to think about. He just pushed it way to the back of his mind and slammed a door tight shut on it. He'd think about it later. Right now he had to keep driving. He had to get away. He never wanted to see Richmond Hills, Georgia again.

Maybe he could get lost in Florida. He already felt lost. He could never go home now. Not after what he'd done. He was lost in every way a person could be lost.

◆   ◆   ◆

In Florida, people were already soaking up the sunshine on the beaches even though it was still March. Nobody paid much attention to one more guy sleeping on a towel on the sand. After he bought some soap and a razor and took a shower in the beach house, he felt almost like a real person again as he sat in the sun and ate some powdered doughnuts. Still he had no idea what he was going to do besides sit there and watch the waves come in and go out and listen to the sea gulls and sandpipers. He couldn't be any place more different than home.

The second day out on the beach, some guy came over and plopped down beside Jerry in the sand. "Hey, what's up?" the guy said. He looked about the same age as Jerry but had longer hair. No soldier for sure. "You from around here?"

"Naw. I'm from up north. It's still cold up there," Jerry said.

"Yeah, tell me about it. I'm from up north, too. New Jersey. It's nearly always cold up there," the guy said with a grin.

"New Jersey? Sure enough. I used to know some folks up there. Harmons," Jerry said.

"Never knew anybody by that name. I'm Richard Chiles." The guy stuck his hand out toward Jerry. "Friends call me Rich."

Jerry shook his hand and said, "Ed." His tongue tripped a little as he said the name even though he'd practiced saying it in case he needed to use the man's driver's license for identification. He cleared his throat and tried to speak more convincingly. "Eddie Baylor from New York."

"The big city?"

"No, New York state. Up a ways from New York City." Jerry had looked up the man's town on the New York map in the car. He changed the subject. "But who wants to talk about the frozen north when we're here soaking up rays on the beach?"

"Not me." Rich said. He gave Jerry a long look. "You got a place to stay?"

"Nope. I just got out of the service a few weeks ago and I've been bumming around ever since. Not too anxious to go back to winter up north. But I'm sort of short on cash so I've just been hanging out on the beach."

"Yeah. I thought I saw you out here yesterday, too."

"It's not too bad as long as the sun's shining," Jerry said.

"I noticed you getting out of a pretty nice car there a while ago. I've got this friend down in Coral Gables. If you want to give me a ride down there, we can crash at his place for a while. I even know a place where you might make some cash doing some modeling over at the college there. You've got an interesting face and good muscles."

"I'm not taking off my clothes for somebody to draw me."

"No, no. Nothing like that. You get to keep your clothes on and it's easy enough money. Think about it. You might want to give it a try when we get there."

It seemed as good a plan as any. He needed somebody to talk to. He needed to get some new faces in front of the dead face of Edward Baylor. And once he got down to Coral Gables, Rich and his buddies had beer and dope. Jerry turned down the marijuana and cocaine, but he was glad enough to swallow the beer and downers. If he passed out, he didn't have to think. And not thinking was what he wanted to do.

He did some modeling. It gave him too much time to think, but as Rich said, it was easy cash money. Then one day Rich said, "Hey, how about we drive up to Jersey? It won't be snowing there now."

"You sure about that?"

"Well, no, but we can give it a try."

They drove straight through. Jerry used the credit cards from the man's wallet for gas. Nobody ever looked even halfway suspicious. Up in New Jersey, they stayed with Rich's folks. When Rich got out his guitar and Jerry sang a couple of songs for him, Rich got all excited and got them a gig at a lodge in the next town. Jerry sang and Rich played his guitar while the people drank and talked. Sometimes they listened to the music and clapped a little. It didn't matter how much they listened. It was just more easy cash money.

Being in New Jersey kept Mama Harmon on Jerry's mind. Mama Harmon might be able to tell him what he should do. It wasn't like he'd be able to keep running from the police forever. Sooner or later they'd catch up with him. And even if they didn't, he couldn't live with what he'd done. He thought about turning himself in. He just didn't know how. Should he just walk up to some policeman and confess? He thought about what he'd say. "Hello, my name is Jerry Shepherd. I think I killed a man in Georgia. No, change that. I did kill a man in Georgia. I've been driving his car, using his credit cards. You need to lock me up."

He thought about doing it, confessing, but he kept running away from it at the same time. He couldn't imagine being locked up. Not forever. He remembered his days in Atlanta when the MP's had picked him up. He couldn't stand that. Maybe he'd just let the police shoot him on the spot. But they wouldn't do that if he gave himself up.

Mama Harmon might be able to make sense of some of the stuff that had been happening to him. Maybe she could read him something out of the Bible that would fill up the empty hole inside him. The beer and pills weren't doing too good a job of that anymore.

He went to the right town. He remembered the stores, the church, but nobody he talked to knew Mama Harmon or Pete. Some of them said they thought the last name sounded familiar but if they had ever lived there, they didn't now. How could that be? The whole family couldn't have just disappeared. Had they even been real? Maybe they'd been angels the Lord had put there to help him and then they'd just disappeared. Gone to some other town to help some other poor sucker.

That was stupid, he told himself. Of course they were real people. Then where were they now? Thinking about it made his head pound as he drove back to Rich's house.

He was glad when Rich suggested going back to Florida. They'd only been in Jersey a few days, but Rich said it was just too cold. He was ready for some more Florida sunshine and they had a little cash from the gig at the lodge.

But it wasn't any better in Florida. Warmer, but no better. Jerry had a bad feeling the police might be closing in on him. He didn't want to cause Rich and his friends trouble, and if the police came after Jerry they'd be sure to see the marijuana and cocaine. He crashed one night at the friend's house in Coral Gables. The next day he dropped Rich off at the college to do some modeling.

"I should be through around six, Eddie. I'll pick up my pay and then we can go get some weed," Rich said when he got out of the car. "Tomorrow we can check around the clubs here to see if they need some music."

Jerry just smiled and waved. When he pulled back out on the highway, he turned the Grand Prix to the north. He had no idea where he was going. He just kept driving. He stopped at a motel in Jacksonville to get some sleep. The next morning he went to the restaurant beside the motel for breakfast. After he ate, he gave them Edward Baylor's credit card. They told him it wasn't any good.

"Gee, I can't imagine what the problem could be," Jerry said. He tried not to look worried, but his heart was pounding inside his chest. "But I've got some cash out in my car. I'll go get it and be right back."

He didn't have cash in his car. He didn't have any money at all. He just got into the car, started it up and drove away. No sirens followed him, but it wouldn't be long. He had one credit card he hadn't used. Maybe it would still get him gas to go home. They were going to catch him, but he wanted to see his folks one more time first.

He turned the nose of the car toward Kentucky and kept the tires rolling north. He was going home one more time. Maybe for the last time.

CHAPTER 15

Jerry thought he wanted to go home. All the time he was driving north, he planned to just drive straight to his parents' house, but then when he was actually on I 64 with the green Shelbyville exit sign before him he couldn't do it. He kept driving and went to Oldham County instead, back to where he'd lived before they'd moved to Shelby County and everything had gone bad. He drove past their old farm. It didn't look the same. The barn roof was sagging a little. The cows looked too skinny out in the field. They weren't their cows. It wasn't their farm any longer.

He drove to Billy's house. Billy had always been a good friend. He'd let him crash a couple of days while Jerry figured out whether he could go home or not. He just needed time to work up the courage to face his mother and father after what he'd done. And he'd have to tell them. They'd want to know what had happened to him, and he couldn't lie to them. But how could he tell them that he'd killed a man? He could hardly believe it himself. There had to be two Jerry Shepherds. Him, the real Jerry Shepherd who wouldn't hurt anybody, and the other Jerry Shepherd, the one who had done that horrible thing in Richmond Hills, Georgia.

He told Billy his folks had bought him the car for a late graduation present, but they were upset at him for getting booted out of the army and so he needed a few days to let them cool off. Billy acted as if he believed Jerry's story, but every once in a while Jerry would catch Billy frowning at him when he thought Jerry wasn't looking.

The third day he was back in Kentucky, Jerry drove over to his folks' house. It was Wednesday night. He knew they'd be at church. They always went to church every time the doors were open, and he thought it might be easier to go in the house if nobody was home. He never thought about there being a note on the door for him. He sat in the car for a few minutes staring at the sheet of notebook paper stuck on the front door. There was writing on it, but he couldn't read it from the car. Maybe the note wasn't for him. Maybe they were expecting company after church. They wouldn't be expecting him. Not unless somebody had spotted him driving around town. Or Billy's folks had called them. That might have happened.

He got out, but left the car running with the door open. He didn't pull the note off the door. It was his mother's handwriting.

Dear Son,

If you see this, please don't leave without talking to us. We can't help you if we can't find you.

We love you so much, Jerry, and this is tearing us to pieces. So I know what it's doing to you. We will help you straighten this out however you think you should. We know a good lawyer.

We love you, so please don't refuse to let us help you.

Mom & Dad

Jerry felt as if somebody had just gut punched him. He stumbled off the porch and ran back to the car. He couldn't go in. He couldn't let them see him. He couldn't tell them what he'd done.

As he drove away the words he'd read kept running through his head. They wanted to help him. They loved him. They knew a lawyer. Did they already know what he'd done or were they just talking about the Army? He had to have time to think, time to figure out what to do.

He drove around a while, not paying much attention to where he was. Finally he went back to Billy's. Billy looked worried.

"Are you sure you're all right, Jerry? I mean you'd tell me if something bad was going on, wouldn't you?" Billy asked.

"Sure I would. You're my buddy," Jerry said. "I'm just worried about my folks. You know how it is."

"Yeah, well, you need to talk to them. You can't keep putting it off."

"I won't. I'll go tomorrow." Maybe by morning he could work up his courage. He spent most of the night staring up at the ceiling in the dark room and rehearsing what he was going to say to his parents. Once or twice he reached over and touched his Bible on the table beside the bed. When the sun came up, he whispered a prayer, "Please don't let this be too hard on my folks, Lord."

So he had been headed home, had just gone across the line into Shelby County when he'd seen the police lights behind him. They'd been waiting for him as if they'd known he'd be coming down that road, as if someone had tipped them off that he was going home. He hadn't stopped. He'd mashed down on the gas and outrun them, could have kept outrunning them if he hadn't been so low on gas. Now he was in the back of the police car listening to the men in the front seat talk in their radios and the crackling sound of the other officers talking back. Sirens were still wailing in the distance. All that noise because of him.

He wished they'd take off the handcuffs so he could put his hands over his ears to block out some of the noise. His head hurt, pounded on both sides where his temples were. If he'd gotten home, his mother would have given him an aspirin and let him rest for a while. They wouldn't have called the police right away.

Jerry stayed quiet and polite. He answered yes sir or no sir every time the policemen in the car said anything to him. He told them he was sorry about the cars he'd run off the road and that he hoped nobody got hurt. He was relieved when they told him that nobody had. "It must have been the Lord protecting them," Jerry said.

The police detective who had arrested him looked around at Jerry. "And protecting you," he said. "They said you were going over a hundred miles an hour."

"Yes sir, that was way too fast. I should have stopped, but I was too scared. And I wanted to see my folks before I got caught."

"You'll get to see them."

"Yes sir," Jerry said. "But it won't be like seeing them at the house."

"No, I guess not. But you should have thought about that before you got into trouble."

"Yes sir." Jerry waited a minute before he asked, "Where are you taking me?"

"LaGrange."

The name hit Jerry hard. That's where the penitentiary was. His father had worked there for a year after the accident that had blinded his eye. Jerry had never heard anybody say anything good about LaGrange. It brought home just how bad things were going to be for him. He might end up there in prison for the rest of his life. Even if that was what he deserved, he could hardly bear to think about it. So he didn't. He thought about the Bible in his pocket instead and about the way peace had flooded through him when the voice in his head had said, "Peace, be still." Was it possible that the Lord still cared about him after all the bad things he'd done? After all the commandments he'd broken?

Jerry leaned back in the seat as best he could and put his head back. He was tired, bone weary. He felt as if he'd been running forever and he was glad it was over. He prayed for his parents. He'd shamed them. They'd tried to bring him up right. They'd taken him to church, taught him the value of honest labor, taught him to read the Bible and pray, and provided his needs through the years. That note on the door written by his mother even said they loved him. What was wrong with him that he'd never been able to feel that love?

And here he was letting them down one more time. He was a total mess up. Had always been a total mess up. Maybe they'd give him the death penalty for what he'd done to that man in Georgia. The idea didn't bother Jerry. The only thing that bothered him was that it wouldn't be soon enough. He'd have to face his folks first.

They took him to an interrogation room at LaGrange. They told him he had the right to contact a lawyer, but he didn't know any lawyers. He remembered his mother's note about knowing a lawyer, but what was the use? He'd done the crime. It was time for him to pay. All he wanted to do was get it over with, so he confessed to everything. He told them about walking away from Ft. Gordon. He told them about being in the motel room and hitting somebody and waking up beside a dead man named Edward Baylor. He told them about stealing the dead man's car and using his credit cards. They wrote it all down.

It was hot in the room. Sometimes he thought he wouldn't be able to breathe. It was as if all the oxygen had just been sucked out of the room. He needed a drink. They got him some water, but what he really needed was a beer. Or a pill. His head was pounding and the black balls kept coming back in front of his eyes.

Nobody cared. They just kept talking, kept telling him to talk. What they couldn't understand was how a lot of what had happened was in some fuzzy corner of his mind where he couldn't see it any more. He didn't know exactly what had happened. He could remember hitting somebody and seeing his mother's face and then the man being dead. He didn't tell them about seeing his mother's face. He could barely stand to think about that much less say it out loud.

They took him back to the Oldham County jail. They were going to hold him there until the sheriff from Georgia came after him. They said he had to be tried where the crime had happened. He didn't care. He just wanted it all over with. He just wanted to be gone before his parents found out he was there. He didn't think he could face them.

It didn't happen that fast. The sheriff or somebody told his parents. They came to the jail to see him. The jailer opened the cell door and let them come in to talk to Jerry. The jailer wouldn't even look at Jerry's father, kept his eyes on the floor as if he didn't want to witness his shame. Jerry wanted to do the same thing. He wanted to just be absorbed back into the walls where his parents couldn't see him.

His mother began crying as soon as she saw him. She wasn't a woman who cried that much. She was strong and determined. She always thought she could fix anything with a little effort and she didn't mind giving the effort. But this time Jerry had done something she wasn't going to be able to fix.

His father's face was grim and there were the beginnings of tears in his eyes, too, as he said, "Son, what they're telling us can't be true. What did they do to you to make you say you'd done such a thing?"

His mother wiped her eyes with a white handkerchief and jumped in with her own disbelief. "We know you couldn't have done anything like that, Jerry. You're a good boy. You wouldn't steal a car. And this other…" She let her voice trail off unable to say the word murder. She mashed her mouth together and pulled in her breath before she went on. "Why would you make up something like that?"

Jerry didn't know what to say. He didn't want to hurt them. He'd never wanted to hurt them, but he always ended up messing things up. He let them talk a few minutes about how they knew he couldn't have done what he'd done before he said, "I'm sorry, Mom, Dad, but I did do it. I don't know how or why. It just happened. I was in there and I couldn't get out. Somebody was yelling at me, standing in my way. They were going to hurt me. I hit him. I know I hit him and kept hitting him, but I don't know what happened after that. I must have passed out or something. All I know for sure is that when I woke up there was a dead man beside me. I tried to get up but big black balls came in front of my eyes and I kept falling back on the floor. Over and over."

His mother was staring at him as if she'd never seen him before, and his dad looked as if he'd just been hit by a train. Finally his father rubbed his eyes and face with both hands before he said, "All right, son. Start at the beginning and tell us exactly what happened from the time I took you back to Ft. Gordon the first of March."

So he tried to tell them. He didn't lie about anything, but he wasn't sure they really heard what he was saying. They didn't want to hear what he was saying. Still he kept talking. He wanted them to understand why he couldn't go back to the school, why everything had happened. He wanted them to know he'd tried, that he hadn't intended to shirk his duty. His father had gone to war, had put his life on the line for his country. Jerry had been willing to do the same thing.

He looked straight at his mother and father and tried to make sure they understood that. "Mom and Dad, I'm not a deserter. I didn't run away from the Army. I ran away from the school. I just couldn't do the school, but I'm not a deserter. I like the Army. I begged them to put me in the infantry or send me to Vietnam or anything but to please take me out of the school. I just couldn't stand the school. I told them I was all mixed up in my mind. The other soldiers were making fun of me and laughing at me. I tried to tell them it wasn't that way, that I didn't want to be a deserter. I wanted to do my duty. But nobody would listen to me or let me explain anything. I got so mad I thought I was going to burn up inside."

"It's okay, son. We know you tried," his father said.

Jerry shook his head. "It's not okay. But I just want you to understand. I really liked Lt. Roberts. He wanted to help me, but he just couldn't. Nobody could help me. But I'm not a filthy deserter the way they kept saying I was." He wanted to get down on his knees and beg them to believe him. "You have to believe me."

They told him they believed him, that they believed everything he'd told them, but they didn't. They told him they'd help him. That they'd pray about it. That the whole church would pray about how best to help him. And that they'd find the right people to talk to, the right people to help. They'd get him a lawyer. Somehow they'd take care of things for him the way they'd always done.

They didn't seem to grasp the fact that he'd already told the police what he'd done. There was no going back. He had to pay for what he'd done. Even the Bible said that. An eye for an eye. A life for a life. After they left, Jerry opened his Bible to try to find that passage. He knew it was somewhere in the Old Testament. He couldn't find it. Instead his Bible kept falling open to Psalms. Somehow as he read the words King David had written centuries before, he felt calmer until he was able to fall asleep.

CHAPTER 16

Those first few days in jail, Jerry thought he was going to die. Then when he didn't, he wished he could. He wanted to just close his eyes and not have to open them ever again. He needed some booze or a pill, but nobody cared. They said he'd just have to deal with it and go cold turkey. They said a kid his age shouldn't be all that addicted to anything anyway and that if he was, he needed to get off the stuff. They wouldn't call a doctor or give him any medicine. They said he'd get over it, that the d.t.'s wouldn't kill him. Jerry wasn't so sure.

He screamed and banged his head against the wall, but he couldn't hit it hard enough to knock out the pain. Clawed hands grabbed the inside of his stomach and tied his gut in knots. Every muscle in his body screamed in protest when he moved. He tried to block out the pain and sleep, but monsters came into the jail cell with him and tormented him. He fought them, but they always won. They ate him alive and then spit him out to lie in the bunk sweating and heaving.

The demons were still chasing him when the sheriff and deputy sheriff from Georgia showed up to transport him to Pembroke, Georgia where he'd be tried. His parents came to visit before he left. They didn't want him to go to Georgia. They kept trying to find a way out, but Jerry had waived his rights. He'd confessed. There wasn't anything to be done.

Even the lawyer they'd hired said Jerry had to go back to Georgia. Mr. York was a nice enough guy. Jerry liked him. He answered all his questions, but the best lawyer in the world couldn't clean up the kind of messes Jerry made.

Jerry's dad was still talking with the Army, going up through the chain of command. He got some promises. They said they'd give Jerry a medical discharge and that they could take over the criminal case, get Jerry straightened out and back home. While his father was with him talking about it, Jerry could almost believe it might happen, but then when he thought about it, he knew it wouldn't. The Army hadn't helped him even when he'd begged them to while he was at Ft. Gordon. They didn't want to deal with a soldier who couldn't fit into the hole they wanted to pound him into. Still there was that hope when his father talked.

"You can come home and go back to helping with the farm. We'll get you counseling for all this other stuff," his father had told him. "But being back on the farm will help as much as anything. You need to be working. Using your head and your hands."

It had sounded good to Jerry. Sometimes when the pounding in his head would ease up, he'd stare at the jail wall and see the farm. He'd think about walking across the fields to check on the cows or plowing the long rows of tobacco. He could smell the fresh cut hay on the ground. He even thought it might be good to feed the pigs again, and he hated pigs.

But the Georgia sheriff showed up to get him while the Army was still talking to his father about what they could or couldn't do. Jerry didn't mind going back to Georgia. It was hard being in jail in Oldham County with his friends out on the street walking around free as birds and his mother coming to visit him and asking him dozens of questions she had written down on paper to try to find some other explanation for him waking up beside the dead man in the motel. She wouldn't believe he'd done it. She said he couldn't have done any of those things. She knew he'd run away from the school, but all the rest of it couldn't be true. There had to be some other explanation. There had to be some other person involved. She even brought in a newspaper clipping about another man found murdered in a Texas motel room as if that might somehow explain Edward Baylor's death in the Georgia motel.

Jerry could hardly bear the look in his mother's eyes when she came to visit him at the jail. She always brought him some cookies or brownies. She'd bring two batches and leave one in the sheriff's office. She tried to anticipate his every need, to figure out something she could do to help him. She was the Martha type, the one who had to be busy about doing something instead of the Mary type who could sit still and wait for a spiritual revelation. She realized Jesus said it was better to be like Mary, but she couldn't help it. She had to be doing something. She couldn't just sit still and wait for whatever was going to happen to happen. Especially not if what was happening was her son going to prison.

If there had been a way, she would have broken down the jail walls and carried him home on her back. But her common sense told her that wouldn't work, that they couldn't hide him from the police. She knew he had to do what the law said to do, but the thought of what might happen to Jerry in prison brought pure panic to her eyes. She knew some about prisons from the stories his father had brought home while he was working at LaGrange. She promised Jerry she'd spend her every waking moment either praying for him or trying to figure out the right person to call to help him stay out of prison. But she hadn't been able to find a way to keep him from being taken back to Georgia to be tried.

The Georgia sheriff, Harry Montgomery and his deputy, Rudy Hackett, were nice enough guys. They didn't even make Jerry wear handcuffs. They'd barely gotten out of Oldham County before Sheriff Montgomery told Jerry he hadn't been at all what they'd been expecting. "We came up here to get a criminal. You're not a criminal." The sheriff had looked at him for an extra long moment before he went on. "What they say you did and what we see of you, there's no way we can put you there in that motel room."

They talked about all sorts of things as they crossed out of Kentucky and through Tennessee. Jerry was carsick. He'd always had trouble with that on any long trip when he had to sit in the back seat. And his head was still pounding when the demons came after him.

After they'd been riding for a few hours, the sheriff and his deputy asked him about Mr. Baylor. Jerry didn't want to answer them. Mr. York had told him not to talk to anybody about what had happened unless the lawyer was there with him, but they kept asking. Jerry had to say something, and he couldn't see what difference it would make. He'd already told the whole story to the first bunch of policemen at LaGrange. The next time he talked to Mr. York, he'd have to ask him what he was supposed to say when the police kept asking him questions.

But now Jerry didn't want Sheriff Montgomery to think he wasn't being cooperative. Being cooperative was important when you were a prisoner. His dad had told him that. They'd read him his rights before he left Kentucky. They knew he didn't have to talk to them, but Jerry wanted the sheriff to like him, wanted him to think Jerry was being straight with him. So he told them what he could remember of what happened.

The day after he got to Pembroke, Deputy Hackett took him to a hearing. His father along with his Uncle Milton and his lawyer, Mr. York, were there with him. Jerry was glad his dad was there. He didn't think he could have stood up in front of the judge and heard the charges against him if his dad hadn't been there with him. Murder in the first degree. Grand larceny. Robbery. Jerry stood there in the courtroom and heard the words, but it was as if they were all talking about somebody else.

The deputy let him visit with his dad and uncle for a little while after the hearing. They didn't talk about the charges or what they were going to do to help him. They talked about the farm and the house. His dad said the house needed painting, but he wasn't sure how to go about it. Jerry jumped at the chance to think about something besides being in jail and he told his dad how he'd paint the house if he got to come home before summer was over.

After his dad and uncle and Mr. York left, Deputy Hackett took him to be fingerprinted. He'd been fingerprinted in Kentucky, but he had to do it all over here in Georgia.

Then the deputy said they wanted to have another interview with him, and he took him into this room where an FBI agent and a state policeman were waiting. They said their names, but Jerry was too scared to keep them in his head. As soon as he went in the room, it was as if somebody was playing back a movie he'd already seen. His heart began racing and he thought he was going to throw up. He'd seen these men before. Not in real life, but in a dream.

Jerry took a few deep breaths to keep himself under control while the FBI guy read him his rights again. Then the man said, "We just want some answers about what happened, Jerry. Just so we'll have it all straight."

"I would like to remain silent," Jerry said. That was part of his rights. The right to remain silent.

"That's fine, Jerry." The FBI man actually smiled at him. "We don't want you to say anything you don't want to say, but we still want to ask you a few questions."

They let Jerry sit down. They started asking their questions. For a while, Jerry kept telling them he didn't want to talk about it, but they kept asking him. Deputy Hackett told him to answer, that it might help him. The deputy smiled and told Jerry that nobody wanted to hurt him, that they just wanted to be clear on what had happened.

The FBI man sat down in front of him and looked straight at Jerry for a long time before he said, "You look like an honest boy. And you've already told your story. We just want to hear it again from you, to see if they got it right up in Kentucky. It's just a few questions."

Jerry wanted to be honest. So he answered them, and all the while it was like an echo in his head. In his dream he had answered the questions, too. He'd been in this room, talking to these men. That scared him more than anything they said. He'd dreamed the future.

It wasn't until they were through with their questions that he saw the tape recorder. They'd put it all on tape. He must have missed that part in his dream.

CHAPTER 17

He was still upset when the deputy locked him back in his cell. They brought him some supper but nothing tasted good. He paced the cell. The place was filthy. It smelled and bugs ran races across the floor. He stepped on a roach, but plenty of others peeked out from the cracks ready to take its place. He tried to read one of the books the sheriff had let him have, but the words ran together and didn't make any sense. He sang a couple of songs and felt a little better. If he couldn't do anything else, he could sing. Even his mother thought he could sing.

He remembered the letter she'd tacked to the door at his house before the police caught him. *We love you so much.* He had never thought his mother loved him. He'd thought he was just a responsibility for her, somebody she had to mold and shape into a decent human being even if it did seem an impossible task. But she'd written the words on the note. *We love you so much.* And she'd looked almost distraught when she'd come to see him at the jail and not just because his arrest was going to embarrass her, make people talk about her. She was worried about Jerry. She wanted to help him.

Jerry picked up the spiral notebook and pencil the sheriff had let him have. His mother wanted him to write a diary for Mr. York. She'd said it would help if he wrote down everything that was happening now and everything he could remember that had gotten him to this place in jail. And she wanted him to write to her and his dad. That was the least he could do after what he'd put them both through in the last few months.

He wrote two and a half pages about everything that had happened since the sheriff had picked him up in Oldham County. He told his lawyer about how the sheriff and deputy had kept asking him questions on the ride down to Georgia. He told him how he'd tried to keep busy that first day after he got to the jail working a jigsaw puzzle and thinking about plans for his dad's farm. He told him how he was nervous at the hearing and how glad he was to see his dad. He told him all about the interview and how he had dreamed about it happening before it happened and how upset all of it made him. He told him he knew it sounded hard to believe, but that it had really happened. He really had dreamed about the future.

Then he wrote his folks.

April 30, 1969
8:25 p.m.
Dear Mom & Dad,

Been trying to keep myself busy by working the jigsaw puzzle and reading and singing. I'm also thinking up plans for the farm which will make it better.

Mom, I don't know if Dad told you about my plan on how to paint the house. If he hasn't he can tell you about it better than I can explain it in the letter. I was pretty happy about that plan cause Dad thought it was a pretty good idea.

I was a little upset this afternoon, when they had me down for an interview. When I was sitting in that room talking with those men, I remembered that I had been in that same room before with the same men talking to me. I had really dreamed about this interview taking place earlier this year, and now it had really come true! It's almost like really reading the future! So this little bit got me upset, but I guess it would get anybody upset.

I have also enclosed some information to my lawyer of my day to day experiences. I want to help in any way I can, and I want to help Mr. York.

Well, I hope to hear from you soon.

Love, Jerry

The days were long in jail. He worked the jigsaw puzzles the deputy brought in for him. He wrote pages to his lawyer hoping it would help in some way even if Jerry didn't know how. He read his Bible. He sang songs, and he slept as much as he could to make the days pass. On Sunday, he would have given anything to be home going to church with his folks. He'd always gone to church on Sundays except when he was on the run, and even then he remembered when it was Sunday if he wasn't passed out from drinking too much.

Since they wouldn't let him out to go to church, he had his own church service. He read a couple of Psalms out loud and sang some hymns. He ended his little service by praying for his folks and for Mr. York and for the sheriff. He just kept going, praying for everybody he could think of until they brought him his dinner.

It was good enough food, but not enough of it. He was hungry. He hadn't had enough to eat for months, and now that he was off the booze and pills, his appetite had come back full force. He couldn't wait till his folks could come to visit and bring him some real food. The food he'd like to have marched through his head. Chocolate chip cookies, chocolate cake with chocolate icing, blackberry pie, pork and beans, bread, crackers, tuna fish, Vienna sausage, potato chips, sour dill pickles. He wanted to pile up the food in the corner of his cell and never have to be hungry again.

But he couldn't keep his mind occupied all the time with thinking about food or working puzzles. What he'd done was driving him crazy and making him sick. Sometimes the jail walls seemed to close in on him, smothering him. His head felt heavy and kind of numb. His eyes hurt. Sometimes it was like an elephant was sitting on his chest. He just couldn't forget what he'd done. It tormented him every minute of the day.

He remembered his mother telling him to write it all down. He had to do something or his head was going to explode. So he wrote everything he was thinking to Mr. York.

May 5, 1969 I got tired of working the jigsaw puzzle, so I decided to rest for a bit. I then got to thinking about what I had done. I'm trying to forget it, but when you're not a killer, you just can't let it drop and forget about it. It's the hardest thing that I have ever tried to live down. It's with me in the day, it's with me when I go to bed, it's with me when I get up in the morning. It's just glued to me.

I've cried myself to sleep a few nights asking myself, why did I do this, why did I do that, and why did I kill that man. I know no reason, no reason at all. I've searched and searched for an answer. Maybe it was the overdose of all those pills that I had taken all that last week. Maybe it was all the tension and strain that had built up inside of me over the past years.

I do know one thing and one thing only. There are two Jerry Shepherds. I don't know the other Jerry and I don't want to know him. But let me tell you this, the <u>real Jerry Shepherd</u> did <u>not kill that man</u>.

If I was a murderer, I wouldn't have gone home to try to get money. If I was a murderer, I would have jumped someone and taken his money or I would have robbed a store. If I was a murderer, I would have killed again. I'm not a murderer. I couldn't have jumped and robbed somebody if I wanted to and I know I couldn't kill anybody. I'm just like my dad. I'm too soft and tenderhearted to hurt anyone. I'm always helping people, not hurting them.

There is one thing I wish I could do. During my court date I wish I could stand up in front of everybody and sing one song that would tell them what kind of person I am, and how I really feel. I really believe in this song with all my heart, mind, body, and soul because it shows my feelings of what I believe in. The name of the song is "Impossible Dream." And if you don't believe me, read the words to the song or listen to someone sing it. Then you will know.

This is a true statement written by
Gerald Warren Shepherd

Jerry read back over what he'd written. Then he stood up and sang the song all the way through as though he were rehearsing for his appearance in court. They'd never let him sing in court. He knew that, but just in case, he wanted to be ready.

The days dragged by. The sheriff and deputy brought in other prisoners for little stuff like drinking too much. They'd stay a day or two and be out. Jerry liked it better when he was alone. It was quieter. He tried to stay busy, but there wasn't anything to do. He talked to the deputy. He talked to the guy who brought him his food. He read his Bible and prayed. He sang until he was hoarse. He wrote his folks and asked them to bring his guitar when they came to visit. He'd never learned to play very well, but now he'd have plenty of time to practice. He stayed so hungry he got worried he might have a tapeworm. He wrote his mother asking her to bring food when she came to visit. He dreamed about food.

He wrote his diary of his day-to-day activities for Mr. York. The second Sunday he was in jail in Georgia, he wrote his life's story for the lawyer.

I was real shy around people for a long time. I guess being the only child had a lot to do with that. I liked to be alone with myself. I didn't care for crowds and I still don't. I liked going places and doing things by myself cause I felt better that way.

I always had a big problem with school, cause I always had trouble with my math which has always been hard for me and still is. I always wanted to please my parents in everything I did, but when I brought bad grades home I knew it didn't please them and it hurt me cause it didn't.

For some odd reason Mom and Dad didn't seem like my parents. They were just two people I was living with which I was always trying hard to please.

My freshman year at Oldham County was the best living year I had since I was born. Everything was going great. I made the honor roll two or three times that year and I was making my parents proud as punch of me. The best thing I liked was music. I was in the choir and I really liked the music teacher. I can sing pretty good which is a God given talent. Our music teacher was taking us everywhere to sing and all the time I knew I was pleasing my parents.

After that one great year, the curtain fell. I had just turned 16 and these three years of high school and living at home were the worst years of my life. I was already 16 my second year in high school and I couldn't drive until I brought my grades up. Well, I didn't get to drive that whole year.

He looked up at the wall in front of him for a long time before he started writing again. He wrote about driving his dad's truck into a tree. He told Mr. York about running away but he didn't write anything about Mama Harmon. That didn't seem to be something the lawyer would need to know. He wrote about thinking he was going to fail when he was a senior and then about being chosen to star in the senior play and getting depressed and wrecking his car. He wrote fast just putting down whatever came to mind.

The big week of the senior play came. We were to put it on three times. My parents and an aunt and uncle were coming to our last performance. The first two performances were really good. The night my parents were there was a flop. So I thought I had let everyone down including Mr. Riddle, the director. That night, the cast and crew, we all went out and had a party of our own. This was the first time I ever did drink. I thought I could drink all my problems down but it just caused me more trouble. I almost didn't graduate because of the trouble at school I got into for drinking.

I worked with dad all summer on the farm and in Sept. I was to go to a business college which I didn't want to go to but I thought it would please my parents. All I wanted to do was stay on the farm and work. But if I did that, I would soon be drafted into the Army.

I withdrew from college and my parents didn't know where I was for a week. I stayed at my old girlfriend's house cause I knew I would be accepted there. I knew Janice loved and needed me and I needed somebody to love. I decided to go back home and face the facts. After that I went back to drinking again. I thought I could drink all my problems away. I got to where I was drinking heavy and one night on my way back home I had a wreck. Well, I really let my parents down this time. Mom & Dad were very upset over this and Mom called me a drunk. Well, I decided to enlist in the army. I wanted to be just a foot soldier and go to Nam cause I felt like I was needed there and if I died, it was for a cause. But Dad wanted me to go to an army school, so I wanted to please him and I entered into an army school. I took basic training at Fort Knox and enjoyed every bit of it. I also was drawn closer to my parents. After basic, I then had to go to Fort Gordon for my school and after I was there a few weeks I felt like I had lost complete contact with my parents and I felt like I wasn't needed here. All I wanted to do now was to be home with my parents and work with Dad on the farm. I hadn't really known my parents at all for 19 years. I felt like they were in one room and I was in another, but those few weeks at Fort Knox had brought us closer together.

As for the rest you know about it. I just wish I could forget it but I can't.

True statement written by
Gerald W. Shepherd

Jerry read it over but he didn't change anything. Then he wrote his mother and dad and told them they could read what he had written for Mr. York before they sent it on to the lawyer. He wanted them to understand, too. He just wasn't sure what he wanted them to understand.

That was the way he was when he prayed, too. He wanted to ask the Lord for help, but he didn't think he deserved any help. His mother and dad told him the Lord loved him no matter what he'd done, but how could he? Jerry didn't think he deserved anybody's love, especially not the Lord's, but he did want it. He wanted everybody to love him. He just hadn't ever been able to do enough of the right things to earn that love. And now here he was in jail. He didn't deserve anything but punishment for what he'd done. He just had to learn to live with that truth.

A Bible verse popped up in his mind. *The wages of sin is death.* That's what he deserved. Death. He'd been chasing after death for years. Maybe this time he'd finally found the way to catch it. He'd committed murder. His punishment could be, maybe should be, the death sentence.

CHAPTER 18

The days passed. Every morning when he woke up, he tried to think of something to look forward to. He'd think about finding the jigsaw puzzle piece that he'd searched an hour for the night before. He'd think about what they'd bring him to eat. They were giving him an extra meal every day, but he was still hungry. He'd lost down to one thirty while he'd been on the run, and now it seemed as if his body was trying to make up for those weeks of never enough food. No matter how much he ate, he wanted more.

He couldn't wait for his parents to make the trip down to visit him. In Oldham County he'd dreaded their visits, but now it was different. Now they knew the worst and they hadn't turned their backs on him. They were working hard to figure out a way for him to get out of this cell and home again. They thought it was possible. Sometimes when they talked about it when he called them or they wrote about it in their letters to him, they almost had Jerry believing it was possible as well.

Then reality would set in. The cell door would still be locked. The four walls would still be closing in on him. His trial date was six months down the road. Six months he'd be stuck in this cell with the bugs and whoever else the sheriff might drag in to lock in there with him.

He spent hours in his bunk wondering how this could be happening to him. And then he'd think about what he'd done and feel like banging his head against the wall the way he had in Oldham County when the alcohol demons were after him. He would try to pray and his prayers would bounce off the ceiling and slam him back in the face. He'd try to read the Bible and the words would run into a black blur. He'd wonder if he was going mad.

But then there would be a quiet time. He'd sing some songs and write a poem. He'd draw some pictures and write out detailed plans for things he could do on the farm when he got out. He'd get a letter from his folks, or Deputy Hackett would come in and ask him to sing a song for him. He'd open the Bible and a verse would jump out at him as if the Lord was saying, "Here, read this. It will help."

For to be carnally minded is death; but to be spiritually minded is life and peace. Somehow hope always resurfaced inside him.

The middle of May Jerry got a letter from Mr. York.

May 15, 1969
Dear Gerald:

Your mother and father have delivered to me all of your recent fine letters which you have composed, addressed to me. I thoroughly enjoyed reading all of your communications and I am so happy to learn that all the town people of Pembroke, and the authorities, are taking excellent care of you while you are with them. They are all real fine people and very much concerned over your welfare and that a good solution can be found for you, that you can be properly treated and assisted in finding out the answers to some of the things that have bothered you.

Keep up the good work and trust in your fellowman and keep your faith in God and I can assure you that in the time to come you will find a complete peace of mind and adjust your life to making the best of your surroundings wherever they may be. As I have pointed out to you, mankind only knows part of the answers, but people everywhere are concerned and basically gentle and want to help each other. As the modern saying goes, "Keep your faith."

Your father and your uncle were here at the office yesterday and we have requested the authorities, through Mr. Cheney, the Solicitor General, to make arrangements for you to have complete medical examinations at the earliest possible date. This will perhaps give you a new surrounding and different people to work with and talk to for a period of several weeks. When they start these examinations in Georgia, you are to have complete confidence in your doctors and to cooperate to the fullest extent and give them all of the fine details of your life as you have related them to me. We are seeking the best of help for you and can assure you that medical science, with all its wisdom, can give you the outline for understanding your mental processes.

I encourage you to continue to correspond with your parents, your friends and myself, and you must be reassured that everyone, and I emphasize "everyone," is working in your behalf. This is the greatest country on earth and it isn't our wealth and material possessions that make it great, but it is our feeling for the individual as the most important thing on earth that gives the American people this real value. Our government and laws are based upon this feeling for the individual and you must remember that in time medical science will find the answers for most of our illnesses. Be patient and continue to take care of yourself.

With kindest regards, I am,
Sincerely,
William F. York

It was a good letter. It lifted Jerry's spirits and gave him reason to think things were going to work out. Nothing about it prepared him for Central State Hospital in Milledgeville, Georgia. That was just as well. If he'd known what the hospital was going to be like, he'd have found a way to escape and run as far away as possible. He'd have run forever before he would have let them take him to that place.

Deputy Hackett had driven him over. When they had turned in through the gates and driven up to the stark gray building, the deputy had looked over at Jerry and said, "Just remember you can take whatever happens and after a while you'll be sent back to us at Pembroke. It'll just be a few weeks here. Anybody can take anything for a few weeks. Right, kid?"

The deputy's words and the very aura of the building had caused a cold fist of dread to grip his insides even before Jerry walked into the building and was taken to the ward for the criminally insane. They took his clothes away from him and gave him tan pants and a shirt to wear. Then they told him the facility was overcrowded with no open bunks in the dorms. They shut him up in a cage something like the one he'd been in when the MP's picked him up at the Atlanta airport, but this time he didn't have to worry about yelling till somebody let him out to the restroom. They'd supplied a coffee can in the corner of the cage for that.

That night as he lay on the mat in the cage and tried to sleep, the jail cell at Pembroke began to look like a luxury hotel. He couldn't believe his parents had requested he be sent here. He wasn't crazy. At least he hadn't been when they brought him in. No telling what he'd be by the time he got out of this place. He wasn't even sure he could get through the night with his sanity.

The guards let him out in the morning to eat with the other inmates, patients, whatever they were. Jerry was trembling inside, but he tried not to let it show. All around him were men who'd done who knew what and they were eyeing him as if deciding what they could do to him. The guards didn't look much better. Jerry wasn't sure some of them hadn't just exchanged their inmate uniforms for a guard uniform for the day.

Jerry wanted to jump up on top of the table and announce to everybody sane enough to understand that he wasn't one of them, to tell them he'd just been sent there for an evaluation, that he didn't belong there. But instead he stayed in his spot and tried to take up the least amount of space as possible. It would be better if nobody noticed him.

After breakfast, the guards herded them out into a bare dirt lot. Some of the men plopped down on the dirt in the middle of the lot as if they didn't even notice the hot sun beating down on their heads. Others prowled the area hunting shade the way lions in the jungle might hunt the best resting spot, ready to kill if another animal got in the way. A few men tried to bounce an almost flat basketball in the hard dirt in front of a basketball goal. There was no net on the metal rim. Here and there a man pulled out a deck of cards. Other men gravitated to the sound of shuffling cards.

Jerry stayed back against the metal building alongside the lot and prayed to be invisible. He'd never wanted to disappear as much in his life. Even the cage with the stinky coffee can was looking good. At least then that weird man on the other side of the lot who kept looking at him with cold blank eyes wouldn't be able to get at Jerry.

The guards came out in the yard and grabbed first one man then another to escort back into the buildings. Jerry started to sit down, then decided against it. He might need to move fast if one of the crazies came after him. Crazy wasn't so bad. He was half crazy himself, but that wasn't the same as being criminally insane. It gave him chills thinking about what some of these men must have done.

Across the way he spotted a man who looked as uneasy as he felt. The man turned and stared straight at Jerry before starting across the yard toward him. He dodged in and out of the other inmates trying to draw as little notice as possible. He stepped up beside Jerry and looked him in the eye. "What you in for?" He was tall with an ample belly pushing out against his loose shirt. His slicked back brown hair was streaked with gray. His greenish gray eyes looked worried, but not weird.

"Evaluation," Jerry said. "How about you?"

"Same here. I wish they'd done it by mail."

"Can they do that?"

"I don't know, but it would have been better than this. These weirdoes aren't just crazy, they're crazy mean. And I ain't necessarily talking about our fellow guests. The guards are just weirdoes in uniforms, but then I guess you have to be crazy mean to take a job working here." The man looked out at the men around them. "But some of us like you and me are just here because some idiot judge wants them to pick our brains. See George over there and Junior." The man nodded toward two men off to themselves across the way. "We hang together and watch out for one another. It's the only way to survive out here."

"Sounds good," Jerry said. "Surviving, I mean."

"My name's Jack. Jack White."

"Jerry Shepherd."

"You look like a kid. How old are you?"

"Nineteen."

"What'd you do?" the man asked, then took back his question before Jerry could answer. "No, don't tell me. It's better if we don't talk about that. Whatever you did, you don't look crazy mean, so we'll watch your back. But it won't be easy for you in here. You're young and cute. Some of these nuts will be hitting on you."

Jerry's face tightened. "I'll kill them before I let them touch me."

"Yeah, kid, you look like you might. At least try to anyway." Jack gave him a considering look. "But you give them that look you just give me and they might just believe you and let you alone. Me and the other guys will do what we can."

"Thanks," Jerry said.

They didn't talk much. They just kept in a group out in the yard and tried to stay under the radar of the guards or the other inmates. Each of them watched a portion of the yard, and when some problem boiled up, they eased away from it. They didn't care about seeing the blood or whatever. They aimed to stay back in the shadows where it might be safe. If somebody bumped against them they ignored it. If the guards bashed somebody in the head, they acted as if they hadn't seen a thing. All they wanted was to make sure none of them was in the middle of whatever trouble the day brought. If they had had shovels, they would have dug foxholes and hidden in them all day.

The hours Jerry spent out of the yard inside with the doctors and his counselor were better. They really seemed to want to help him. They listened when he talked about all the problems he'd had growing up. His social work counselor, Alison Atwood, was especially easy to talk to. He could tell her anything and she never acted as if he was disgusting even when he felt disgusting himself. He hadn't been able to talk to anybody like that since he'd talked to Mama Harmon in New Jersey. At night before he went to sleep, he'd thank the Lord for helping him make it through another day and he'd thank the Lord for Miss Atwood.

He remembered how he'd wondered if Mama Harmon was an angel, somebody the Lord had put in his path to help him. Maybe that was the way it was here, too. The Lord had put Miss Atwood on his case to help him make it through this hall of horrors. Jerry smiled at the thought. Miss Atwood didn't much look the way he'd always imagined an angel would look. She was tough and no nonsense with no kind of fuzzy or saintly aura, but she was just what Jerry needed.

He told her all about his childhood and how he'd always felt off to himself and alone even when his parents were there. He told her how he'd tried so hard to please everybody and how he'd never been able to please anybody, especially his mother. Miss Atwood tried to explain to him that there was more than one kind of abuse, how a person could be emotionally abused as well as physically abused and she thought that might be what had happened to him even if his mother hadn't really intended to hurt him.

After he thought about what she said, Jerry told her about seeing his mother's face when he was hitting the man in the motel. He hadn't told anybody that before Miss Atwood, but it had been boring a hole inside him. It was a great relief to hear her say it wasn't all that uncommon after years of emotional abuse. He still didn't quite believe it could be anything approaching normal, but at least he wasn't the only person who'd done something so horrible.

Miss Atwood didn't even act surprised, much less shocked. She just accepted whatever he said and tried to help him see why it had happened. She didn't say it was right, just that it was understandable considering his state of mind. She understood about Jerry not even knowing that other Jerry Shepherd who had killed that man in the motel. And even more important, she didn't think the rest of his life had to be a total mess up like the first part had been.

CHAPTER 19

Jerry felt as if he'd gotten a reprieve when they gave him his clothes back and let him go back to the Pembroke jail. The doctors had picked every bit of information out of his head. They would send their findings to his lawyer and the judge. Jerry didn't care what they found as long as he never had to set foot inside Central State Hospital again.

He was grateful to Miss Atwood and Dr. Mike for talking to him and helping him understand things, but he didn't need any more counseling. He knew what his problem had been now, and he could handle it himself. Had already handled it. He was facing forward and not looking back.

Deputy Hackett came to pick him up. Once they got out to the car, the deputy said, "I sure am glad to see you looking so good, kid. I have to admit I was a little worried about what might happen to you in there. They've got some real bad cases up here."

"You won't get no argument about that from me," Jerry said as he leaned back in the seat and let out a long breath. He could feel his muscles springing loose. He had been stretched tighter than a guitar string ever since he'd walked into that chamber of horrors. He should have broken a dozen times, but he hadn't. That surely meant he had learned to handle things better.

It felt like coming home being back in the cell at Pembroke. It was hot, the middle of July. He'd been at Milledgeville for over a month. He didn't even mind the roaches and mosquitoes in his cell at Pembroke for a few days.

He hadn't written his parents at all while he was at the hospital. He didn't want to take even the slightest chance the hospital people might read something he wrote and decide he sounded crazy enough to have him committed at that place. He told his mother and dad as much when he wrote to them his first day back at Pembroke.

July 15, 1969
Wed. 5:00 p.m.
Dear Mom & Dad,

I am now back at Pembroke and I have never been so glad to get away from anywhere as I am to get away from that stinking, rotten, good for nothing place. I could add a few more, but they are not for writing.

As for someone straightening and helping me with my personal problems, I don't need it. I have already been straightened. I know now what my problem was but it's in the past.

I'm very sorry I didn't write to you while I was at Milledgeville. It's not because I didn't want to. I was just being on the safe side.

From now on you will be getting a steady shipment of letters from me. Want to hear from you soon.

Love, your Son

He read over the letter. It didn't really explain anything. He said his problems were in the past, but what did that tell his folks? Nothing. And ideas were blowing all over the place inside his head. He needed to let things out, to tell people what he was feeling. Miss Atwood said that way maybe things wouldn't get so crazy they exploded in all the wrong ways. Miss Atwood said he should have told his mother and dad how he felt a long time ago. So maybe now was a good time to start. He picked up his ballpoint pen again.

P.S. Just about every time I didn't do something perfect, I punished myself. I just thought about that. Maybe by going AWOL from the Army I was punishing myself. Also when I was in that motel room with Mr. Baylor all I wanted to do was get out of his room and away, but he didn't see it that way. I was scared and didn't think, cause the Army teaches you not to think when your life is in danger. When I fought Mr. Baylor, all the pressure, strain and hate that had built up in me was being released and I think I killed Mr. Baylor just to punish myself. This may not sound like me, but I was sick at the time.

It's something to think about cause I didn't have any other reason to hurt him. Why didn't I leave him instead of keeping on beating on him? I believe it was because I wanted to punish myself for everything that I had done wrong. This may sound crazy but this came across my mind and I had to tell somebody to get it off my mind.

He folded the letter. He hoped it wouldn't upset his folks, but he thought Miss Atwood would have been proud of him trying to think things out like that. She'd been the one who had told him that a lot of the things he'd done had been because he wanted to hurt himself. But he had ended up hurting someone else.

The days passed. His mother came to see him and brought him a box of food. They locked her in the cell with him since that was the only place they had to visit. They didn't talk about anything much, just what his dad was doing on the farm, about the new dairy operation and how hard it was to get good help with the farm work. They talked about the moon shot. Jerry hadn't gotten to see it, but he had heard it on the radio. She caught him up on all the family news and told him about the people at church and how they were praying for Jerry.

She told him everybody wanted him home again and that when that happened, things would be different. She really believed she would find a way to get him out of there and home again. She told him that next spring he could help with the plowing and Jerry could almost smell the rich dark dirt turning over behind the tractor and plow while she talked. She told him to keep writing down how he felt and not to worry about it bothering her. She just wanted him to be well and happy. And home.

A few days after his mother was there, he wrote another long letter to Mr. York. His mother had said it might help with his case if he explained to Mr. York some of the feelings Miss Atwood had helped him understand.

July 29, 1969
Dear Sir,

I'm going to try to write down the things that have happened and what my responses were. I hope for my sake this will be very helpful.

As you know during my life I had this thing of perfection to be accepted. I did this because I thought I would be rejected if I didn't. During my early part of life I was around my mother more than my father because he was working most of the time. If I had done something wrong Mom was the one who did the scolding. I just couldn't take the scoldings she gave me and I became afraid of her. I felt that when I was scolded, Mom was rejecting me and I was not wanted. So I was determined to be perfect so Mom wouldn't get on me.

During my four years of high school I still had this perfection to be accepted and when something went wrong she would get on me. By now the pressure and strain of this was beginning to get to me and so I started fighting back. She would get on me and I would scold right back which didn't do any good at all, but made matters worse.

By not being able to do a lot of things to perfection I did a lot of punishment to myself. There were some places I would have liked to go to and things I wanted to buy and needed, so I wouldn't go to these places or buy anything just to punish myself.

The pressure and burden of this was to the limits my junior and senior year in high school. During the first part of my senior year I left home to get away from Mom. And everything was at its best, but I missed the farm. So I came back home and tried to start all over again. Instead things got worse but I still hung around.

At the end of the year I just barely passed and during the summer I started drinking to punish myself for everything that I did wrong. I didn't want to go to college. I wanted to stay on the farm, but Dad said I would be drafted into the Army. I then enlisted and took basic at Fort Knox. Everything went to perfection and no trouble at all and I was really feeling closer to my parents for once.

Well, I came down to Fort Gordon and went to a school I didn't want and I ended up making bad grades and I felt like this was going to cause trouble and the Army was going to reject me so I decided to get away from everybody and get lost. I left the army because I didn't think they would help me but instead, reject me. Every time I went AWOL and came back they would rush me right back into school when I wasn't even settled down yet. I couldn't keep my mind on school because of the things that happened. I didn't believe the Army believed anything I told them and I just couldn't face the things that I had done, so I just tried to run from it like I've been running for the past 18 years of my life. I just couldn't face reality.

I needed help of some kind but I didn't know what for at the time. It was like walking into a brick wall. So the problem of perfection to be accepted and not being able to face reality was so much of a strain, pressure, and burden that I just lost all self control of myself.

Gerald Warren Shepherd

◆   ◆   ◆

The bugs in the jail got worse. They were in the bed with him, crawling on his face when he slept. They got in the food his mother shipped down in his care packages. They were everywhere. He had so many bug bites he couldn't count them all. His mother sent insect repellant, but when Jerry smeared it on his arms and legs, he broke out in a rash all over. So Jerry decided to get something done about the bugs.

He complained to everybody who came up to the jail—the deputy when he came to put somebody in jail, the old guy who brought his food, even the visitors of the other prisoners. They all heard about the bugs and how mad Jerry was. It took a month, but Sheriff Montgomery finally came up to see what he was complaining about. When the sheriff opened up the wall to the space between the cells, hundreds of roaches scattered everywhere, covering the sheriff's shoes and running up his legs. From the dance he did stomping and beating his legs, the sheriff didn't appear to like bugs a bit better than Jerry did.

Jerry didn't even mind the smell of the insecticide they sprayed all around the place. At last he could sleep without roaches crawling on his face waking him up. And he found out something else. He could get things done if he kept trying and didn't give up.

Nearly every day, Willie, the little man who brought up the food for the prisoners, smuggled in some special treat to Jerry like an extra dessert or dinner roll. Then he'd hang around to talk to Jerry or get him to sing an old Elvis song. Willie liked to sing along even though his voice sounded sort of like a rusty hinge on an old gate screeching back and forth in the wind. Sometimes when Willie hit a particularly bad note, it was all Jerry could do not to hold his ears.

Willie liked him. Jerry knew that, but he wasn't as sure about the sheriff until he overheard Willie talking to somebody in the next room. "Yeah, everybody likes that Shepherd boy. Ain't nobody down here can hardly believe he done what he said he done. I heard the sheriff talking just the other day that a boy like Jerry don't belong in jail and that if it was up to him he'd turn him loose and not make him serve a minute's more time. The sheriff says Jerry ain't the kind of boy who needs to be locked up. That we got plenty of them. Some that we ain't even got locked up yet, but that Shepherd boy ain't one of them."

Jerry did everything he could to keep the sheriff thinking well of him. He even scrubbed down the walls and floor of his jail cell without being asked. He didn't know how old the jail was, but Jerry doubted if it had ever been cleaned, really cleaned like his mother cleaned. While he'd rather be working out on the farm back home, it still felt good to get his hands dirty with work whatever kind it was.

After that the sheriff let him out to clean the courthouse offices on the weekends. Jerry never thought cleaning something would turn out to be such a treat, but any way he could get out of that cell was good. Sometimes he didn't know how he stood being locked up, but somehow he stayed on an even keel. Even when they locked a real nutcase in the cell with him, he was able to deal with it.

His mother told him it was the way he was maturing and all the prayers everybody was saying for him at home. And he was praying, too. He'd never quit praying.

He tried to pray the right things. *Dear Lord, thank you for this day. Bless the sheriff and deputy and Willie. Help the black guy over in the next cell to quit yelling. Give Mom and Dad good crops. Thank you for my parents and help me and Mom keep trying to understand one another. Give me a special song to sing. Forgive me.*

Even though he didn't pray out loud, sometimes he prayed as if he thought the sheriff or his mother might hear the prayers. Jerry still wasn't sure the Lord would take time to listen to any prayers from somebody who'd messed up the way he had. He wasn't sure he had the kind of feeling a person was supposed to have inside when he was a Christian. He wasn't sure what God wanted him to do.

He knew God expected a Christian to go to church, to pray, to read the Bible and to do right things. He knew God had given him a singing voice and he should use it for the Lord. And he wanted to. He wanted to go to church and sing. He even asked the sheriff to take him to church so he could sing a special for the people there.

The sheriff looked sorry as he turned him down. "I'd like to, Jerry. I really would, but I don't think I can. It'd cause too much commotion with the other prisoners. Everybody would be trying to get out by saying they wanted to go to church. I mean I know you aren't saying it just to get out, but some of these others would. Tell you what. I'll ask my preacher to come see you in here."

That was okay with Jerry. He didn't mind the preacher coming to see him. He'd even be glad to sing a song just for him, but it wasn't the same as getting up in front of a whole church full of people and singing "Amazing Grace" or "The Old Rugged Cross." He could make people cry singing those two old songs. Stuck there in the jail, he was the only one who ended up crying.

CHAPTER 20

August slid by. The middle of September, Jerry's lawyer flew down to Georgia to meet with Mr. Stedman, the district attorney. After the meeting, Mr. York came to the Pembroke jail to catch Jerry up on what was going on in his case. In June, the court had returned three indictments charging Jerry with murder, with robbery, and with larceny of a motor vehicle. In August, the hospital at Milledgeville had sent their findings to Judge Paul C. Rutherford who would be hearing Jerry's case. The Board of Doctors found Jerry able to distinguish right from wrong and therefore, mentally capable of being tried on all charges. They'd had no word from the Army about Jerry's discharge or any possible help from that quarter.

After the deputy had ushered Mr. York into the jail cell with Jerry, the lawyer shed his coat and tie. "This weather in Georgia is a killer. It ought to be getting cooler by now," he said as he wiped the sweat off his forehead.

"It is cooler," Jerry said. "You should have been here in August."

"If it was hotter than this, no thanks." Mr. York hitched up his suit pants and sat down in the chair the deputy had put in the cell for him. He smiled at Jerry. "Your parents tell me they've been taking turns coming down to visit."

"Yes sir. Dad was down a couple of weeks ago. It's always great when I get to see them and Mom always sends food."

"Your mother is a great cook. A good woman. She and your father are both working very hard along with all of us at the firm to help you, Jerry. And I know you're doing everything you can here to help your case as well."

Jerry watched the lawyer's face and didn't say anything. He was waiting for the chit-chat to be over so they could get to what was important—how he could get out of here and back home to the farm.

The lawyer dabbed his forehead with his handkerchief again and fingered some papers in the briefcase on the floor beside his chair, but he didn't pull anything out. "The district attorney has your confessions, so there's not really much we can do about that. We were in hopes the hospital report would rule you couldn't stand trial, but that didn't happen."

"I'm glad they didn't decide I was crazy," Jerry said.

"Well, of course," Mr. York said. "But you were under a great deal of stress and mentally unstable at the time of the crime. When you tell me about what happened now, there are a lot of murky areas, things you can't remember well. All of that is an indication of your mental state at the time."

"But my mental state is better now," Jerry said.

"And we're grateful for that, but it does mean you won't be able to avoid being tried for the charges against you."

"I understand," Jerry said. "Will I get the death penalty?" The question was easier to ask than he'd thought it would be.

"No, certainly not," Mr. York said quickly and firmly. "But there is a good possibility you will have to serve some time in prison. Murder is a very serious charge. The state of Georgia has minimum sentences for stated crimes the same as Kentucky does."

"What does that mean?"

"It means that if you are found guilty as charged, the judge would have to sentence you to prison for at least the minimum time for that crime. He wouldn't be able to shorten the sentence due to your age or other extenuating circumstances."

"So you think I'll have to do time?"

"I'm afraid so. If you're found guilty as charged."

Jerry kept his eyes straight on Mr. York's. "That's all right. I did the crime. I should have to pay for it."

"That shows maturity, Jerry. And we're proud of you for being ready to take responsibility for what you've done, but this entire unfortunate situation is difficult for everyone involved. Naturally your parents want to obtain the best possible outcome for you as do I," Mr. York said.

"That would be me going home to help Dad on the farm."

"You'd get agreement from your parents and me on that one, but the judge on your case may be harder to convince." Mr. York fingered the edges of the papers in his briefcase again but still didn't pull anything out. After a long moment of silence, he went on. "Your parents have been consulting with some doctors in Louisville to see the best way to proceed as your trial date approaches. Mr. Stedman says the judge on your case, Judge Rutherford, has a reputation for toughness."

"Have they set a date?" Jerry asked.

"The middle of October. October 16th."

The day hung in Jerry's thoughts like a heavy storm cloud getting ever closer. It colored his every thought. Before Mr. York had visited, he'd written his folks a letter talking about setting his feet on free ground again and helping with the farm with the hope the people in Georgia would give him a second chance. Mr. York had pushed reality at him and made him realize he might be facing years in prison, that perhaps he might never be a free man again. Maybe the death penalty would be preferable to that.

Deputy Hackett frowned when Jerry told him he'd be going before Judge Rutherford. "Oh, man, that's not good news," he said. "Any judge but him."

One of the prisoners in the other cell heard them talking and yelled, "Yeah, boy, you done got the hanging judge. He gonna done throw the book at you. You'll be lucky to ever see daylight again."

Deputy Hackett made him shut up, but it was too late. The storm cloud hanging over Jerry's head got blacker. He poured out his heart to his parents.

Sept. 17, 1969
Dear Mom & Dad,

I can't help but worry about what's going to happen. I know my lawyer is doing his best, but I know I'll get time and I'll be lucky if I get out in five years which I doubt very much. In my case it's life or the death sentence. I know I won't get death but I'll have face a few years or more. I hope that you and the farm will still be there but things will probably change a lot while I'm serving my time.

I was sick both physically and emotionally. I thought my life was in danger. At the time it happened I don't really believe I remembered everything that went on and what I really did do. It's just so confusing I can hardly stand it. All I know is at the time I didn't know if I was coming or going or what and at the time I just had a nervous breakdown.

It's still very hard for me to believe that this has happened to me and I get so blue and discouraged that I feel like throwing it all down the drain. I have lost some weight since Dad was here, it's just that being locked up like this and what has happened and that I know I'm going to have to serve time in prison makes you lose your hunger for food. Well I guess I could write a few more sad lines but I guess this is enough for right now.

Love, Gerald

For a week he stayed in a dark funk. All he could think about was being put away for life. He couldn't eat. He couldn't read. The only thing that helped was singing and he sang through twenty or thirty songs every night. He wrote another letter to his parents. He needed to talk to somebody. He needed somebody to shine a light into the darkness enveloping him.

Sept. 21, 1969
Dear Mom & Dad,

I can't really think of anything to say. Right now I'm so depressed that I feel like giving up and ending it all and I won't be on anybody's hands and this would be one case the court wouldn't have to put up with. It would also save the prison of putting up with me.

The closer it gets to Oct. the sicker I get cause you can bet the court is going to try to bury me for good. I just wish you wouldn't be there to see it happen. The day Mr. York was here I tried to make him think I was in great shape, but to tell you the truth, I was nearly in tears so I guess that I'm not a man after all. It's just so hard for me to face up to all that's happened. I've gone through so much already it's very hard for me to stand on my own two feet.

The really important thing that keeps me going right now is I hope that I'm given a chance to give you my love and loyalty and I want to give you both that so much that my heart aches for it. I don't have to decide to come back to the farm. "I want to." Farming is something I like and I think I could become good at. It really makes a person feel he is accomplishing something.

With your love, the farm, and my singing I can have the happiness and peace within myself.

With Love Always,
Gerald, Your Son

His appetite didn't improve much, but his spirits lifted a little when the sheriff let him and one of the other prisoners out to clean the courthouse. Work felt good. He liked being too tired to think about what was going to happen when he lay down at night. Still in another way he looked forward to the date in October. He wanted to get it over with however it went. And when he got a letter from his parents late in September telling him they had arranged a special private trial in front of the judge with no jury or anything, he almost believed that one more time they were going to pull off some kind of miracle and find a way to get him out of trouble. He wrote back that night.

Sept 29, 1969
Dear Mom & Dad,

Your letter came today and I was very surprised about this informal trial. There are a lot of things I would like to ask you about this special trial, but I guess I can wait till you come down. The people down here must be on my side, too, cause I don't believe you could have gotten this thing to take shape without their help and approval.

Yes, it has been very hard on me down here behind these bars, but I wanted to prove that I could stand on my own two feet and show these people what I'm really like.

I'm really looking forward to seeing you the 15th and I'll really need you the 16th cause when we see the judge you'll probably have to hold me up cause my legs will be knocking together so hard I won't be able to stand up. I just hope all things go well that day. I guess the only thing I can do till then is pray a little harder and <u>hope, hope, hope</u> and have faith in God so strong that it will knock anyone down.

Love, Your Son

Jerry was trying to have that kind of faith. His parents had always had that kind of faith, the unshakable sureness of knowing God was in his heaven and watching out for them. His mother had been bombarding heaven with prayers and everybody else with letters to help him. She believed he'd come home. Jerry wanted to believe it, but secretly, down in a spot inside him where he was afraid to look, he didn't think he'd ever be free again. He didn't think he deserved to be free. Not after what he'd done.

CHAPTER 21

When his parents came down for the hearing, they brought his navy blue suit from his high school days to wear. It felt good getting into dress clothes again. He just wished he was going to a church somewhere to lead the singing at a revival or to sing a special instead of going before a judge who might lock him up for the rest of his life.

Jerry couldn't sit down while they waited for the minutes to inch by before the hearing. His insides were all atremble and once or twice he thought he might throw up. His parents had on their brave faces, but his mother's smile looked as if it might shatter any second and she kept twisting her handkerchief into a tight spiral. His dad kept sitting down and then popping right back up to walk around again while the top of his bald head turned bright pink.

All of them tried to pretend they were calm and in control as they chatted about the cows and the crops. There wasn't any need in talking about the hearing. They could talk it to death and it wouldn't make any difference. It was up to Judge Rutherford now.

And to the Lord, his father reminded Jerry. "Remember, me and your mother have been praying non-stop, and the folks at church are all praying. The Lord will get us through this."

They met with Judge Rutherford in a side room at the courthouse. Mr. York stood beside Jerry as the prosecuting attorney, Mr. Stedman, presented the charges and the case against Jerry. Mr. Stedman didn't talk long. He didn't need to. Everything he needed for a conviction was in Jerry's confessions he put before the judge.

Mr. York made a short appeal for mercy due to the extenuating circumstances—Jerry's age and mental condition at the time. Then the judge asked to hear the story from Jerry. Looking stern in his black robes, Judge Rutherford kept his eyes unwaveringly on Jerry.

Jerry tried to be as straightforward and honest as he could. He'd already pleaded guilty to all three charges. It was what Mr. York had told him to say. Guilty. And he was guilty. He had killed the man. He had stolen the man's car. He had used the man's credit cards. He deserved whatever the judge gave him.

Still when the judge handed down the sentence, it was like looking at a thermometer from inside a warm house and knowing the temperature outside was ten below but until you stepped out into the wind you couldn't quite believe it. That's the way he felt. He'd known it was going to happen, but at the same time he'd believed his lawyer, his parents, the Army, somebody would find a way to let him go home.

That hope died when Judge Rutherford pronounced his sentence. "Gerald Warren Shepherd, I sentence you to life in prison, ten years for robbery and five years for grand larceny. These sentences are to run concurrently with credit for time already served in the Pembroke jail. You will be eligible for parole in seven years." He looked almost sorry as he said it.

Seven years. 1970. '71. '72. '73. '74. '75. '76. And then he might not get parole. That was just when he could go before the Parole Board to seek parole.

After they went out of the room, Mr. York told Jerry and his parents the sentence handed down was the minimum for the charges under Georgia law. So really there was no need for any of them to be surprised. Still they were. They'd looked at it. They'd known what the law said, what the punishment was. Still they hadn't believed it would apply to Jerry.

His mother and father kept looking at each other as if they'd just lived through a bomb exploding in their laps.

It was hard telling his parents goodbye. His mother kept staring at Jerry as if she might never see him again. For a minute he thought she might just start screaming, but then she drew in her breath, set her chin, and mashed her mouth together in a thin line before she said, "This isn't the end of it, Jerry. We won't give up until you're home again. We'll never give up. The Lord has a plan for your life and it isn't in prison. He'll help us. We just have to put our faith in Him." Her eyes looked as fierce as Jerry had ever seen them.

"Yes ma'am." Jerry tried to look hopeful for her even if he did feel as if he'd just been buried under a truckload of rocks.

His mother moved to the side and let Jerry's dad move in to talk face to face with Jerry. He gripped Jerry's arms as if he would never turn loose as he said, "I'm sorry, son. Maybe we shouldn't have asked for this kind of hearing. Maybe there might have been a better way."

"It's okay, Dad. I told you all along I had to pay for what I've done. I'll be okay."

His father pulled himself together. "Sure, you will, son. You just do what they say and settle down and you'll get trusty status before you know it. The trusties don't have such a hard time. At LaGrange they were almost like the hired help except they didn't get to go home at night. And there will be a chaplain. Soon as you can, you go see the chaplain. He might even need a helper. There are ways to help yourself inside, son. The good Lord will help you find them. He'll send a guardian angel with you right into the midst of the prison to watch over you. I know he will, and your mother and I will be praying every morning and every night for you."

Behind his father, his mother nodded and dabbed her eyes as she whispered, "Not just in the morning and at night. Every minute. We'll pray every minute." Jerry could feel his mother's eyes on him long after Sheriff Montgomery ushered him away.

On the ride back to Pembroke, Jerry asked the sheriff more about what he should do in prison and how to earn trusty status. The sheriff said the same thing as Jerry's dad. Jerry just had to be a model prisoner the way he'd been at Pembroke. The men in charge at whatever prison he was sent to would want to help him.

"And most prisons have church services every Sunday," the sheriff said. "You'll like that. You've been wanting to go to church ever since you came down here."

"Yes sir. And I sure do appreciate how kind you and everybody down here has been to me."

"Well, fact is, Jerry, we're gonna miss your singing when you're moved out of here. We get plenty of singers but most of them are drunk as skunks. Not that that matters. They probably couldn't carry a tune in a bucket even if they weren't. Not a thing like you. You've got a fine voice. A gift. So you just keep on singing and getting your life back on track. Maybe there'll even be a chance for you to do some singing in whatever facility you end up in. If they have church, they're bound to have hymns and that kind of thing."

It was funny, but now that he knew what was going to happen, the black cloud lifted a little. It was still hovering up there somewhere, but Jerry could see below it now and plan and think about the best thing to do. Prison would be different than the cell at Pembroke. They'd let him work. The sheriff told him all the inmates had jobs. That was something to look forward to. Something real to do to pass the time besides working jigsaw puzzles and doing bad sketches. And each day would bring him closer to the end of his sentence.

In a letter to his folks the day after he got back to Pembroke, Jerry vowed to do everything in his power to make the most of each day with the Lord's help.

Oct 17, 1969
Dear Mom & Dad,

I'm still at Pembroke but I may be gone by the time you receive this letter or I might still be here for another week. I don't know. As soon as I leave, I'll let you know as quick as I can so the mail will get to the right places.

When I get to prison I'm going to try to fit myself in as soon as possible and the sooner I do that the sooner I'll get to be a trusty and a trusty has a lot more freedom than the other prisoners do.

The other thing I want to do is try to become a chaplain's assistant and if I get to do that, I'll be able to study religion and the word of God and to be really able to understand better and also study religious music and with my working at this and with the chaplain's help I might turn into a good speaker and be able to preach the Word of God. When I'm dismissed from prison I'll have better knowledge of the Bible and in my spare time when I'm not farming I'll be able to go out and preach to people who need help and who want to follow God's way and to go down the path of righteousness in His Name's sake. God gave me a voice to sing with to use me to reach the heart of the people. So that's what I'm going to try to do, help those that need help and sing my heart out to reach their hearts till they understand the kind of feeling I have when I sing religious music.

You won't have to worry about me down here cause with God's help and me helping myself I'll hold up my end and when everybody gets to know me as well as Pembroke did, everything will work out just fine.

Just take real good care of the farm while I'm away and then before too long I'll be able to take care of the farm and you all, too. Can't beat that, can you?

I love you both very much.

Love, Your Son

He wrote his last letter to his parents from Pembroke on October 24, 1969. He explained to them that he didn't want to limit his reading and studying just to religious material and that he intended to study other music besides just religious music.

Just put it this way, I want to broaden my mind on all kinds of material that I can get my hands on. I can also brush up on my English and math and expand my vocabulary and figures.

The big thing I want to do now is just to get as busy as I can so the time will go faster until it's time for the people down here to give me a chance to be a free person again.

He didn't let himself think about how long seven years was. He'd never been good at math. There was no sense in starting now to figure up how many months and days and hours that would be. He just had to figure how best to use them, to take the sheriff's advice and his father's advice and to use this time to improve his mind and voice.

He didn't understand how it could happen, but the closer the time came for him to be sent to whatever facility they assigned him to, the calmer he got. He spent hours thinking about the things he would do while he was in prison and writing down plans.

He was going to step closer to the Lord. He was going to find out what the Lord intended for him. The Lord hadn't let Jerry die when he kept trying to end it all by driving into trees when he was in high school. When he ran away to California, the Lord had led him all the way back to New Jersey and Mama Harmon to help him go back home. The Lord had put Miss Atwood in his path at Milledgeville so he wouldn't go completely nuts. The Lord hadn't let Judge Rutherford, the reputed hanging judge, sentence him to death for killing Mr. Baylor.

Maybe they were all angels the Lord had put at the crossroads of his life. He hadn't always recognized the angels even as they'd guided him and pushed him down the right roads instead of the wrong ones. Maybe the Lord even had angels in prison. That sounded crazy, but then it could be true. Jerry just had to look for them and listen to them when they found him.

The Lord must have a purpose for his life the way his mother was always telling him. Maybe it was singing. Maybe it was preaching. Jerry still wasn't all that sure. He still sometimes felt as if everything he did was because that was what his parents said the Lord wanted him to do. What Jerry wanted was to find that feeling that the Lord was there inside his heart because Jerry had put him there and not because his parents told him the Lord was there. Jerry loved the Lord. He loved to sing for the Lord, but sometimes that place in the center of his heart just stayed empty. It was as if he was loving the Lord through everybody else's heart and not his own.

CHAPTER 22

In November, he said goodbye to Sheriff Montgomery and Deputy Hackett at Pembroke. They looked as if they wanted to hug him, but instead they just shook his hand and wished him luck.

His next stop was Jackson, Georgia where he would be tested at the Diagnostic and Classification Center to determine where he'd be sent to serve out his sentence. Jerry didn't know what to wish for or even pray for except for a place where he'd be safe. He had enough sense to know he wasn't going to summer camp, but at the same time, he had no real idea of what to expect in prison. People in his family didn't go to prison. They went to church.

The center in Jackson was a new facility. Everything was white and clean, almost antiseptic, so he didn't have to worry about roaches crawling on his face while he slept like at Pembroke. He just had to worry about bumping his head on the john when he turned over in his cot. The cubbyhole cell was so small the john and the cot practically touched. They wouldn't let him sleep with his feet down by the john. The guards had to see his head when they peeked through the window in the door. He didn't complain. He just slept with his face toward the wall. He was out of the cell most of the day anyway. It was almost like being on a college campus and going to classes all day, except of course, this campus was locked up.

Jerry did whatever they told him to do. He slept when they said sleep. He got up when they said get up. He ate when they said eat. He didn't cause any trouble as they kept him busy with counseling and testing, but with the truth of his future hanging over him, he felt as if he was walking down a narrow hallway that kept getting darker and darker. He couldn't stop walking and he couldn't turn around. He had to keep going until the black swallowed him up.

He was nineteen years old and he was going to be in prison at least until he was twenty-six and maybe forever. Even if he got paroled, the best years of his life were going to be lost behind bars. Those were the years when a man started out on his life's work, fell in love, married and started a family, moved off on his own. He was moving off, but hardly on his own. He was a captive of the state of Georgia.

He kept praying. His parents told him that prayer could help everything, but sometimes he didn't see how. Still when he opened his eyes in the mornings and had to face another day, he looked up toward the ceiling and prayed, "Since I'm not dead, thank you, Jesus. I'm locked away and the key's thrown away. So even though this is where I'm going to spend the rest of my life, I'll try to remember to say praise God." Most days he remembered, but he wasn't able to put much enthusiasm into his praise.

The first few weeks in Jackson he wasn't even able to write his folks. It was just too hard to pick up a pencil and write anything on the special stationery they'd given him with a heading at the top calling for the inmate's name and state serial number. He'd become a number in the system, D-1902, one peg among many to be stuck in a hole somewhere and beat down to stay.

They gave him tests to see which hole he fit in. He didn't like tests. They told him there was no failing these tests, but sometimes as he stared at the paper on the written tests, his heart would start pounding and his hand would get so sweaty the pencil would slide sideways in his fingers.

Still as the days passed, he adjusted to the place. The commode next to his nose at night was way better than roaches. He did miss the way Willie and Deputy Hackett had bragged on his singing back in Pembroke. There they'd asked him to sing for them. Here every time he started singing some voice beyond the thin wall of his cell would yell at him to shut up and go to sleep. So Jerry had to whisper sing himself to sleep.

He was really blue on Thanksgiving Day as he thought about the turkey and cornbread stuffing and pumpkin pies his mother would cook and spread on the big table at home. He imagined her setting a plate for him even though he wasn't there. He wished he could just pop out of this place and be home for a couple of days.

That was all he wanted. Just a couple of days of freedom. He wanted to eat until he was as stuffed as the turkey on his mother's table and then walk out with his dad to the barn where he could smell the cows and the hay. He wanted to get up the next morning and hear the crunch of early morning frost under his feet. If it rained and brought the tobacco into case, he wanted to climb up in the barn and throw down the sticks of tobacco and help his father bulk it down to strip. He wanted his ears to ring from the loud whir of the chainsaw as they cut wood for the fireplace. He wanted to get up with the sun and do something, anything on the farm as a free man.

Inside this prison he felt totally removed from the natural world. It was hard to keep up even with what time it was since he didn't have a watch. The hours rolled into one another and stretched out too long. He knew daylight and dark, but the weather didn't seem to have any meaning to him. What difference did it make if it was hot or cold, if it was rainy or dry, if the wind was blowing or it was still?

The only storms he could feel were the ones inside him. He'd let his family down. He couldn't imagine what his mother and dad were going through at home, good Christian church folk with a convict for a son. Some of the time while he was in the Diagnostic Center he wished they'd just disown him, say they'd done their best and leave him to his just desserts.

But they didn't. They kept writing, kept telling him they loved him and were working every way they knew to help him, that they would never give up or stop praying for him.

Finally after Thanksgiving one of the counselors told him if he didn't write to his parents to explain the rules of correspondence, they were going to start sending their letters back. Prisoners couldn't get just any old letter from whoever took a notion to write him. In fact, at the Diagnostic Center he could only get letters from his parents and nobody else. Later he might be able to add more names to his mailing list as long as everybody followed all the rules. And everything he wrote or his parents wrote him would be read and censored.

Thinking about some guard reading what he was writing to his folks made the words dry up in Jerry's head. Besides he couldn't think of much to write that wouldn't upset his folks. He'd done enough of that already. So he just wrote the rules and a stiff *how are you and I am okay.*

Still after he wrote the first letter, it was easier to put his prison number on the top of the letter paper and write again. Things were going better anyway. They were holding him at the Diagnostic Center, and he was beginning to hope they might just make him a permanent inmate there since it was a new facility and clean. That way he wouldn't have to be sent to another prison. He could just serve out his time there. He went to church, and the chaplain let him sing "The Old Rugged Cross" the Sunday after Thanksgiving. Jerry put everything he had into singing the old hymn. He wanted to knock their socks off so they'd let him sing every week.

Before they decided where to send him, they brought in the Board of Doctors from Milledgeville. Just the sight of those doctors brought back the horrible memories of his time at the State Hospital locked up with the criminally insane. He could barely hold off the panic that they might decide he needed to go back there for more evaluation. He did his best to answer their questions the way they wanted, but the questions sounded stupid to Jerry. He didn't know what they were trying to figure out about him, and he was petrified he might say the wrong thing. At the end of the session, one of the doctors asked him if he remembered their names.

Jerry said, "No sir, I did my best to forget everything about that place. I didn't want to remember anything about my time there."

The doctors acted half mad about that, but he'd been as cooperative as he could be. He'd just told them the truth. Politely. He didn't remember their names. He remembered Miss Atwood's name, but not the doctors. She'd been the one who'd helped him the most. The night after he talked to the doctors he wasn't sure what would happen, where they might send him. He didn't know why the prison officials had to get the mental hospital people involved again. Miss Atwood had helped him understand his problems while he was there, but that was all in the past. Whoever that other Jerry Shepherd was who had done that horrible thing to Mr. Baylor was gone. Gone along with the need for alcohol or pills. Gone forever.

The next day the word came down that he was being sent to the Georgia State Prison in Reidsville to serve his time. A maximum-security facility. Where rapists and murderers and repeat felons were sent. Where lifers were incarcerated. That's where Jerry was going to spend at least the next seven years of his life if he could survive that long. There were no guarantees. Bad things happened in prisons like Reidsville.

It was the middle of December when he got to Reidsville. At home the churches would already be putting on their Christmas pageants. Little kids would be dressing up in bathrobes to be shepherds and thinking about the presents they might get on Christmas morning. Just a couple of years ago, he was one of those kids, still in school, looking forward to singing "O Holy Night" at church, shaking packages under the tree in the living room to see if he could guess what was inside. That seemed like a lifetime ago.

Now he was in a dorm with about a hundred other men waiting to be processed and assigned a spot in the prison and a work duty. He didn't know enough about what was going on to even know what exactly to be worried about. He was in a holding pattern, mentally and physically. He tried not to think too much about going into the prison population. He tried not to think about the kind of men he'd meet inside there.

He told himself there were sure to be others like him who had done terrible crimes but were ready to reform, ready to learn and ready to get as much from their time in prison as they could. Sometimes he could keep his mind on how he hoped to improve himself, to take advantage of whatever learning programs they had inside, but other times he just fell into a deep pit of depression and could hardly bear to think of anything at all.

Still he kept his letters home cheerful. He didn't write about how scared and lonely he was. He didn't write about how he cried himself to sleep when he thought about spending Christmas locked inside a prison. He didn't write about how he might have wasted every chance he had of making it as a singer. And sometimes when he was writing his letters to his mom and dad or reading the letters they wrote him, he could almost believe there was still some chance for him to get out.

He'd get up and put on the prison uniform of white shirt and pants with a blue stripe up the side of the pants and down the button placket of the shirt, and he'd think about pulling on his black leather boots and his old green coat with the tear in the elbow where he'd caught it on some barbed wire and going out to feed the cows. He didn't need a coat here. He wasn't going out anywhere.

In their letters, his parents kept asking what he wanted for Christmas. Jerry didn't want to think about Christmas. He wanted to shut his eyes and open them again in January after Christmas was over. He didn't care whether he even got a gift, but they kept asking so he finally told them a watch. It drove him crazy not knowing what time it was.

A few days before Christmas he wrote his mom and dad a letter telling them the results of the tests he'd taken at the Diagnostic Center. He hoped just knowing he'd done well on some of the tests would be a kind of gift.

The Social Worker at Jackson showed me the results of my tests and I came in above average and scored high normal. The test scores showed that I had the ability to be a Chaplain's Assistant, Office or Clerical Work, the ability for the art of drawing and designs and being a teacher, actor and singer.

It wasn't much of a gift, but it was all he had. Then since he was thinking about Christmas and how when he was a kid he'd gotten this great bike when his dad had kept telling him they couldn't afford it, Jerry decided to ask for something that sounded even more impossible. But weren't all the preachers always telling people to pray big? So he added another paragraph to his letter.

The next time you see Mr. York, ask him if it would be alright if I could write a letter to the Governor of Georgia. If I can get enough people to back me up and write letters to the Governor and to the Warden of the prison, they will take notice of my case, knowing that people are interested and wanting to help me, then I can start the ball to jumping down here. Let me know what you think and what Mr. York thinks about this.

Christmas morning Jerry woke up early. He thought about last Christmas when he'd gone home after basic training. He'd done his folks proud winning awards in basic, and that Christmas had been one of the best they'd ever had together. The tree had been nearly up to the ceiling and his mother had bought new gold bells for it. They'd opened presents and he'd probably downed a dozen of his mother's sweet rolls for breakfast. He'd gotten a black leather wallet with a twenty in it. He tried to think what had happened to the wallet. He must have left it in the barracks at Ft. Gordon.

Jerry rolled over in his bunk, pulled the cover up over his head, and willed his body to stop breathing. His lungs betrayed him by continuing to pull in air and let it out. The get up signal was going off. The guards would be around to roust out anybody who didn't pay attention. There weren't any Santa Clauses in prison.

Jerry sat up and gave himself a talking to. Christmas had never been about Santa Claus. Christmas was the day Jesus was born. The Christ's birthday. Jerry wished he had a Bible to read the Christmas story the way his dad always did on Christmas morning, but they'd made him leave all his things at Pembroke. Still he'd heard it read a million times. He didn't need a Bible. He could remember it.

He stared at the wall and whispered the words, "And she brought forth her firstborn son, and wrapped him in swaddling clothes and laid him in a manger because there was no room for them in the inn. And there were in the same country shepherds abiding in the field, keeping watch over their flock by night."

Shepherds. As a kid, he'd never wanted to be Joseph or one of the wise men or a donkey. He'd always wanted to be a shepherd. Jerry Shepherd, one of *the* shepherds who heard the angels sing on that first Christmas Day. "And an angel of the Lord appeared unto them and the glory of the Lord shone round about them and lo, they were sore afraid."

He used to wonder exactly what it meant to be sore afraid, but now he was beginning to find out. He was sore afraid of what was ahead of him. He moved his mind away from his fear and tried to come up with the next verses. It was something about not being afraid.

When he was a little shepherd in the church pageants, he had never wanted to act afraid like the play directors told him to. Jerry had wanted to see an angel. He thought it would be the greatest thing to get to sing along with the angels. Sometimes late at night on Christmas Eve, he would go outside and look up at the sky and imagine angels there singing.

His voice got a little louder as he went on with the next part. "And the angel said, Fear not, for behold, I bring you good tidings of great joy, which shall be to all people, for unto you this day is born a Savior."

There was something else. Something about the swaddling clothes and the manger but he couldn't remember the words well enough to say it. He remembered the multitude of angels appearing and singing. "Glory to God in the highest, and on earth peace, good will toward men."

Did he have any chance of peace in this place? Good will toward men in prison was surely a joke. These men didn't have any good will toward anybody. He didn't know whether it was the Lord's voice or his mother's voice echoing in his head. *You don't have to worry about what the other men feel. It's your good will that matters.*

"But what if I never get out? What if I'm here every Christmas for the rest of my life?"

The answer was clear in his head. *Daily the Lord will give you grace sufficient enough to meet the challenges of the day.*

"But I'm not strong enough," Jerry said. "I can't do it."

This time he knew it was his mother's voice, perhaps some memory from the past when she was pushing him to do more, to be perfect. *You can't, but the Lord can. His strength is made perfect in weakness.*

That's how Jerry felt. Weak. Not good enough. Not strong enough. Not able. Never able. As he joined the line for breakfast where they'd be sure to plop those globby grits on his plate yet again, he silently said a prayer. *Thank you, Lord, for being born. Forgive me for wishing I wasn't.*

Then in a very quiet whisper he sang, "Happy birthday, Jesus."

After he was through with every line of the song, he thought about singing happy birthday to himself. His real birthday, January third, when he would turn twenty was still ten days away, but this Christmas was his first as a convict. Of course that didn't seem like a very good reason to celebrate.

CHAPTER 23

The days in quarantine dragged by. He had a watch now. His folks had sent it in the Christmas package he'd gotten a few days after Christmas. The watch was great, but now he knew exactly how long it took the hour hand to make a circle. If only they'd go ahead and assign him to some kind of work duty. If he had something to do, some real work, the time would surely pass faster.

He'd gotten some cards from the people back home even though they weren't on his mailing list The mail censors must have had a fit of Christmas spirit.

The day after he turned twenty, he got a letter from Mr. York. Mr. York wrote how he was sure Warden Stamper and the other officials at the institution already knew how much Jerry wanted to fully rehabilitate himself. The lawyer told him to work hard, not become discouraged and make the most of each hour of the day.

Jerry stared at the words. It was easy enough for Mr. York to write about not being discouraged. He wasn't locked up. Jerry kept reading.

Make the most of each day by involving your mind and take care of your health by getting as much exercise as possible.

Jerry was all for that. He'd run all the way home if they'd just open the door. The lawyer wasn't very hopeful about getting a quick pardon from the governor.

As you know, the Governor of the State of Georgia has the power to grant you a pardon; however, I encourage you not to build up your hopes that this can be brought about overnight. The odds are that it will never happen, and I am sure that you understood this as you made your decision to pay your penalty when you were at Pembroke. This does not mean that you should not continue to try; however, at this point, I think it would be unfair to yourself and to the authorities, which includes the Governor of the State of Georgia, to request them to take this under full advisement until you have proven yourself as a model individual at Reidsville.

At first Jerry didn't think it was a particularly encouraging letter, but the more he read it over, the more he did feel encouraged. Mr. York thought he could handle being in prison. Mr. York thought he could show everybody how well he could be rehabilitated. Mr. York thought they'd give him some kind of work that would make a contribution to his fellow man. He didn't just say fellow inmates. Mr. York told him to keep up the good work and promised to keep working on his case at home. They hadn't forgotten him. All he had to do was prove himself a model prisoner and then he could write the governor.

Finally in the middle of January, he got out of quarantine and was assigned a new number, 50687, and a spot in Dorm G-1. The West Side of the prison was mostly black inmates with one integrated dorm. The East Side was mostly white inmates also with one integrated dorm. Jerry was in the integrated dorm on the East Side. He was told it was a good assignment, the safest place for him since the hundred and twenty-five men in that dorm were mostly older inmates with good prison records.

Double bunks lined the wall. Each man had a small gray metal locker for personal belongings. Jerry didn't have much to put in his yet. Some letters from his folks. Paper and pencil to write his letters back. He still didn't have his Bible. His life had been stripped down to the bare necessities—whatever food they dished out on his tray when he went through the food line, water, a narrow cot to sleep on, an open shower in the middle of the dorm area, a square patch of dirt yard to stretch his legs in at assigned times.

He went out on the work detail. He dug ditches. Sometimes he just dug them to fill them back in. Jerry didn't care. He was glad to be using his muscles again. And he wouldn't be on the ditch digging detail forever. Come spring they'd plant a garden to raise vegetables for the prison kitchen, and in six months or a year he'd be able to request a transfer to a different duty, maybe something using the aptitudes and talents they'd said he had at the Diagnostic Center.

As soon as he could, he met with the chaplain. Jerry tried to impress him by saying how he hoped to use his time in prison to study the Bible and take classes and improve his singing. "I want to take advantage of every opportunity during my time here to improve myself and try to convince the authorities that I deserve a second chance," he ended up.

"That's admirable." Chaplain Chatham smiled at Jerry, but he looked like a man who'd heard too many promises from too many men who failed to keep them. "We'll certainly do everything on our end to help you. Are you interested in attending church services here in the prison?"

"I'm looking forward to it. I've always gone to church ever since I can remember and I want to keep going to church in here."

"Good. Your records say you are a member of the Baptist denomination."

"Yes sir. Where my folks live in Shelby County up in Kentucky, there's a Baptist church just across the field. When we moved there, we changed over from the Christian Church. My mother didn't much want to, but Dad and I didn't see any reason to drive a long way to church when we could see one right there beside us," Jerry said. "But I've sung specials and led the music at revivals in lots of different churches. I'd like to be part of any kind of choir you might have here."

"You sing tenor?"

"Yes sir, ever since I was in high school. Before my voice changed, I sang bass in a barbershop quartet at my junior high school."

"Well, that's different. A boy usually goes from tenor to bass, not the other way around." The chaplain smiled again.

"I have a way of doing things backwards," Jerry said. "You want to hear me sing?"

"I don't know that it's necessary. Your aptitude tests show singing ability, but why not?" Chaplain Chatham leaned back in his chair and put his hands together.

Jerry sang the first verse of "The Old Rugged Cross," the song he'd just sung a few weeks back while he was at the Diagnostic Center.

"Nothing backwards about that," the chaplain said after Jerry sang the last word. "I'll arrange for you to come out for choir practice this week and you can sing with the choir next Sunday."

Sometimes Jerry thought as long as he could sing, everything would turn out all right. The blisters on his hands turned to calluses as he kept digging ditches. He sang while he dug as long as the other inmates digging around him didn't yell at him. Sometimes they sang along just like in the old prison movies he'd seen when he was a kid. They'd sing everything from kids' songs to the old hymns to the latest pop song somebody had heard on the radio.

Other times one of the men would get in his face and tell him to shut up. Jerry would square off with any of the inmates, toe to toe, and stare them straight in the eye no matter how big they were. Jerry never backed down. He'd flirted with death. No, more than flirted. He'd chased after death more than once, but he wasn't about to let anybody else push him over the edge. Not the tough guys who just wanted to make noise. And not the homosexuals who told him he was a pretty boy and they could make everything easy for him if he'd just cooperate.

Jerry should have been expecting it. His dad had warned him in a roundabout way. The guards had told him to watch his step. A couple of older men in the dorm had pointed out some inmates to shy away from. Even the warden must have known what might happen to Jerry. They'd put him in the safest dorm where they had the best chance of protecting him. But still the first time one of the men hit on him, it was like somebody had thrown ice water in his face to wake him up.

He didn't go down. He fired up. He stared the man right in the eye and told him to take his business elsewhere, that nothing like that was ever going to happen.

"I've got friends," the inmate said. "We can take you any time we want."

"Maybe you could. If your friends are big enough. But you'd never do it but once," Jerry told him.

For some reason the man backed off. Jerry didn't know whether it was the crazy look in his eyes or if the Lord was holding his hand over Jerry because of his mother and dad's fervent every minute prayers.

The last Friday of January his mother along with a church friend, Mrs. Williams, and his Aunt Adele came to visit. Since they had to come from out of state, the warden had granted them permission to spend the day with Jerry. His mother brought a basket of food and Jerry ate until he couldn't stuff another bite in his mouth. His father had stayed home to do the milking, but he would make the trip the next time. Best of all the captain of the guard let his mother give him his Bible, a hymnbook, his dictionary, and a shaving kit, which was completely against the rules. Everything was supposed to be mailed in. But then nobody could stand up against his mother for long, not even the Georgia State Prison guards. Especially when she was plying them with her homemade brownies.

Being in Reidsville was like being in a new world where he had to learn the rules of existence. He watched to see who the troublemakers were so he could stay away from them. He kept his mouth shut no matter what he saw. He didn't do anything to give the guards reason to notice him when he was out digging ditches. He learned to eat whatever they put on his tray in the food line. He bought cigarettes every week even though he didn't smoke. Cigarettes were money in prison, and he wanted to get enough to trade for a radio. At least if he had a radio, he would have some connection with the outside world and he could hear music.

Sometimes he thought music was the only thing keeping him sane. He wrote his mother and asked her to send him a book that would teach him everything about music so he could learn to read music the way he could read a book. He wanted to be the best singer in the prison choir.

He put in his hours on the work detail. He read his Bible and whatever else he could get his hands on. He studied his music books. He wrote letters home. He sang songs in his head. He did everything he could think of to stay too busy to think about the days and months and years that would have to pass before he would be a free man again, but it was always there in the back of his mind.

The time stretched out in front of him like a row of tobacco with no end in sight. When he was a sophomore in high school, they had raised tobacco in a field with rows that must have been two miles long. He remembered chopping out the tobacco and trying to see ahead to the end of the row, but all he could see were more tobacco plants. He'd wanted to drop down in the middle of the field and just sit there because he didn't think he could ever get to the end of the row. Instead he'd kept hoeing each plant, then stepping up to the next one to start pulling the dirt up around its roots to make it grow better. And eventually he'd come to the last plant in the last row.

That's the way it was in prison. No end in sight, but all he could do was step forward and do whatever it took to get through the next minute. And maybe someday there would be a last minute, a time when they opened the door and let him leave on his own and not just with a shovel to dig ditches while an armed guard stood watch.

That's what Everett kept telling him. To just keep moving through the days and the years would pass for him the way they had for Everett. Everett slept two bunks down and he'd been at Reidsville for eight years so he knew what he was talking about. Jerry reminded Everett of the little brother Everett hadn't seen since he got sent up. He wouldn't let his brother come see him or write to him. He wouldn't even let his mother send him a picture of the brother when he got married a few years ago. Everett didn't want his little brother to get close enough to get the slightest whiff of prison.

"I always hate to see babies like you come into the system," Everett had told Jerry the first time he'd stopped by Jerry's bunk.

Jerry's hand had tightened on his pencil as he looked up from the letter he was writing to his folks. The man had looked okay, but it was always best to be ready for whatever might happen. "I haven't been a baby for a long time," he had said.

Everett had just shaken his head a little. "You're a just born baby in here. And you never know which way babies like you are going to go—to the bad or to the good."

"I'm not aiming to go bad. Least no worse than I already am," Jerry had told him.

"Maybe you won't, kid, but it'll take some doing for you to get through the years here with no scars. You're a pretty boy."

Jerry had sat up straighter as his eyes narrowed on the older man. "You hitting on me?"

Everett's smile had been almost sad. "Nope, just trying to help you out a little. The way some other guys helped me out when I first came in. You need to get a good job, something away from the hard cases who'd just as soon hit you over the head with a shovel as look at you. Or catch you alone in the showers. Or out in the yard. You need to keep your head up and stay out of trouble. Bad things can happen awfully fast in here."

"I'm on outside duty. They say you can't ask for another assignment for six months. That won't be till June or July," Jerry had said.

"If you make it that long." Everett had given him another long look. "You can't ask, but that don't mean somebody else can't. I work in the shipping department. It's not a bad assignment. One of the guys over there is getting out next week. I'll see what I can do."

Everett had headed back toward his bunk. "Why would you do that?" Jerry had asked him before he got too far away.

"You remind me of my little brother."

"He in prison somewhere, too?"

Everett had whirled around and stared daggers at Jerry. "Don't ever say that again."

"Sorry," Jerry had said quickly. "It was just a question."

"Well, the answer's no. Always and forever no."

"That's good to hear."

"Yeah, it is good." The anger had drained out of Everett's eyes. "He's a preacher up in Knoxville. Got a big church. I hear him on the radio sometimes when the signal's extra strong."

"I sometimes think about being a preacher," Jerry had said. "But I'd rather be a singer."

Everett's lips had twitched up in a little smile. "Yeah, I heard you in the choir last Sunday. You not only look pretty, you sound like a girl."

Jerry had clinched his fists and sprung off his bunk to face off against Everett. Some of the other guys in the dorm had looked over at them expecting a fight.

Everett had stepped up close to Jerry and kept his voice low. "First lesson, kid. Learn to tell who's a friend and who's not. I'm a friend telling you the truth.

You're pretty and you sound like a girl, but I like you anyhow and I'm going to help you even if you are stupid. So back off and live. Okay?"

Jerry had stared straight into Everett's eyes a second before he had relaxed his hands. "Okay," he'd said. "Sorry. I am stupid."

"Nearly every kid your age is. But most of them don't know it, so you're one step closer to smartening up. Just stay out of trouble and don't be so ready to fight. You ain't mean enough to fight in here. With God's help, you'll never get that mean."

"Are you that mean?" Jerry had asked.

"No, but I'm that smart." Everett had smiled again and walked away.

CHAPTER 24

Jerry sang in the prison church choir two Sundays. Then the choir director quit and the chaplain called Jerry into his office and gave him the job. Jerry was in hog heaven. He was still digging ditches during the week, but on the weekends he was getting to sing. He wanted to make the choir the best ever, and he had the voices to do it. They just needed some encouragement to reach down and pull out their best efforts.

The first practice on Friday went great. The choir members listened to him. The tenors sang higher. The basses sang lower. All of them put feeling in their voices.

After the practice, Chaplain Chatham threw his arm around Jerry's shoulders and said, "That's the best I've ever heard any choir here sing. You've been able to pull out some hidden talents we didn't even know were there. Talents the guys didn't even know they had. Great job, Gerald. I'm looking forward to hearing the music on Sunday."

Some of the choir members came by to talk to Jerry before they reported back to their duties. "Hey, man, I like the way you give it all you've got," one of the basses said. He'd hit notes so far down the scale Jerry didn't even know they were there.

"Yeah, Shepherd, we like the way you bounce around and listen at the same time. We're going to blow them away on Sunday." This was a big tough looking black guy named Rawlins who'd sung his solo part with a voice straight out of heaven.

By the time Jerry went back to the dorm, he was practically floating. He was doing something good. Men ten times tougher than he was were paying attention to him, listening when he told them they could do better. And they had sounded good. He'd even seen a couple of tears in a few of the men's eyes while they were singing "Amazing Grace."

You couldn't direct emotion like that, but at the same time, Jerry couldn't let himself get carried away by emotion. He had to listen to each note to make sure it was on key. He had to concentrate on the harmony and the music. He couldn't think about the words all that much. He just wanted it to sound good. He wanted to give the men who showed up for church Sunday the best music they'd ever heard. If the Lord wanted to use the music in some special spiritual way, then that was up to him. Jerry just wanted it to sound good.

And on Sunday it did. They had two services with about a thousand men at each one. Jerry had led a lot of revivals, but he'd never sung to so many people at one time. And the inmates seemed to like it even if they were a captive audience. He was a captive performer. His parents had written to ask if they could come to church with him when they came down to visit, but no visitors were allowed at the prison church services. So he could only share with them how the choir was going in his letters.

He kept writing lots of letters. He even wrote to Judge Rutherford. His mother said it might help and she didn't see how it could hurt to keep the judge from forgetting about Jerry locked up there in Reidsville. His mother said Judge Rutherford had told her how interested he was in Jerry's case. His mother must have been right because the judge answered Jerry's letter. He told Jerry to keep taking advantage of every opportunity to improve himself while he was in the prison system until he had the chance to be paroled. Jerry turned his mind away from how many years that would be. He had to try to take things one day at a time.

Everett put in Jerry's name for the job in the shipping department. There was plenty of work since Reidsville made the prison uniforms for all the institutions in the state. Jerry got the job. A few days after he started working on the line packing uniforms in boxes to ship to other prisons, Everett pulled him aside.

"You know how to type, Shep?" he asked.

"No, but I guess I could learn," Jerry said. "Why?"

"Well, I got good news. The Parole Board has finally decided I've paid my due to society and they're letting me out of this place in a couple of weeks."

"That's great, Everett." Jerry made himself smile. He was happy for Everett, but he hated the thought of losing a friend so soon.

"Yeah, it is," Everett said. "And you'll make out just fine without me. You know some of the ropes now. You just need to keep your temper under control and not be so ready to fly off the handle. Stay calm and live."

"That's what my dad keeps telling me, and I'm trying," Jerry said. "I haven't socked anybody yet."

"And make sure you don't. You don't want to get written up and sent to the hole. You need to keep your record spotless." Everett frowned and shook his head a little. "But I wasn't meaning to give you no sermon. I was just wanting to know about you typing. I've got a typing book and you can practice on my typewriter some in the afternoons. You learn fast. I know you can do it, so I'm putting you in for my job."

"Shipping clerk?"

"It ain't all that hard. You just have to watch the numbers."

"Numbers?" Jerry felt his stomach sink. "Numbers aren't my strong suit."

"You can do it, Shep. It don't take a math genius. It's mostly just record keeping stuff, what's shipped out and where, what needs to be shipped out, that kind of stuff. And you'll be back here in the warehouse away from the hard cases. I'll get you in. All you got to do is learn to type."

"I'll learn to type." Jerry took the typing book. He'd practice till his fingers were sore.

"Good," Everett said. "Come on back to my desk now and you can practice on some shipping slips."

Everett sat beside him while Jerry hunted and pecked the keys. It took him three times as long as Everett but he got it done. "See I told you it wasn't so hard," Everett said.

Jerry sat back and looked at the man. He had no idea how old he was. He just had that worn prison look that said he'd spent a lot of his life locked up. "What are you going to do when you get out?" Jerry asked him.

"First thing, I'm gonna take a big lungful of free air. Then if that don't make me cough too much, I'm gonna go to some restaurant and order all the peach pie with ice cream on it that I can eat. After that I'll go see my family."

"You have a wife and kids?"

"Nope. Not yet, but who knows? Maybe that's what I'll do after I get full of peach pie and ice cream." Everett smiled. "No, I just have my mother waiting for me. She'll be glad to see me."

"What about your brother? You going to go to his church when you get out and hear him preach in person?"

"I don't know." Everett looked over at Jerry. "What do you think, Shep? It hasn't been so long since you went to church on the outside. You think those good Christians would want an ex-con sitting in their pews? I wouldn't want to cause my brother no trouble."

"The people back at my old church pray for me all the time. I think they'd be glad to see me sitting in the pews there again. And I'll bet your brother would be glad to see you in his church. Besides, the Bible says we're all sinners, doesn't it?"

"Some more so than others."

"Not in the Lord's eyes. At least that's what my father always said."

"We aren't talking about the Lord here. We're talking about the good folks at my brother's church."

"You won't have to wear your prison uniform when you get out." Jerry pulled out his button placket to show the blue stripe. "Won't nobody know you're an ex-con if you don't tell them."

"Maybe not," Everett said. "But I've heard some that got out and came back claim that free world people can smell you or something. That they always know. But one thing you can count on. When I get out of here, I ain't never coming back. If they throw up bets in the dorm the day after I leave on how long before I'm back, you bet on never."

Jerry learned to type, and he got the job. Everett had a few days to train him before he walked out of the prison a free man. The first week after Everett left, Jerry had a run in with the prison boss over shipping. Nobody had told the boss that Jerry needed Fridays off to work with the choir. He informed Jerry the shipping clerk job was a five day a week job and that was that. It didn't matter if Jerry worked extra the other days to keep his work caught up. It didn't matter that all the uniforms were getting shipped out on time and the orders were written up without the first mistake. Nothing mattered except what the boss man said mattered.

It was Jerry's worst week in prison up till then. He wasn't giving up choir director. He couldn't give up choir director. Music was his life. And it could be the Lord wanted him to do the choir. That's what he told himself anyway even if he didn't exactly open up the conversation with the Lord. Some things you didn't have to pray that much about. You just knew already. The choir was like that. Jerry wanted to stay with the choir. He told his parents in a letter home that he'd go back to digging ditches with work detail 22 before he'd give up leading the choir.

And it wasn't just the choir and the job conflict. Everything was going wrong. Everett was gone. He was out breathing free air and eating peach pie with as many dips of ice cream on it as his plate would hold. Jerry was glad about that, but he didn't have anybody to talk to, nobody to tell him to stay calm and clean.

Other guys talked to him, told him not to get jumpy, told him not to be expecting everybody to be sweet and kind. After all if they were all sweet and kind, they wouldn't be locked up behind barbed wire fences with guards on every corner. They told him bad things happened in prison. All he had to worry about was not letting the bad, the really bad things happen to him.

Things like happened to Bobby Joe. He wasn't much older than Jerry. Had only been there a week when they found him in the showers half dead. Things like happened to Jimmy who was always ready to take Jerry on one on one on the basketball court out in the yard. The other guys told Jerry that Jimmy must have stepped on the wrong people's toes. Tuesday night Jimmy was in line four men up from Jerry for supper. The next thing Jerry knew, Jimmy was on the floor with a pool of red spreading out around him toward Jerry's feet.

Somebody pulled Jerry away. He didn't know who. He heard somebody talking in his ear, telling him not to look too close at anything. That some things were better not seen and they weren't talking just about the blood.

The guards locked down the prison. Nobody got to eat. Not that Jerry felt like eating after that. He stared at the ceiling above the bunk and listened to Oscar snoring below him. Oscar was a scrappy looking black man around forty. He was in on a life sentence for killing some white guy in a fight. Everett had told Jerry Oscar was innocent, that he'd gotten a raw deal, but Oscar didn't talk about it. He didn't talk much about anything. He mostly slept all the time, but tonight before he'd pulled the blanket up over his head, he'd told Jerry, "You'll get used to it, boy."

Jerry didn't see how anybody could get used to somebody getting knifed three feet away from him. He kept his eyes wide open in the dim light. It was never completely dark. The guards wanted to be able to see the men in their bunks. It hadn't been the least bit dark in the supper line, but that hadn't made any difference. Jimmy had still gotten a knife in the gut. Jerry was locked up in here with a bunch of animals. It was a joke the guards saying they could protect him. There had been guards in the cafeteria.

Funny, all those years when he was a teenager he'd wanted to die. He'd driven into trees. He'd drunk himself into a stupor. He'd swallowed handfuls of pills. But now, with death stomping all around him, he wanted to live. He wanted to do something with his life even if that life was spent behind bars.

He wondered if Jimmy had wanted to live. He didn't know much about Jimmy except that he had a great jump shot. He'd been in for a while, they said. Would have been up for parole in a year or two. Now he was dead. Paroled to heaven. Or maybe not. Jerry tried to remember if he'd ever seen Jimmy in church. He wished he could remember seeing his face staring up at the choir from one of the pews, but he couldn't. All he could see was the desperate fear on the man's face as he crumpled to the floor while his blood spread wider and wider around him before the guards pushed everybody back.

Jerry wondered if somebody stuck a knife in him, he'd be paroled to heaven. His mother told him he was going to heaven. He'd asked her after he joined church. But there were times he wasn't sure. Preachers said you were supposed to be sure. That you weren't supposed to wonder about that. Not if you were right with God.

But how did you get right with God? He'd done everything the preachers and his parents had told him to. He'd walked the aisle. He'd prayed. He'd sung hymns, was still singing hymns, was willing to go back to digging ditches rather than quit directing the choir that was singing hymns. Then why did he still have questions?

And if he'd been right with God, he would have never done all the things he'd done. Not even if he was sick the way Miss Atwood said he was when he beat poor Mr. Baylor to death. He wished he could talk to Everett so he could tell Jerry how to survive in this jungle. He wished he were out in the field with his father planting something. Anything. He didn't care. He just wanted to hear his father's voice. He wanted to hear his father telling him that he could survive prison. No, not could. Would. He wanted to survive. He wanted to live.

He would write his folks in the morning and tell them how bad things were. They surely didn't know how bad things were or they would find some way to get him out. And even if they couldn't get him out, then at least they'd know he wasn't just having some walk in the woods here. They'd know he was in a jungle with a bunch of wild animals who could jump out of the bushes and kill him any time they wanted to.

He started writing the letter in his head. *My lawyer says sit back and wait and you say take it easy and everything will be all right. Well, you know good and well that everything isn't all right, and I can't sit back and wait for time to pass. I'm under pressure. I can't plan ahead because I don't know what's going to happen from one day to the next. It's like a jungle. I'm alive one day and I may be dead the next. Just like Jimmy.*

Of course his folks didn't know Jimmy. They didn't know anybody here.

He mentally scratched out Jimmy's name. The censors wouldn't let it go out anyway. It might make the prison look bad if the free world knew people were dying in here.

He shut his eyes to try to go to sleep, but then the body sinking down into the pool of blood wasn't Jimmy's. It was his. Jerry popped his eyes back open wide. He began trying to lay out the typewriter keys on the ceiling above his head. He was trying to decide if the *y* was on the top line under the numbers or on the bottom line when he finally fell asleep.

He wrote the letter to his parents the next morning before he went to breakfast. The lines were just the same as always with the men shuffling along fussing about the food. Jimmy's blood had been scrubbed up off the floor.

CHAPTER 25

Chaplain Chatham worked things out with Jerry's prison boss in the shipping department so Jerry could keep his job there as shipping clerk and still direct the choir. It was a bit of a reprieve but not a complete one. The boss kept piling extra work on Jerry as if trying to make sure Jerry messed up, but Jerry worked at a run every minute of the day and kept things caught up.

It helped that the work was getting easier and that he was getting better at typing every day. He wasn't going to let the boss man win. Every time Jerry felt like exploding and shoving the papers down the man's throat, he made himself think of Everett. Everett had gone out on a limb pushing Jerry for his job. And while the boss couldn't do anything to Everett now since he was out there somewhere breathing free air and eating peach pie, Jerry still wanted to prove Everett was right about him and he could do the job. It didn't matter that he was only twenty. Age didn't make the first bit of difference. The chaplain thought he was doing a great job directing the choir, and he was only twenty there, too.

Everybody was always telling him to keep his prison record clean, to stay out of trouble, to keep his nose clean. He was trying. He really was, but the boss was ready to jump on any little mistake. He wanted him to fail. He wanted to find a reason to write him up and send him to the hole.

Still the days passed. Jerry wrote letters home. He got letters back from his mother telling him to sit back, stay calm and wait. She didn't understand about waiting. She wasn't inside this jungle with people shoving him toward some big hole with stakes in the bottom to skewer him. She didn't see Jimmy's blood spreading out at her feet every time she closed her eyes. She meant well, but he was just as glad it was his father's turn to come visit in March. And he couldn't wait. He wanted to unload on him. He wanted his father to tell him how to make it in a place where there was no one to trust, no one to help, where people were trying to block him every time he tried to do something good, where people were trying to beat him down.

Even at night he couldn't rest. He'd go to sleep but then faceless monsters would be trying to mash him, spiders would be crawling on him, or he'd be trying to write down orders and the numbers wouldn't add up. Finally one night he jerked awake after a particularly bad dream to see Oscar had climbed up on the edge of the bottom bunk to put his face right in front of Jerry's. Jerry swung at him, but Oscar caught his wrist and held it in a vice grip.

"You gonna have to get hold of yourself, boy. You're messing with old Oscar's sleeping time," Oscar growled.

Jerry took a deep breath to calm down. "I can't help what I'm dreaming."

"You gonna have to learn to. This fighting bears and yelling all night right above my head is gonna stop one way or another. You understand what I'm saying, boy?" Oscar's fingers loosened on Jerry's wrist, but he didn't let him go.

"You tell me how to stop it and I will," Jerry said. What did the man expect? Jerry didn't plan to have nightmares.

"You think too much, boy."

"I can't quit thinking," Jerry said.

"Maybe not, but you can quit always thinking ahead or behind. What you got to learn to do is think right now. Think I'm eating now. Think I'm working now. Think I'm breathing now. Think I'm sleeping now. Don't let none of that other stuff come in while you're thinking them things. Especially on the sleeping one."

"I can't…." Jerry started, but Oscar tightened his grip on Jerry's wrist and didn't let him finish.

"I ain't hearing no can't. Think I'm sleeping now. Better yet think old Oscar's sleeping now. Think I ain't bothering poor old Oscar who don't like mad dogs fighting in the bunk over his head."

"I'll try," Jerry said.

"Good." Oscar turned loose of Jerry's wrist. "Cause you a nice enough boy, but fact is, I done been accused of snuffing out one white boy. I could do it again. They can't add no time on to a life sentence. They might put me in the hole, but leastways it'd be quiet down there and a man could sleep."

"Everett said you didn't do it," Jerry said.

Oscar smiled a little. "Then maybe the State of Georgia owes me one." He ducked back down to his own bunk. Two seconds later, he was snoring.

Oscar knew how to sleep. Most of the men in the dorm knew how to sleep. Snores were echoing all over. Maybe it was something Jerry could learn. Just shut his eyes and think sleep. Not worry about the boss man. Not worry about falling in a pool of his own blood. Not worry about a gang catching him alone in the showers. Not worry about anything but this moment.

That's all the Bible said a person had anyway. The minute right now. Wasn't there something in there, something Jesus had said, about not worrying about tomorrow because there was plenty enough to worry about today? And nobody even knew if they'd have a tomorrow. A person's heart could explode inside his chest. A tornado could come along and blow the whole prison to kingdom come. Oscar could get tired of getting woken up in the middle of the night and put a pillow over Jerry's head. Jerry didn't think the old man could take him, but he was pretty strong. Jerry rubbed his wrist.

The kids' song "Jesus Loves Me" popped into Jerry's head. He hadn't sung that song since he'd helped with the music in Bible School four or five years ago. *Jesus loves me this I know for the Bible tells me so. Little ones to him are weak. They are weak but he is strong.*

That was Jerry. Weak. But the song said Jesus was strong. Maybe he should ask the Lord to help him sleep without nightmares. That was surely easier than bringing Lazarus out of the tomb, and he'd done that.

What was it everybody was always saying? When all else fails, pray. Jerry wondered why people didn't pray before all else failed. He wished he had done more praying and less failing and then he might not be in this place. He moved his lips silently as he repeated the Lord's Prayer over and over. He didn't figure it was the best time to pray out loud right then. He didn't want Oscar back in his face.

◆   ◆   ◆

It helped having his father visit. His father talked sense to him. His father knew how things were in prison from his year of working at LaGrange. When his father said to just keep holding on, just keep doing his best, and staying out of trouble, he made Jerry believe he could take whatever happened. He could get the boss man off his back. He could handle the men in the choir that just came to practice so they wouldn't have to go out on their work details. He could block out the bad things and think on the good things like the delicious food his mother had sent down with his dad. He could plan new songs to sing. He could concentrate on how to improve the choir. He could stay too busy to think about the years stretching out in front of him. After all, what didn't kill a person made him stronger and so far Jerry was still breathing.

He was surprised when his mother wrote to him that she was going to visit Miss Atwood at the Milledgeville Hospital. He thought all of that was in the past. He'd been mentally ill, but he understood his problems now. So those problems were gone. For one thing, when things went bad, he'd used alcohol and drugs as a crutch. That meant he was an alcoholic. He'd been looking into joining AA here in the prison. If he ever did get out, he didn't want to fall back into the same hole.

But his mother said she realized now that she was part of Jerry's problems and while she couldn't do anything about the past, she didn't want to hold back his progress in any way in the future. She wanted to be the right kind of mother for him, and she was willing to listen to whatever Miss Atwood had to say about it all. She wrote that there was no shame in making a mistake unless a person didn't try to correct the things they were doing wrong. She said she'd gladly go back and do everything over again if she could have done something different that would have kept Jerry out of prison. She was proud of all the good things he was doing in prison and the way he'd decided to improve himself in every way possible. The least she could do was the same and try to improve her mothering skills. After her visit with Miss Atwood, she would come on down to Reidsville to visit Jerry, and she promised to bring all his favorite foods again.

The days passed. The boss man got off Jerry's back when he finally opened his eyes and saw how hard Jerry was working to do everything he asked. They let another inmate start helping Jerry get the uniforms ready to ship. Things got so much better in the warehouse after T.C. started working there that Jerry almost decided the man might be one of those angels Jerry had wondered if he'd find in prison.

The thought made Jerry smile. T.C. looked like anything but an angel. Instead the big, ugly, rawboned man looked as if he'd been on the bottom of a pile of football players a few too many times. T.C. said he'd been on drugs outside and held up some banks. Never killed anybody. Never even shot at anybody. The judge had gone easy on him the first time he got caught since he remembered T.C. playing football at the local high school. He got light time, but once he got out, he'd just gone straight back to doping again and started hitting banks again.

"Folks always did say I was a slow learner," T.C. told Jerry with a laugh. "But I've learned this time. If I ever get out again, I ain't never going in another bank. They tell me filling stations have more cash anyhow."

One day T.C. came in from the dock area where they loaded up the trucks carrying this pitiful excuse for a kitten in the palm of his hand. "Did you ever see such a sight?" he asked Jerry. "It don't have but two legs and no tail. Looks like it was born that way."

Jerry stroked the kitten's head with his finger. He used to pet the barn cats back on the farm. He'd rub them all the way down their back so fast their fur would crackle. Sometimes his mother would name them, and sometimes they just called them kitty. When they moved, they usually left the cats at the old barn. Jerry looked from the kitten to T.C. "But how does the poor thing get around?"

"Wait. You got to see this." T.C. put the kitten on the floor. The little animal picked itself up off the floor, balanced on its back legs and jumped like a rabbit over to Jerry to get another rub around his ears.

"That's the funniest thing I ever saw. It must be half rabbit." The kitten began purring the minute Jerry touched its head. The week before he'd gotten a letter from his dad saying he had a new pup, and Jerry had been extra homesick ever since. He wanted to be there at the farm watching the pup to figure out if it was a Chief or a King, a Jerome or a Hugo. He wanted to feel the pup licking his fingers. He wanted to get mad when the dog chewed up his shoes. A two-legged, tailless cat might not compare to a German shepherd pup, but it was alive and breathing. It was surviving when odds said it shouldn't.

"You think we could keep it here in the warehouse?" T.C. asked. "I could sneak it a little food now and again. And it might be able to catch a mouse."

"I wouldn't bet on that. But then I wouldn't have bet on it being able to walk either."

"Or hop," T.C. said.

"Let's call it Cabbit. Part cat, part rabbit."

The cat helped Jerry settle down into the routine of the prison. He still sometimes felt like a baby goat turned loose in a jungle with hungry beasts ready to sink their claws in him and devour him, but when he came into the warehouse and saw Cabbit hopping toward him, it was proof anything was possible. He could survive. The choir members might get more dedicated. He might sing higher than he'd ever sung before on the new song he was practicing. The years might pass. The Governor might look at his case and give him a pardon. Anything was possible.

The choir did the best they had ever done the next Sunday morning. Inmates kept coming up to him that afternoon in the exercise yard to tell him how much they liked the special music. Some of them said the music was the only reason they came to church. They told him that if it weren't for him being stuck in prison, he'd be on the radio for sure.

And then the letter came.

CHAPTER 26

The letter came in to Warden Stamper. He didn't give it to Jerry right away. When he called Jerry in and handed him the fat brown envelope, he told Jerry he had discussed with Chaplain Chatham whether to give it to him at all, but they'd decided he could handle what was inside.

Jerry couldn't imagine what that was. He'd never heard of Joletta Ballard, the woman the warden said had written the many pages of the letter inside the envelope. The name didn't ring the first bell. Why would a woman he didn't even know write him such a long letter?

And why did Warden Stamper look so uneasy as he told Jerry he'd best read what the woman had written and decide for himself what he wanted to do about getting any more letters from her or letting her visit? Visit? Jerry didn't even know who she was. If they were going to let anybody visit, he had some better candidates. Maybe Amanda Sue, the girl from back home who had been getting letters through the mail censors to him in spite of not being on his mailing list.

Jerry didn't pull the letter out of the envelope until he was on his bunk after supper. Somehow he sensed it wasn't something to be dipped into lightly. He read the first two words, and it was as if somebody had reached into his chest and wrapped an icy hand around his heart.

Dear Son. What did that mean? It wasn't his mother's handwriting. Why was this woman calling him son? He made his eyes go back to the words on the page. The cold hand squeezed his heart tighter as he began to read again.

You may not remember me. Your father never wanted you to know who I was, but I am your mother. Your natural mother. The woman your father has told you is your mother all these years is your stepmother, not your real mother. I gave birth to you on January 3, 1950, and I almost died doing it. I'm not telling you this to make you think more of me, but just as a fact. I had a difficult pregnancy. Your father, he never gave me the first bit of notice when I would tell him what a hard time I was having carrying you. His mother had a whole pile of kids and he thought it was easy as baking a cake or something. He even told me she did bake a cake or canned beans or something the day she gave birth to him. But I wasn't his mother, and I came close to dying when you were born. He didn't know what was going on half the time anyway because he was always gone driving his buses. I was stuck home alone most of the time. I mean I was just a kid. A 19 year old can't handle things like that alone. I had a sister that wanted to help me but she was all the way down in Tennessee and your daddy got mad whenever I went down there. So there wasn't anybody close by to take care of me and it's not easy having a first baby. Especially when the daddy don't care about nothing but making more money taking on another run for Greyhound. You'd have thought that Greyhound bus was his wife.

But I did have you. I walked right through all the dangers of childbirth to have you. You were my first. And even though we haven't seen each other for a heap of years since you were four years old, I'm still your mama and a mama always has a special place in her heart for her first baby, especially her first born son. There wasn't no way I could ever forget you even if your daddy did try to get you to forget about me. Your daddy and that woman that taught you to call her mama when she never was your mama. I am your mama.

I remember the day you were born. There was a little snow and it was cold, but we made it to the hospital okay. Then when you were born, you were so tiny and precious. I haven't ever stopped loving you even though I wasn't able to come visit you. It was just too hard seeing you there with another woman pretending to be your mama when I was your real mama.

Jerry quit reading. He kept his eyes on the papers in his hand, but he quit reading. The handwriting was big and loopy with frilly capital letters at the beginnings of the sentences and circles instead of dots over the i's. The strokes of ink looked flamboyant. Nothing like his mother's no nonsense script. His mother. Which mother? Both of them said they were his mother. Just like in the Bible story about Solomon's wisdom.

This had to be some kind of crazy joke. How could he have a mother named Joletta? He'd never heard of anybody named Joletta. He shut his eyes to see if that would stop his head spinning, but it just made it worse. His whole world was spinning. He felt as if somebody had just picked up his life and was shaking it around like one of those hand held games where the little balls roll into the holes except his life was opening up new holes he didn't even know were there.

A mother he couldn't remember. A mother he didn't even know he had. The mother he thought he had wasn't his mother.

Little bits of memories edged into his mind. Some lady at church telling him how lucky he was to have a woman like Hazel to be his mother as if he could choose who his mother was. His mother—Hazel—telling him how much his father had sacrificed to give his son a good home. *His* son. Not *our* son. His mother—Hazel—always looking at him as if he could never measure up when he was a kid. His feeling that if he didn't do everything right nobody would love him. The feeling that he didn't belong to anybody, that he was just a visitor in his parents' house.

Jerry licked his lips and made his eyes start reading again. The woman, this woman who said she was his mother, went on and on about how much she loved him, about how she'd just been so young when she and his father had married. She wrote a whole page about how she wanted to see him, had been wanting to see him for such a long time but didn't know how to go about it, but now with Jerry in prison, it seemed a good time since maybe she and her husband could help him.

She had remarried. Actually for the second time. The man she was married to right now worked on golf courses getting the grass and everything just right and he had done well for himself. They had money. They could hire some new lawyers to help Jerry get out of prison.

She wrote another page or two about her sister and her brother-in-law and how surely Jerry remembered them since they had doted on Jerry from the day he was born until Jerry's father quit letting Jerry visit them after he married Hazel. She wrote how it was all Hazel's doing. That Hazel didn't want Jerry to have anything to do with his mother's family. She didn't have anything good to say about Hazel. Jerry read the words, but he didn't really let them sink in. He couldn't get angry. Not at this woman who said she was his mother. Not at his mom and dad who should have told him. Not at anything. At least not yet. He had to figure out what it meant before he got mad.

Jerry read it all, every word on every page and then he read it over again. He thought if he'd known what her voice sounded like he would have almost been able to hear her shouting in his ear. The words looked like they were shouting. But he didn't know. He had no idea what her voice sounded like. His own mother's voice.

She ended up begging to come see him. She said he was an adult now, and he could make his own decisions. He didn't have to let his daddy decide everything for him, and she thought it was time he got re-acquainted with his mother. She knew it was time she got re-acquainted with her son. She had another son from a different marriage and she loved him, but there was no love like the love of a mother for her first born son.

She wrote some more about this other son, Charles. She called him Charlie. Jerry skimmed over the words. He didn't care whether or not he had a half brother. He didn't want to hear about Charlie and how good he was doing. This woman who said she was Jerry's mother had been a mother to the half brother. She hadn't just pushed that son off her lap and forgotten about him for years.

Jerry folded the sheets together and put them back in the envelope. Then he stuffed the whole thing under his mattress as quietly as possible since Oscar was already snoring below him. Jerry didn't expect to do much sleeping that night. He needed a telephone to call his father and demand to know what was going on. He needed a jet plane to take him home to confront his mother—to confront the woman he'd always thought was his mother—and ask why she'd pretended to be his mother all these years. He needed this Joletta to take a lie detector test to see if anything she had written was true.

How could a mother just walk away and leave her son for sixteen years and then out of the blue write a letter saying *Hi, it's me, your mama*? What kind of mother was that? Perhaps the kind of mother he had. And she wanted to see him. She wanted to help him. As if his folks hadn't already done everything they could to help him. She was going to fly in here from nowhere and save the day like Superwoman or somebody.

Did he even want to see her? He didn't know. He felt all jumbled up inside. He could tell the warden that he didn't want to get any more letters from Joletta, and they would send her letters back unopened. She hadn't ever wanted to see him before. She could have if she'd wanted to. His folks hadn't kept him in a locked room. She could have found him. Why had she found him now? What did she want?

He shifted a little on his bunk. Old Oscar's snores kept going. Jerry shoved his pillow up into a little ball and lay down. What was it Oscar had told him? That he did too much thinking behind and ahead. But how could he keep from thinking about this new mother who'd popped up out of nowhere?

A million questions were spinning around in his head without the first answer. He didn't have any answers. His parents had the answers, and he'd just have to wait until he saw them to find out what they were. His mother was coming next week. Well, at least the woman he'd always thought was his mother was coming next week. She had a way of fixing things.

While she might never have been able to exactly "fix" him the way she'd wanted him to be when he was a kid, she fixed other things. Something needed to be done in the church, she did it. They needed a job done on the farm, she took care of it. For years, she'd worked for Greyhound taking care of things there, too, before she married his father. His father said the whole company was sad when she quit. She'd bought their first farm while Jerry's dad was away on a Greyhound run, and then just told him they owned a farm when he called home. She'd taken care of everything.

Jerry would show her the letter when she came. She wouldn't like this Joletta writing to him and telling him she was his mother, but she'd know what to do. She always knew what to do. She'd take care of it. He wasn't sure how, but she would. He was glad she was coming alone this time. They'd be able to talk without worrying what his aunt or his mother's friend thought.

He punched his pillow a few more times and shut his eyes. He ran a stream of words across his mind like a plane pulling a sign over a football stadium. *I'm not thinking about anything but sleeping. I'm sleeping now. I'm sleeping now.* Old Oscar gave good advice.

The next day he told the warden he'd read the letter and he'd take care of it. He told him he wanted to talk to his folks about it all before he decided about the woman coming to visit him. The warden seemed to think he was handling it all well. Jerry didn't tell him that he was going to let his mother, his stepmother, Hazel, whoever she was, handle it for him. It was good that the warden thought he was being mature and sensible, and maybe he was being. He just threw himself into his work and stayed too busy to even think about Joletta's letter. He thought about what new songs the choir might sing and how he could get more music and if some of the songs he used to sing in one key he might try to sing in a higher key now.

He didn't even look at the envelope again until he pulled it out of his locker to take with him to the visiting room the day his mother came.

CHAPTER 27

The envelope lay between them on the table in the visitors' room like a coiled snake. His mother looked at it once when he first put it there and said what it was. That had been awkward, too.

He'd practiced in his head what he'd say walking down to the visitors' room. *This is a letter from my mother.* He couldn't very well say that, because this woman he was going to see was his mother, the only mother he'd ever known. *This is a letter from Joletta.* He couldn't say that because it made it sound like he and Joletta were on a first name basis and he wouldn't know the woman if he bumped into her on the street. *This is a letter from my birth mother.* That's what he finally decided on, but it sounded strange when it came out of his mouth with his mother looking at him as if the floor had just dropped out from under her and she had absolutely nothing to catch hold of to keep from falling.

She looked at the envelope, tightened her lips into a thin line, and pulled in a deep breath before she said, "Why don't we talk about it later?" She pushed a smile across her face and started lifting plastic bowls and tinfoil wrapped packages out of her basket. "First, how about some food? I brought some of those fudge brownies you like so much. I had to be careful what I brought this time since I went to see Miss Atwood yesterday and everything had to sit in the car. I kept the cooler full of ice, but still I wanted to be sure I didn't bring you anything that might give you food poisoning. Here's a can of Vienna sausages. I know you like them. And I found a Kentucky Fried Chicken restaurant on the way down here this morning. I knocked on the door and got them to open up early so I could bring you some chicken."

She tried to sound relaxed and easy, but Jerry caught the tremble in her voice and her hands were shaking a little as she unwrapped the tinfoil around the brownies. He'd almost forgotten about her going to see Miss Atwood. He grabbed on that as something to talk about other than the letter. "How was Miss Atwood?"

"She was fine," his mother said. "She had nice things to say about you and told me to tell you hello and that she hopes things are going well for you. I told her that, of course, everything isn't exactly great, but that you were directing the choir and hoping to get on as a chaplain's assistant soon. She said that sounded wonderful, that you must be taking advantage of your opportunities. How is that coming? The getting on as chaplain's assistant?"

"I'm still hoping." Jerry dug a chicken leg out of the box his mother sat in front of him and took a bite. He chewed a while before he went on. "But I don't know if it's going to happen. Seems like something always goes wrong."

"Maybe not this time. We're, your dad and I, have been praying extra hard for you these last few weeks because you sounded upset more than usual in your letters home."

"Things happen in here that upset you," Jerry said.

"We know they do, Jerry. We worry about you all the time. Reverend Jacobson says not to worry, just pray, but it's hard not to worry." She popped the top off a bowl of baked beans and stuck a plastic spoon in it for him. "I didn't think beans could ruin, and I kept them in the cooler. I tasted them before I brought them this morning and they tasted fine."

"Yes, ma'am," Jerry said as he dug in. "They're better than fine. You can't imagine how good all this is after having to eat prison food every day."

She sat down to watch him eat. It was the one way they'd always been able to connect. She loved to cook for him, and he loved to eat. Carelessly, almost as if by accident, she dropped one of the dishtowels she'd had in the food basket on top of the envelope to get it out of sight. They had all day to visit. Because his parents lived out of state, the prison officials allowed them to stay all day instead of just a couple of hours.

They chatted about the farm and how much milk the cows were giving while Jerry ate. They talked about the new pup his father had named Hugo after Jerry had suggested that name in one of his letters home, and how fast the pup was growing. "You can't leave a shoe anywhere on the porch or it's gone. Chewed up and gone. Your father learned that the hard way. Lost one of his barn boots. You'd think he'd never had a pup before," his mother said with a smile. "But I don't guess either one of us has ever had a pet like your Cabbit. I can't imagine how that cat gets around."

"I wish you could see him, Mom. It's the funniest thing." Jerry stood up and gave a little hop to demonstrate.

They both laughed and when he sat back down, his mother put her hand over his. "You always were a funny thing," she said. Her smile disappeared. "I'm sorry for all the things I did wrong when you were little. I don't know what I was thinking, but I really was trying to do what I thought was best for you. I don't know that I even realized how much I was on you fussing all the time. I just wanted to make sure I did the right things, that I raised you right. I didn't want you to grow up wild. I wanted to do what a mother was supposed to do."

"I know, Mom."

"And your father and I didn't aim to keep any secrets from you about Joletta." Her tongue tripped a little over the name. She cleared her throat and went on. "We thought you remembered her. You were four years old the last time you saw her. We didn't think you'd forget that, but Miss Atwood says that it's unlikely you'd remember much about anything before you were five or six. Especially since you were getting moved around a lot and probably spent a lot of time feeling abandoned and lost. She says you might remember a face or some special thing that happened from those years. Of course, if you did remember a face it would probably be Carla's instead of Joletta's."

"Carla?" Then Jerry remembered the name from the letter on the table between them. "Oh, Joletta's sister."

"Right. Your daddy says she kept you more than Joletta did when you were a baby. Your daddy says she wanted you for her own. I guess I shouldn't find fault in her for that. I did, too."

"I've been trying to remember her, but I can't."

"I guess you were too young. And you stayed some with Mama and Papa Shepherd, too, before Dewey and I married. I mean we never told anybody in the family not to talk about it. We just never did talk about it ourselves. We did try to explain some of it to you that last time you came home from the army."

"I don't remember much about that weekend."

"I know," she said and squeezed his hand. "You were so tired and sick I don't think anything we said got through to you that weekend. But as for when you were little, I guess we didn't talk about it then because we didn't want you to feel sad about Joletta never coming to see you or calling or anything. She could have. We wouldn't have stopped her. We couldn't have stopped her. Your daddy got custody of you when they got the divorce, but she had legal visitation rights."

"Maybe you should read the letter," Jerry said. "It's long, but it'd be better if you read it than me trying to tell you what she said. She said a lot."

His mother looked at the tea towel covering the letter as if somebody had just thrown up on the table and she was going to have to clean up the vomit. The lines of her face tightened as she said, "All right. Do you want anything else to eat?"

"Yes ma'am, I do, but I couldn't stuff in one more bite right now. Just cover it up and I'll eat the rest of it before you leave. Or at least as much as I can hold. Wouldn't want any of it to go to waste." They wouldn't let him take any of the food back to his dorm. They'd search him when he left the visitors' room to be sure he didn't try to smuggle something into the prison, and as much as he loved brownies he didn't want to get a black mark on his record. He was still planning on making it to trusty status.

His mother covered up the dishes and picked up the tea towel off the envelope as though the envelope might have hatched little snakes that had crawled up into the towel. She shook the towel a little before she spread it over the brownies. "You might want to snack on these while we talk," she said.

"I really want you to read it, Mom."

"All right." She sighed and picked up the envelope. "My word, how many pages is it?"

"Thirty some."

"Good heavens. I wouldn't have thought Joletta could have written thirty pages about anything. She must have been trying to make up for lost time."

Jerry watched his mother's face as she read the letter. Color rose in her cheeks and she mashed her lips together so tightly Jerry thought they'd surely be bruised. Once or twice she looked angry, but she didn't say anything as she read through Joletta's words. Then, still without a word, she carefully straightened all the sheets, folded them, and slid them back into the envelope.

Jerry waited for her to explode, for her to tell him none of it was true, that Joletta wasn't his *real* mother the way she'd claimed, but she surprised him. She just looked up at Jerry and said, "Well, that was interesting."

"But is it true?"

"It's true that she's your birth mother. As for the rest of it, I think your father needs to answer that question. I never knew Joletta. I met her that one time she came to see you when you were four, but I didn't know her. I do know some of the things your dad told me about her when we first got married." She mashed her mouth together again as if to keep from saying any of those things out loud. After a minute, she went on. "You know I wouldn't agree to marry your daddy until he gave me his word that I could raise you and be a mother to you. I wanted to raise you. Even if I didn't always do it right, I wanted to. You're a wonderful boy with a good heart and I've known right from the very first time I saw you with Dewey that the Lord has a purpose for your life."

"In prison?"

"Maybe here too, but for sure when you get out. And you will get out. We, your father and I, are doing everything in our power to keep your case in front of the people that matter. We were so happy to hear that Judge Rutherford had written back to you. We can't be sure what good might come from that in the future, but it has to mean he's still interested in your case and that he hasn't forgotten you. He wants you to do well. And since he's the one who sentenced you, it might make a real impression on the Parole Board if he recommended an early parole."

"Do you think he might do that?" Jerry asked.

"I don't know, Jerry." His mother reached across the table and put her hand on his arm. "But I do know that I'll never give up till you're out of here. I'll do anything, go anywhere. I'd write the President himself if I thought it would help. And I'll pray till my knees are raw to get you home again. I'll be like the woman Jesus talked about in the Bible who kept worrying the judge till he granted her petition. And I know the Lord is hearing our prayers. He'll make a way out of no way, and he'll help you straighten this other out, too." His mother gestured toward the envelope. "Just don't worry overly about it until your father writes you. He'll tell you the truth. He's always told you the truth. You know that, don't you?"

"Yes ma'am."

"Good." She smiled. "Well, let's talk some more about the farm or tell me the songs you're going to have the choir sing next Sunday. And you say the men here in prison are flocking to church to hear all of you sing?"

They didn't talk any more about Joletta. She was there hovering in the background, but Jerry couldn't ask any more about her. He couldn't ask what she looked like. He couldn't ask if he was like her. He couldn't ask if it was something he'd done that had made his birth mother abandon him. He couldn't ask if any mother had ever loved him.

But a couple of days after her visit, his mother answered that question. She'd written him a letter in the parking lot before she left the prison.

Dearest Son and you are my son, the son of my heart if not my womb. I've always been better at saying what I feel on paper rather than in person. That's not good. I should have told you I loved you a million times when you were a little boy. I should have told you I loved you even more times when you were a teenager trying to hurt yourself with alcohol and by driving too fast. I should have told a zillion times how proud I was of you instead of always finding fault.

I was and am proud of you. I've never done anything in my life to compare to the honor of being able to raise you as my son. I love you, Jerry. Forgive me for not saying that more often. You are a wonderful person and I'm proud you are my son.

Jerry put his mother's letter on top of the letter from Joletta in his locker. That somehow seemed to help him forget about Joletta's letter. He wasn't going to make up his mind about any of what she said until he heard from his father anyway. He was going to remember old Oscar's advice and think on what he wanted to do right now. He wanted his trumpet. A little trumpet music would add some pizzazz to the church services. So he pulled out some paper and wrote to Warden Stamper to see if he could have his trumpet sent to him. Then he wrote his mom and dad and assured them of his love by signing the letter *your loving son*.

He didn't mention Joletta. He wasn't Joletta's loving son. He didn't even know Joletta. At this point he wasn't even sure he ever would. But he did include her in his prayers at night before he went to sleep. It wouldn't hurt to ask the Lord to bless her. The Lord surely had plenty of blessings to go around.

CHAPTER 28

He had to wait a long week before his father's letter came in the mail. The letter had been typed single-spaced. Jerry's mother must have typed it up for his dad so that the letter would fall into the prison's two-page limit on letters inmates could receive. Joletta's letter had exceeded that by a bunch, but they'd passed that letter on to Jerry. It might have been better if they'd only given him two pages of it so he wouldn't have had to get in the middle of this "he said, she said" situation. Still he needed to know his father's side of the story.

His father started out by saying he wished he didn't have to write the letter at all, but that Jerry needed to have the *actual* facts. After that Jerry's dad didn't pull any punches. It might be a letter he hadn't wanted to write, but once he'd warmed to the task he'd had plenty to say about Joletta and none of it good.

His dad had met Joletta on one of the buses he was driving. She'd told him she was eighteen, but she had looked twenty-one. He'd have never guessed her seventeen, which was actually how old she was when they got married in November. His dad had been twenty-four and home for two years from the war. Thirteen months later, Jerry had been born, but Joletta wasn't ready to be a mother, something that she had admitted herself in her own letter to Jerry.

As Jerry read the letter, he could almost see his father's mouth getting tight and the smile disappearing from his eyes. His father was strong, rock solid in what he believed was right and wrong, and he had never had much use for anyone who tried to make excuses for some weakness or for failing to do the right thing in life. Jerry had seen that look himself often enough, but at least behind it he'd always known his father loved him even when he was upset about whatever Jerry had done wrong. If his father had ever had any love for Joletta, those feelings had died a long time ago.

You were born Jan. 3, 1950 at Good Samaritan Hospital in Lexington, Ky. She had no problems and did not nearly die when you were born. She had the best medical help available. She did not want the responsibility of a baby and left you with her sister (against my strict order that you were to be kept home where you belonged), but I'd come home from my Greyhound run and you'd be at Carla's house 180 miles from home. You were gone so much you didn't know where home was nor who she was. I have seen you sit in her lap and cry for your mother.

Jerry looked up from his father's words to stare at the wall for a moment. His stomach was in knots and he felt queasy. Even if Jerry had never actually known his mother, he didn't want to read bad things about her. Better that a missing mother had fallen in a river and drowned or nobly given him up to be raised by his father and Hazel because she thought they could provide for him better. Jerry didn't want to know his mother was a loose woman who hadn't honored her wedding vows and hadn't wanted to be a mother.

But that was what his father had written. He accused Joletta of leaving Jerry with her sister so that she'd have more time for her boyfriends. He said he'd even caught her with another man once when he came in early from a run. Even with all that going on, his father said he'd tried to make the marriage work.

She was given every chance to straighten up and make a home for you and me. She promised dozens of times, but never did it. She continued to have one affair after another and was dating four (4) different men in Jackson when I divorced her Nov. 3, 1952.

Jerry could see his mother's fingers on the typewriter keyboard emphasizing the number four to make absolutely certain Jerry got the full impact of what Joletta had done. He was surprised the word wasn't underlined. Jerry shut his eyes. He didn't want to think about his mother typing the letter. He wanted this to just be the truth from his father and not a doctored up indictment of Joletta. Jerry made himself open his eyes and start reading again.

After the divorce she cried and threatened and tried to make me take her back. The day after this outburst she went up north and married a Perkins. It was at Jackson where she left you several nights by yourself to cry all night while I was on a bus run. I didn't find this out until after the divorce.

Had she really done that? Just put him in his crib and gone off and left him? His father said so. Jerry turned his eyes back to the letter. All the noise in the dorm faded away as he concentrated on the typewritten words in front of him. It was as if he had been transported somewhere out of this place to a strange place he thought he'd never been before but then when he looked around he wasn't so sure. Something about it all felt familiar.

He'd been two and a half years old when his parents divorced. For the next year he'd been shifted about between his dad, his dad's parents, and the Dugans, Joletta's sister and her husband. His father said he had to let them keep Jerry because they kept threatening to take him to court and take Jerry away from him. And he feared they could. Those weren't good times for a father to win custody of a child in court, so he hadn't wanted to chance another hearing and another judge. He wanted his son with him.

The only reason you were ever at the Dugans or anywhere else except with me was because Greyhound doesn't allow drivers to raise children on buses, and I had to make a living for us.

Then the accusations against Joletta got even worse.

You were about 6 months old when she and her current boyfriend tried to kill me with my own car for my Navy and Greyhound Insurance. In Jackson, she tried to have me shot.

Maybe that's where the other Jerry Shepherd had come from, the one who had done that awful thing to Mr. Baylor in the motel room in Richmond Hills. Maybe it hadn't been a Jerry Shepherd he didn't know after all. Maybe it had been his natural mother coming out in him. Jerry wasn't sure if he wished his father had written more about that or if he was glad he hadn't elaborated on it. He had stated it as fact without the first line of proof or explanation. He hadn't even said how he had stayed alive with Joletta and her boyfriends trying to kill him. Instead his father had gone on to write about Joletta trying to force him to give Jerry to the Dugans after he married Hazel. His father said Joletta never once asked for Jerry for herself.

Jerry wanted to quit reading. Why hadn't his mother asked for him for herself? Why hadn't she wanted to be his mother? At least Hazel had wanted him. At least Hazel claimed to have loved him even if Jerry hadn't always been able to feel that love.

But Joletta had also claimed to love him in her letter and had gone on and on about how cute and smart he'd been when she last saw him when he was four and how it had nearly killed her to leave him there with Hazel. His father's description of the visit was nothing like Joletta's.

> In the fall of 1954, Joletta came by one night and stayed about fifteen minutes. She didn't tell you who she was and you didn't know her. She never showed up, called or wrote again until last May.

That must have been after Jerry had been arrested. Joletta must have seen his name in the newspaper, but what about him being arrested had made her want to contact him again after so many years of not caring? His father hadn't forbidden her to come. He'd even copied two paragraphs verbatim out of the divorce decree in the letter as if the legal sounding words would show the court had been on his side.

> Dewey W. Shepherd is hereby granted the permanent custody and control of the infant child of plaintiff and defendant, namely: Gerald Warren Shepherd, with the privilege of the defendant seeing said child at all reasonable times so as not to interfere with his health and education.

Well, Jerry thought she hadn't done that. She hadn't interfered with anything as he was growing up since he didn't even know she existed. His father should have told him who she was when he was four. His father should have told him about her when he was six and when he was sixteen. It might have helped Jerry understand why he never felt as if he quite belonged anywhere. But his father didn't believe talking about Joletta would have made a difference. And he wanted to make sure Jerry knew he was nothing like his birth mother.

> Son, these kind of character traits are not traits people are born with. They pick them up because they want to. You are certainly _not_ like her. You are a decent, self-respecting, fine young man, and I and your Mom are very, very proud of

you. I would give anything if I didn't have to write this letter, but we know you have the intelligence and ability to handle it.

Don't let this worry you, Son. It is all in the past and they can't hurt you now. I love you and so does your "real" Mom.

Jerry shut his eyes after he read his father's signature. He didn't need to read the letter again. It was burned on his brain. Why couldn't his father have just said that Joletta left and went too far away to visit? Why did he have to set out to prove she was such a bad mother? Was it so his "real" mom, Hazel, would seem like a better mother?

Why couldn't he have just written the bare facts? Joletta gave birth to him. Joletta was too young to be a mother. He divorced Joletta. He couldn't take Jerry with him on his Greyhound runs. After a while he married Hazel and they tried to make a good home for Jerry. Maybe Joletta didn't come see him because she didn't want to confuse him. Maybe she moved to California or Maine. Maybe she lost their address.

She had contacted him here in prison—not exactly when a long lost mother might most want to show up to claim kinship. Why not just stay away instead of admitting she had a convict for a son? Then again maybe she wanted to show up to prove she could have done better or at least her sister could have. Jerry tried to delve deep into his mind to pull out an image of either one of them, but he had no idea what Joletta or Carla looked like.

What was it his father had said? *Don't let this worry you, Son.* Good advice if he could do it. It sort of went along with Old Oscar's advice to not think about things that he couldn't do a thing about. He'd sleep on it. Maybe next week he'd read Joletta's letter again and then his father's letter again and try to figure out what was what. Maybe he'd never read either one of them again. Maybe he'd write back to Joletta and tell her she could come and see him if the warden gave her permission. At least then he'd know what she looked like. Didn't a man have the right to know what his birth mother looked like?

Maybe he'd even tell his folks he was going to let her come visit him if the warden gave permission. He wouldn't keep secrets the way they had. He couldn't see what it would hurt to meet Joletta. It wasn't going to change anything in the past. His parents were still going to be his parents. Joletta couldn't get custody of him now. He was an adult. An adult in prison. He wasn't going anywhere for years.

Of course she'd promised to help him get out. Everybody was always promising to help him get out, but so far he hadn't gone anywhere. And it didn't look as if he was going anywhere for a long time. Why not see what Joletta had to say? What could it hurt?

His father had thought he was intelligent and had the ability to handle the truth about his birth mother, and he had handled it. His whole past had blown up in his face. He wasn't who he thought he was, but he was getting used to the idea. He was handling it. So he also had the intelligence and ability to handle meeting her.

He wanted to meet her. He was curious about her. So what if his mother used to tell him that curiosity killed the cat? Jerry hadn't seen the first cat actually killed by poking its paw into a black hole or climbing on top of a stack of hay bales to see what might be there. The hay might topple, but the cat could spring to safety. That's the way Jerry would be. Ready to spring to safety. That's the way he already was, tense and ready for whatever might jump out at him next.

He hadn't expected a new mother to jump out at him, but now that one had, he'd write to her and tell her to contact the warden and ask for permission to visit. He didn't have the least reason to feel as if he was betraying his parents. If anybody had betrayed anybody, they had betrayed him when they hadn't made sure he knew the truth about his birth.

Jerry punched his pillow and tried to get comfortable. It was just April but already beginning to warm up in the prison. He couldn't imagine how bad it was going to get in August stuck in here with a hundred and twenty other men trying to breathe in the heat. Some of the men already had fans running.

At home on the farm, Jerry had kept a box fan in the window right beside his bed to draw in the cool night air. That damp air had felt like night licking his face as it blew past him to rustle the calendar on the wall by his door. He remembered lying in bed whispering prayers and imagining the fan blowing them right up to heaven.

His prayers now sometimes just seemed to get stuck in a little cloud right over his bunk. For sure, there was no wind to carry them up and out through the prison roof. He whispered, "Dear Lord, bless my mother and father and Amanda Sue. Bless Chaplain Chatham and help me do the right things to get the job as chaplain assistant. Give our choir strong voices Sunday. Help me, Lord, to live in here, one minute at a time so I won't go crazy with worry over everything. Bless Joletta and help me know what to say to her if I ever do meet her." He lay there a few minutes before he added, "And help me not disturb Old Oscar's sleep.

Amen." Then he blew softly into the air above his head. Maybe that would move the prayers on toward heaven.

He grinned a little at how silly he was being. God heard his prayers no matter where he was when he prayed them. Every preacher Jerry had ever heard preach on prayer said that. They might disagree on how a person should pray or what a person should pray, but they were always in agreement that the Lord heard the prayers no matter what. There was even something in the Bible about the Holy Spirit praying for you when you were in too much misery to come up with the right words to pray yourself. Jerry had been miserable plenty of times, but he hadn't ever felt the Holy Spirit praying for him. A person ought to be able to feel that.

Sometimes after he'd sung a song in church, people would tell him that he'd been full of the spirit, but all he'd ever felt full of was the song. His mother had always told him the Lord had something special in mind for him, but Jerry had never known what. He'd played with this idea and that. Nothing had ever really seemed as if it was God's plan. It had always just felt like Jerry's plan or a plan his mother or father had for him or something a preacher somewhere along the way had thought might be a good idea.

One sure thing, all their plans must have gone bust. It couldn't be the Lord's plan for him to end up in prison even if he was singing here and leading the choir. The Lord was good. He hated sin and Jerry had sinned big time. How could God have a purpose for somebody who had done what Jerry had done? Maybe the best Jerry could hope for was entertaining the other inmates, putting on a show. If that was it, then he'd knock himself out and sing every chance he got. It didn't have to be church singing. He'd sing anything.

Singing was what was keeping him alive in here. Singing was what was keeping the prison from winning and turning him into a man who belonged here. He didn't belong here. He was going to get out. Someday. Some way. Somehow.

CHAPTER 29

Jerry told Warden Stamper he would see Joletta if she wrote and got permission to visit. Then he wrote Joletta telling her the same thing. He didn't write much. The words didn't flow out on the paper the way they did when he wrote his folks. He wasn't sure what to say to a mother he hadn't even known existed a month ago. He also wrote his mom and dad to assure them he wouldn't let Joletta upset or hurt him in any way. He didn't know whether that was true or not, but he thought he could make it true.

Then he sort of forgot about it. He was getting like Old Oscar told him he'd have to get to survive inside. He was in this special little world, this prison world. Out in the free world, life kept happening the way it always had. People had babies. People died. Girlfriends forgot to write. Some girlfriends got married to somebody else. People sold farms and bought new ones. Fields were plowed and crops were planted. Kids started school. Kids graduated. Dogs died. It rained and it snowed. The sun came up in the morning, and the moon slid across the sky at night.

Life went on, but it went on without the men stuck in the prison. There was nothing they could do about any of it. They had a whole different world to deal with behind bars. Jerry had been inside long enough to begin getting a feel for the power of the place. It was trying to swallow him. Some days it was hard to hang on to the hope that he'd someday be a free man again, but then he'd wake up the next morning and hope would be flickering within him once more. He'd see other men getting their chance at the Parole Board. Some of them came back beaten down and defeated, swearing to not even try for parole again, but others came back with a release date floating in the air a few weeks away.

Even when that happened, even when they walked out the front gates as free men, the prison kept an invisible elastic band connected to them and often as not yanked them back inside. Any time one of the men was paroled or released the dorm started a betting pool on how long they'd stay free. Many of them didn't. They came back into the prison world they'd grown used to. The free world outside was too hard.

Jerry was determined not to let the prison absorb him, but then he'd notice more loose hairs in his comb and peer into the mirror over the sink to see if he was going bald like his father. He was only twenty, but his heart would sink at the thought that he was growing old in prison, spending his best years locked up. Nobody liked a bald singer.

He tried to explain some of the way he was feeling to his folks since his mother was always on him to write whatever might make him feel better.

You want to know what prison's like. Let me tell you. Prison is a place where the first prisoner you see looks like an All-American boy, and then you find out different. Prison is a place where hope springs eternal, where each Parole Board appearance means a chance to get out, even if the odds are hopelessly against the prisoner. It's where the flame in every man burns low. For some it goes out. But for most, it flickers weakly, sometimes flashes brightly, but never seems to burn as bright as it once did.

Prison is a place where you learn to hate through clenched teeth, where you want to beat and choke and kick and scratch but you don't know who you want to do these things to. It's a place where you feel sorry for yourself, then you get disgusted with yourself, then you get mad for feeling disgusted, then you try to mentally change the subject. Prison is a place, but the wrong kind of place.

I have seen what prison can do to a man, but it is not going to do me that way. I'm going to stand up against it till my last dying breath. I'm not going to let it get hold of me like it does others. I won't give up, but I will fight till I get my freedom. Prison is a place, but not a place for me and it knows it won't be able to hold me.

The weeks passed. It got so hot he would have paid triple price in cigarettes for a fan, but nobody would sell. Finally his folks shipped one down to him. At least with air blowing against him he had the illusion of cooling off when he went to sleep. Then the Georgia mosquitoes started sneaking into the dorm and adding to their misery. Even Old Oscar had to slap at them when they started sucking out his blood. Pretty soon the whole dorm smelled like bug repellant, and the mosquitoes kept up a constant whine in his ears as they searched for a spot of skin he might have forgotten to spray.

He got up early and worked hard every day. T.C. got transferred to another prison, so he lost his helper in the shipping department, but he managed to get the work done. He wanted to be busy. He wanted to be so busy that the only thing that could sneak into his head was a snatch of whatever song the choir was singing the next Sunday.

He didn't make it as chaplain's assistant. He didn't dwell on it long. He just sat down at the typewriter with Cabbit in his lap and thought up a new goal. He liked thinking up goals with the two-legged cat there to prove nothing was impossible. He set his sights on the jazz band.

Every Sunday afternoon, the prison put on entertainment programs. Free world bands and singers would come in for half the program and then inmate bands would put on the other half of the program. Big name Southern Gospel groups and country western groups came through to do their bit for mankind. Jerry didn't know much about either of those kinds of music, had never listened to country western and hadn't even know there was such a thing as Southern Gospel—trios and quartets that harmonized on songs about the Lord that got up and moved, but he liked it. Radio disc jockeys came in to run the shows.

Jerry had been watching from the crowd, but he wanted to be on the stage with the other performers. He wanted to have the chance to get to know the disc jockeys. He wanted to find out how to get started in the music business so that when he finally did get out of prison he'd know how to launch his singing career. Jerry set his sights on the jazz band since he didn't know the first thing about country western music. At least he'd heard some of the stuff the jazz band sang. All he had to do was convince Mr. Brodson, the prison official who ran the extra-curricular activities that he could sing better than anybody else in prison.

Jerry started praying that Mr. Brodson would come to the church services and hear his choir on Sunday mornings, but he didn't just depend on prayer. He wrote Mr. Brodson a couple of letters so he'd know how interested Jerry was in singing in the band. He'd never actually seen it in the Bible, but all his life he'd heard people say the Lord helped those who helped themselves.

He was glad he had his singing plans to think about. It kept him from worrying too much about the soap opera going on in the letters coming in from his folks and Joletta. His folks didn't want him to see Joletta. They said no good could come from the woman wanting back into Jerry's life now. Then when Joletta broke the first date she'd gotten permission to visit Jerry, his parents said that was proof she wasn't the kind of woman a person could depend on.

Jerry got to the point where he didn't even want to open his parents' letters and have to wade through more accusations against Joletta. The least they could do was wait till he met her and had a chance to make up his own mind about her. He told his folks to drop the past and not worry about it. He had the present and future in his mind and was doing his best to clear the past completely out of his mind. That had to be the best path to sanity, and they all knew where insanity had got him.

But his mother just couldn't let it alone. She had to keep harping on how Joletta was no good. Maybe Joletta had had problems back when she deserted Jerry, but maybe she'd changed. Jerry had had problems, but he was doing his best to change. And he was changing. He had goals. And one of the goals was to meet Joletta.

Jerry still hadn't gotten in the band when Joletta finally showed up the end of June. It was hot. The fans in the visitors' room were humming, but not doing much but moving hot air around. Jerry's shirt was sticking to his back even before he went in the room. His heart was beating too fast. He told himself there wasn't any reason to be nervous, but his hands were sweating and his mouth felt dry the way it did sometimes right before he had to start singing in front of a crowd. Then after the first line or two of the song the nervousness would fade right away. Maybe after the first hello and how are you his nervousness at facing his birth mother would fade, too.

That is, if he could figure out how to say hello. He couldn't call her mother and certainly not Mrs. Ballard, her married name now. Joletta. He'd just have to call her Joletta although that felt awkward on his tongue when he tried it out before going into the visitors' room where she and her husband, Bob, were waiting for him. He wished there had been a way from him to peek in at them before going in to meet them. He needed some way to get used to the idea of seeing her right there in front of his eyes instead of just imagining what she might look like the way he had when he'd read her letters. He should have asked her to send a picture.

He'd halfway expected to feel a sense of recognition when he first set eyes on Joletta. After all, she was his mother, and he had seen her. He just couldn't remember seeing her. But there was nothing, no recognition at all. The man and woman at the table waiting for him were strangers.

This woman with the bouffant black hair looked like she might be somebody's sister, but certainly nobody's mother. Or maybe like one of the country music singers they'd been bringing in from the free world to entertain on Sunday afternoons. Her hair was dark like Jerry's She was small, petite and even more nervous than Jerry. Her hazel eyes darted to Jerry's face and away as if she couldn't bear looking at him for long and the tips of her red painted fingernails chattered against the tabletop. The man beside her looked quite a bit older than her with thinning hair and a paunch hanging over his belt. Still he had broad shoulders and looked like a working man. He put his hand on top of Joletta's to stop her fingernails bouncing.

Of course Joletta was only thirty-eight. Years younger than his mother who was older even than his dad. Jerry stopped a few feet from the table and said, "Hello."

Joletta glanced up at her husband who was standing behind her now with his big hand on her shoulder as if to give her his strength. Then she pushed a big smile across her face, blinked away the tears threatening to spill out of her eyes and make her mascara run, and said, "Hello, sweetie. Come on over and sit down." When Jerry hesitated, she added, "I promise not to bite."

CHAPTER 30

He didn't know her. No echo came up from deep inside him at the sound of her voice. Still, even though it all felt a little awkward, he'd always been able to talk to anybody whether he knew the person or not. He could come up with some kind of chitchat to fill the visiting time. So he sat down across from her and said, "Thanks for coming. In here, a visitor is a big deal."

"I'll bet," Joletta said. She glanced up at the man behind her again. "This is my husband, Bob. I wrote you about him, remember."

"Sure." Jerry stood up and shook the man's hand. "Good to meet you, Mr. Ballard."

"Call me Bob," Joletta's husband said as he gripped Jerry's hand. Then he squeezed Joletta's shoulder again before he sat down beside her.

"Bob," Jerry said as he sat back down, too. He looked back at Joletta. "Are you a singer?"

"A singer?" Joletta said. "What makes you think that? Because you sing?"

"No, just curious."

"It's the hair, Jolie." Bob laughed and looked at Jerry. "She looks like Loretta Lynn, don't she? Except, of course, Jolie's lots prettier."

They all laughed and that seemed to break the ice. Joletta reached over and put her hands on Jerry's. He had to make himself not pull away. He'd come here to see what she had to say. He wasn't going to run out of the room just because she touched him, but she could have waited a few minutes before she latched onto him and tried to make him acknowledge her as his mother.

She kept her eyes on his face as her hands tightened on his and she started talking. "First off, I want to say how sorry I am that I didn't come around more when you were a little kid. It just seemed to be for the best to let you alone. I knew your daddy and that woman he married would take care of you. I knew they were church people who'd raise you right. Probably better than I ever could. My sister, Carla, you remember her, don't you?"

"I've been trying to," Jerry said.

"Well, anyhow, she was into church. Still is. And me and Bob go some now, don't we, honey?" She glanced over at her husband again as if drawing strength from him. "As long as Bob doesn't have to work. You know he does the grass on those big golf courses and if something needs doing, the folks that run those places don't like to wait till Monday. Especially if they're having a tournament."

"Sounds like interesting work," Jerry said just because Joletta seemed to expect him to say something.

"Yeah, I think you'd like it," Joletta said. "Bob says you can work with him when you get out. When we get you out."

"That's right, son," Bob said.

Jerry had to bite his tongue to keep from telling the man not to call him son, that he wasn't his father even if Joletta was his mother, but he managed to stay quiet. If Jerry had learned nothing else in prison, he'd learned there were benefits to keeping his mouth shut or at least thinking first before he talked. After a minute, he said, "I would like to get out."

"You shouldn't have ever been put here in the first place," Joletta said. "Any fool can see that you're not a murderer."

"I did kill a man," Jerry said.

"But there were extenuating circumstances. There had to be. Like I said, anybody could look at you and tell you wouldn't hurt a fly under normal circumstances. They should have let you have a trial where that kind of thing could have been brought up." Joletta squeezed his hands a little.

As if he suddenly had an itch he couldn't ignore, Jerry eased his hands out from under hers to scratch his nose. Then he put his hands down in his lap under the table and away from her reach before he said, "My folks are working with our lawyer to get me out."

"Sure they are, but we might be able to do some things they can't," Joletta said. "We've got a little money. Bob's business is good, and the truth of the matter is that sometimes money can make a difference. We'll hire you the best lawyer we can find down here. The lawyer you had from Kentucky probably was fine, but it could be that he just didn't know enough about the law down here. Everybody I've talked to says you should get a local man, somebody who knows the judges and the people on the Parole Board."

"He'd still have to go through my lawyer, Mr. York," Jerry said. "Mr. York knows about my case and everything."

"No problem. All we want is the best for you, honey, and all of us, even your daddy and Hazel, know this—being here in this place—isn't the best for you. You're barely out of your teens. You don't need to be in here with a bunch of hardened criminals."

"I'm managing," Jerry said.

Tears welled up in Joletta's eyes again. "You've always had to manage, haven't you, sweetie? You can't imagine how bad I've felt all these years, just going off and leaving you the way I did. I was just too young to be a mother when you came along. I told your daddy that. He was so serious, ready to settle down and do the grownup stuff, but I wanted to have some fun. I guess we should've never married. We weren't a thing alike, but your daddy was so cute sitting up there in that bus driver's seat and he took a shine to me. I'd never had a man like him looking at me. I mean he'd been in the war and there was something different about him. So we probably shouldn't have got married, but people are always doing things they shouldn't."

"I can't argue with that," Jerry said.

"But I'd give a lot if I could know you weren't harboring any ill feelings about the way I didn't take as good of care of you when you were a baby as maybe I should have," Joletta said.

"I can't really remember any of that," Jerry said.

"I know, sweetie. You were just a little bitty thing, but now that you're all grown up and everything, you might be able to understand." Joletta glanced down at her watch. "We've got quite a bit more time. Let me tell you about what went on the way I saw it. I know I wrote a lot of it to you in that letter I sent down here, but sometimes it's easier to explain things in person. Or harder. But I want to try."

And so Jerry listened as she went through it all again, a lot of the same stuff she'd written in her letter. Some of it sounded rehearsed. Some of it didn't. She kept going over and over how young she was and how she and Jerry's dad just didn't see things the same way. She didn't say the first thing about having boy-friends or trying to run his father over to collect his insurance money. Jerry didn't think it was the best time to ask her about that. Maybe his dad had misunderstood. Maybe she had never intended to hurt him.

She certainly claimed to have never intended to hurt Jerry. She said he was a sickly baby who cried a lot and that her sister, who was older and more settled, just seemed to be able to calm Jerry down better. And then with him down at Carla's, Joletta would get lonesome at the house by herself while his father was driving that infernal bus. Sometimes she'd thought he was next to married to the bus.

"He was just trying to make a good living," Jerry slipped in when Joletta paused to take a breath.

"I know that now, but I was too young to know anything then. Sort of like you were when you got into trouble. Too young to know better."

"I wasn't too young to know better," Jerry said. "I've known the Ten Commandments since I was seven. Thou shalt not steal. Thou shalt not kill."

"Yeah, I know some of them, too," Joletta said. "Honor your mother and father. I might not have been much of a mother to you before, but I want to try and make it up to you now so you'll have some reason to think I might deserve just a smidgen of honor."

"You aren't my mother." Jerry didn't intend to sound mean or anything, but she had to know that she couldn't just show up on the scene after sixteen years and pretend she'd never left. He tried to soften it a little by adding, "At least not the mother I've always known. Hazel's that mother. But I appreciate you giving birth to me, Joletta." Her name wasn't as hard to say as he'd thought it might be. It just rolled right off his tongue without the least bit of trouble. "And like you say, it was probably for the best that Dad married my mother, Hazel. She's been a good wife to Dad and has tried hard to be a good mother to me."

Joletta's smile faded for a moment before it came back brighter than ever. "I made mistakes, Jerry. Lots of them. And believe me, I'm sorry for them, especially the ones that have to do with you. All I'm asking is that you let me try to make it up to you by helping you get out of prison."

That sounded good to Jerry. He didn't think she could do it. When he thought about his case in the stark light of reality, he wasn't sure he'd ever get out of prison. He was supposed to serve seven years before he could even get a hearing with the Parole Board and other inmates told him that hardly anybody got out on their first hearing unless whatever they were in for was some nickel and dime stuff. The State of Georgia was tough on making men serve out their terms and Jerry's term was life. He'd served a little over one year counting the time at Pembroke and sometimes when he thought about it that seemed like a lifetime. He couldn't imagine six more years in prison and then maybe six more after that on and on until one day he just didn't get out of the bunk when the guards started banging on the cells.

So it sounded good hearing somebody say he was going to get out. Of course, his folks said that all the time, but nothing they'd done had worked. Maybe the lawyer Joletta could hire with her husband's money might know a way out nobody had thought of yet. It was worth a try.

Even after visiting time was over, Joletta's voice kept echoing in his head. But now that he'd met her, he wasn't mad at her about it all. What good did it do to mope around and be resentful? She'd been young. She'd made mistakes. She was sorry. It had taken courage for her to come and tell him that. When he thought about it, he wasn't sure he could say he loved her, but he might learn to have some kind of affection for her.

He'd never had much luck with women in his life. As a child, he'd never been able to do anything to please his mother. She'd always wanted him to be better than he was. She could never seem to find a way to love him the way he was. Even teachers kept having a way of either expecting more from him than he could do or simply disappearing from his life. He'd loved his first grade teacher, but then she'd gotten pregnant and the school system had made her quit at Christmas.

Then there was Mrs. Gravitt in the fifth grade. She'd liked Jerry. He liked going to school and seeing her smile at him, hearing her tell him that he'd done a good job on whatever assignment she'd given him. But then one morning he'd gone to school and the principal was standing beside another woman sitting in Mrs. Gravitt's chair. Mrs. Gravitt had died the night before. A heart attack, the principal said. Jerry had wanted to quit school, but of course, his parents made him keep going. The new teacher didn't smile at Jerry. He could never do anything good enough to please her. She was always giving him back papers with lots of red marks. That made his mother yell at him, too.

And now Joletta had found him, promised him she'd be there for him. Jerry didn't know whether to believe her or not. Either way, his folks weren't going to be happy about him seeing her. He worked a couple of hours on the letter he sent to them telling about Joletta's visit. He called her visit *rewarding* and wrote how he felt better about the whole situation of suddenly discovering he had a mother he didn't know about. Surely they'd understand that he wanted his natural mother to love him even if she had deserted him. He told them he and Joletta were friends and that he wanted them to share his feelings, that he was even praying that they do so. Then he wrote a whole paragraph about how Joletta could never take the place of the only mother he remembered.

Of course I have made it plain to my natural mother as I will to you, Mom. She or no other woman can begin to take your place or be worthy of the love I have for you. The love I have for you is the love a son has for his blessed mother. My love for my natural mother is a grateful love for giving birth to me. Whether you can understand this or not, I do not know. But please always know this, Mom. You are, always were and always will be my mother. And I thank God for you.

He hoped he hadn't poured it on too thick. Hazel was his mother and he did thank God for her even if they'd had their hard times. He turned his thoughts to his father. His father didn't have any use for Joletta. That was more than plain in the letters he'd written since Joletta had come back into Jerry's life. Still he needed his dad on his side. Jerry desperately wanted to believe Joletta could help him, but she could only do that if his parents and his lawyer, Mr. York, cooperated with her and whatever lawyer she found. He chewed on his pencil a while before he started writing again.

I know, Dad, that you may not feel as I do, and your feelings in a way are justified. But it is in the past, Dad, where I'd like to see it stay.

So I ask you, son to parents, to let the past be and accept the help and friendship they are so willing to give. As you know, I need all the help and support I can get. Please don't fight against Joletta, but work as a team for me.

Your loving son, Jerry

Jerry said a prayer and sent the letter the next day. He tried to imagine his mother and dad reading it and nodding their heads with a little smile as if they were finally understanding everything and agreeing with Jerry, but he couldn't hold on to that image. They were too against Joletta being back in his life. They weren't going to be swayed all that much by Jerry's sweet words.

Sometimes Jerry just wished people had knobs like a radio so you could just tune them into a happy station with nothing but good music. That's what he decided to do to himself after he sent the letter. Just tune out all the static and find a good station of hope. Besides, he had enough things to worry about here on the inside. He couldn't stand to pile on a bunch of worry about what his folks were thinking. So he just pushed it all aside till he got the next letter. He'd worry about staying out of trouble. He'd worry about not waking up Old Oscar. He'd worry about getting in the band. Three things. That was enough for a while.

What he forgot to worry about a few days later was his footing as he loaded one of the trucks to ship uniforms to one of the road camps. One minute he was up on the loading dock. The next minute he was on the ground several feet below with his foot in a funny twist.

"My ankle's just twisted," he told the boss when he came to check on him, but he couldn't put any weight on it. They had to carry him up to the hospital floor.

CHAPTER 31

His ankle was broken. Just when everything had seemed to be going so well. Mr. Brodson had come to church, heard him sing, and had even talked to Jerry about the bands. He wasn't in yet, but he'd thought he might be soon. He'd even written and told his mother he was practically in the band in hopes she'd start writing about that and quit harping on and on about Joletta in her letters.

His job in the shipping department kept him hopping, but he was getting everything done and getting it done right. The boss man hardly ever got on his case any more, and a new inmate had just started working in there with Jerry. Keevin had taken to Cabbit the same as T.C. had. Jerry wouldn't have to worry about the cat while he was laid up. Besides the cat was a survivor. Just like Jerry.

Cabbit would make it as long as he stayed out from in front of the trucks. Jerry was the same way. He just had to avoid the "big trucks" that could smash him here in the prison. He sure hadn't noticed many angels ready to help him out, but then maybe angels came in all shapes and sizes. Old Oscar might even be a kind of helping angel to set him straight on how to survive inside. Maybe the angels were there around Jerry. He just had to open his eyes and pay attention so he could spot them.

He had to stay in the hospital until they could bring in some doctors from Augusta to make sure the fracture was properly set. The days dragged by with nothing to do but lie there. Jerry begged them to let him go back to work, but the prison doctor just shook his head at him.

"Take it easy, Gerald," he told him. "Most of the guys would be happy for a week or two to lay around and do nothing. Fact is, even if these bone specialists say the set is fine and we don't need to do anything else to your ankle, you're going to be on crutches a good while. You won't be able to go back to your shipping room job until you get the cast off."

So Jerry lay in the bed and fidgeted. He did leg lifts to keep his muscles from melting away. He read sports magazines that were over a year old. He sang until he was hoarse. He prayed for everybody he could think of, but still the time crawled by. He hated not having any work to do. He couldn't even write his folks to tell them about his ankle since he didn't have any paper or stamps. It felt funny being laid up in the hospital and his folks not even knowing about it. It made him wonder how long it would be before anybody told them he was dead if some day he ticked off the wrong people inside these walls and somebody stuck a knife in his gut.

He was still in the hospital when Mr. Brodson asked him to be in the country western band. All that extra time he'd had for praying must have paid off even if the country western band wasn't the one he'd been praying for. Still he was willing to sing any kind of music if it meant he got to be up on the stage.

So once he got out of the prison hospital, singing became his job. He was still in prison. He still had to worry about the beasts in the jungle devouring him, but from eight o'clock in the morning until four o'clock in the afternoon he didn't have to worry about anything except hitting the right note and planning the band's act for the next week. He sometimes sang the solo part and the other guys backed him up. Sometimes he backed up one of the other singers, usually Jesse, who could not only sing a great song but also wrote some lonesome prison songs that were as good as anything that was playing on the radio. At least that's what the disc jockey, Lyle Keller, told them.

"You boys are good. If I could just get you all out of prison at the same time, I'd take you on the road and we'd make something happen," he'd tell them every week.

Lyle was so skinny he looked like a scarecrow in fancy clothes. His narrow face practically disappeared behind his dark rimmed glasses. He was just a big nose and glasses. But he had a smooth voice and a fast wit and hosted a popular radio show aired out of Nashville where he played all the big time country hits. Sometimes he made a tape of Jerry and the other guys singing and played it on a local program he did in Augusta, but he had them half believing that someday they'd make the Nashville show.

In September they put on a show for a special meeting of the Alcoholics Anonymous organization in the prison with between two and three hundred free world guests. A few months earlier Jerry had gone to his first AA meeting after Chaplain Chatham had pushed him to join the group. The first thing Jerry had had to do was own up to the truth that he was addicted to alcohol and that when he got out, he could never take another drink or he'd find himself in the same old sorry, hopeless state he'd been in before he was sent to prison.

At the AA meetings, the men were encouraged to look to some higher power to help get them through bad times. The literature didn't actually say the Lord. Each individual had to decide on his own higher power. And while Jerry still didn't know what the Lord wanted from him or even if the Lord could want anything from somebody who'd messed up the way he had, he did know, without a doubt, that there was no higher power than God.

Jerry had never quit praying, never quit reading the Bible, never quit being grateful that his folks, not just his parents but his whole family, were praying for him, never quit singing church songs, but his heart still felt strangely empty. He kept trying to shove some convictions in there, but somehow nothing he came up with ever felt like his own convictions. He was just leaning on everybody else's beliefs.

Now as he learned more about AA and thought more about the Lord as his higher power, the door of his heart began to creak open a tiny bit. Maybe the Lord did have a purpose for his life. Even if he never got out of prison, maybe he could do some good things inside and be an example to others. Maybe someday he might even point out the right direction to someone like one of those angels that kept stepping into his own path.

The show for the AA meeting went great. After Jerry sang "Danny Boy," the crowd cheered him back on stage to sing "I'm So Lonesome I Could Cry." The only way Jerry could have been happier was if it had all been happening out in the free world instead of inside the prison walls. Still the band's fame was growing. Everybody was always telling them that the free world bands the prison officials brought in weren't a bit better than their own Rebel Band. They worked hard the whole week to come up with new programs that would have the men laughing and cheering.

Mr. Brodson was always after Jerry to sing his heart out at this or that show because of all the free world people who would hear him. He said if enough people got to talking about Jerry maybe it would help get him noticed by the men who had the power to get him an early parole. Jerry had told his folks once he was going to sing his way out of prison, and now it looked like that might be going to happen.

For sure, the lawyers Joletta and her husband had hired hadn't pulled any rabbits out of any hats. They had come up with the same answer Mr. York and his parents had come up with. Stay out of trouble, keep a good record in prison, and wait for the Parole Board to review his case. In five plus years. Jerry liked the idea of singing his way out better.

So he put his heart and his soul into his singing. He polished his gospel songs and pushed his voice to the upper limits in the tenor range. The band sang all sorts of songs, but when they sang gospel music, Jerry was always the star. Mr. Brodson even brought in a free world piano player, Perry Patterson, for Jerry since Perry had a way of banging out gospel music that seemed to especially fit Jerry's gospel singing style.

So everybody kept telling Jerry he was great—the free world groups, Mr. Brodson, Perry, the girls who came in from the free world to listen and make eyes at him after the performances. Some people he'd gotten to know in Pembroke even came down every week just to hear Jerry sing. So he could do it. He could make it in the singing business. He knew he could if he could only get out of prison.

He'd sing so great that they'd have to let him out. Jerry could almost feel it happening, feel himself walking out the gates of the prison as a free man and straight into some studio in Nashville somewhere to make a record.

The days passed, turned into weeks, then months. Christmas came to the prison again, Jerry's second Christmas locked inside. Every morning in December when he woke up with the bars holding him inside, he thought of something new he missed about Christmas outside. The shopping, the anticipation, the carols at church, the great food, seeing family he hadn't seen since the last Christmas, singing "O Holy Night" at a dozen different churches, the decorations, the smell of cookies and pies baking, everything. His folks sent him boxes of food, but no matter how well the candy and cookies traveled, it wasn't like gathering around the table with family and saying grace before enjoying a holiday feast.

Not that he didn't enjoy the care packages and Christmas gifts. For one thing he got to gorge on sweet things. For another it made him popular in the dorm and with the guards because he always got way more than he could eat by himself. Sometimes one of the guards would stop him as he went to his job and ask when his mother was coming to visit.

But no amount of cookies could make up for missing Christmas at home. Still there was nothing he could do about it. He was stuck there. He'd done the crime, and the State of Georgia was making him pay the price for that. For months, he'd sung his heart out and he wasn't one bit closer to getting out.

Jesse got out. He'd been a short timer anyway, and he'd gotten the good news from the Parole Board right before Jerry turned twenty-one on the third day of January.

Twenty-one. Jerry remembered talking with Billy, his old friend from Oldham High about turning twenty-one back when they were fifteen. It was like a door they could hardly even imagine up ahead where they would pass through into adulthood. They would legally be of age. They'd talked about how they wondered if they'd be married, where they'd be working, what they'd be doing. Never in a million years would Jerry have ever thought he'd spend his twenty-first birthday behind bars.

The day after his birthday he got a letter from Amanda Sue saying she thought the world and all of him, but there was this guy at her church and they'd been going out some. Jerry told himself he didn't care. He told himself he could barely remember what Amanda Sue even looked like unless he pulled out one of the pictures she'd sent him. He told himself he had plenty of girls wanting his attention at their shows or at the big AA gatherings with all the free world people. Still his spirits took a nosedive.

So did the fortunes of the Rebel Band. Jesse had been a big part of the band and with him gone, it just wasn't the same. Jerry was happy for Jesse, glad he was free to go out and make his name in the music world, but he wanted to be out there with him. He'd done everything they'd asked. He'd sung his heart out. He'd prayed. He'd read his Bible. He'd gotten past the shock of finding out about his birth mother, Joletta. He'd forgiven his mother and father for keeping him in the dark about his past. He'd made peace with them and had gotten them to make peace with one another or at least to quit pulling him into their fights. He'd kept out of trouble in this prison jungle. He'd kept an iron grip on his temper even when people were doing their best to push him over the edge. But he was still in prison with long years stretched out in front of him. He wasn't going to be able to sing his way out.

So he looked squarely at another year in prison without putting on the blinders of hope that a miracle was going to happen just because he wanted it to. The governor wasn't going to suddenly pardon him. He was going to be in prison for a long time.

Jerry lost his enthusiasm for the choir. They were just singing words. None of it meant anything. The chaplain started pushing him to do things that he couldn't do, that the men in the choir couldn't do, so he quit. His parents weren't happy with him, but then that was far from a first. They didn't understand how it was inside. They couldn't. Nobody could who hadn't been there, who hadn't crept through the jungle searching frantically for a way out only to have more jungle vines growing up to choke him.

But then he bumped right into another angel, Millard Cleveland, assistant warden at Reidsville. Mr. Cleveland reached out and grabbed Jerry before he could take the first step down the wrong road in prison. He pushed Jerry to get involved in a couple of new programs in the prison, R-inc and Guides for Better Living.

"R-inc or Reclaim, Inc. was started by some inmates who wanted to stop the same old revolving prison door. Their intent is to help men who want to change. Men like you, Gerald, who want to break the cycle and get off the treadmill of going to prison over and over." Mr. Cleveland sounded like a preacher trying to convince people to get saved at a revival. He even sort of looked like one of the preachers Jerry had known when he was a kid. He was about six feet tall and wide, not fat but stocky and strong. His suits always looked too tight in the arms and half the time he had his tie pulled loose at the neck. He was young looking and had a fire in his eyes as if he really thought he could make a difference in the world around him.

"If I ever get out, I'll never come back," Jerry assured him.

"That's what everybody thinks," Mr. Cleveland said. "And believes on the day they leave here, but things happen. Things you can't do anything about. A man has to be strong."

"Yes sir, I'm working on that."

"I know you are, Gerald, and I know you've got good parents who are doing everything they can for you and supporting you while you're here, but there are some things that nobody can do for you. Things you have to do for yourself. This course can help you succeed not only when you get out, but inside, too. I've kept tabs on you the last few months. I've seen how the AA meetings have helped you and how well you've done with the band, but sometimes you're too ready to throw it all in when anything goes against you."

"You're talking about the choir, aren't you? It all just got too stale. And I was always losing my best singers."

"I'm not talking just about that," Mr. Cleveland said. "You have to keep focused, Gerald. You have to keep moving forward and not let yourself slip back because of things you can't control."

"Yes sir," Jerry said.

"Keep your eyes on the mountain."

"I want to, sir. I try to, but sometimes it's like I'm walking and walking and I look up and God has moved the mountain back a few miles until I'm even farther away than I was when I started," Jerry said.

"The Lord doesn't work that way, Gerald. That mountain's closer no matter how it looks to you." Mr. Cleveland leaned forward in his chair and pinned Jerry down with his eyes. "You just keep walking. Keep moving your feet and trying to improve yourself. This might not be the best place for a young man to grow up and get educated, but it's the place you are. Don't give up and take the easy path. If you do, prison can swallow you. Don't let that happen to you. Keep growing so that when you are set free, whenever that is, you'll be ready to face the challenges of life on the outside."

CHAPTER 32

So he stepped back on the high road in prison. Bad things happened all around him. One kid about the same age as Jerry, somehow tore his blanket into strips, braided them together, and hung himself one night while everybody was sleeping. The boy had just been there two weeks and hadn't said the first word about anything or anybody tormenting him. He'd just picked dying over learning to survive inside.

Jerry thought that could have been him. He'd courted suicide often enough, but the Lord had always held his hand over Jerry and protected him even from himself. What Jerry had never been able to figure out, still didn't know, was why. Was it his parents' prayers for him, his mother's absolute certainty that his life was important to the Lord even when Jerry hadn't felt his life was worth two cents? Maybe it was just their strong unshakable love, or maybe it was simply because his mother couldn't stand to be wrong. Jerry had no problem at all imagining her storming heaven's gates and demanding the Lord give Jerry another chance, that she knew Jerry could do better, that she'd see to it that he did better.

Whatever the reason, the Lord had kept giving Jerry more chances. Even in prison the Lord was giving him chances to improve, to learn, and the most amazing thing was that here in prison Jerry had grabbed hold of the will to live so strongly he couldn't even imagine what he might have been thinking when he'd tried to drive his car into a tree so he could stop living when he was a teenager.

He was working so hard on the Guides course that he hardly had time to write to his folks, but he could feel a difference in his life already. The words of the instructor and in the books about keeping a positive mental attitude seemed to be spiraling into Jerry's brain and taking root there. He could eliminate the kind of negative thoughts that kept him down. He'd done bad things, but he could be, no he was, a worthwhile person.

Even if he never got out of prison, he could do good things, help others keep from making the mistakes he had made, step closer to his parents. And if he did get out, he could be successful even if he had to start with nothing. He had his abilities and his energy and he could obtain the true riches of life and make his way in the free world. He vowed to learn everything he could and use it all to make sure he did get a chance to be part of the free world again.

The band took an upswing along with Jerry's spirits once he enrolled in the Guides course. Mr. Brodson found a new singer that fit in with their band, and The Rebels were on the rise again. It wasn't Jesse with his original songs, but there were plenty of other songs to sing. Mr. Cleveland began taking a special interest in the band. As their free world crowds grew, they got donations of new equipment and offers for radio time.

Out in the yard, there was some grumbling that the jazz band, now all blacks, wasn't getting equal time on stage. The disc jockeys weren't making tapes of their performances to air on the radio. Mr. Brodson tried to smooth it over. The prison was in the south. Country music was all the rage. The jazz band was getting just as much chance to play as the Rebel Band.

It was impossible to keep everything perfectly equal. As Mr. Brodson said, all singers weren't equal and right now the Rebel Band was made up of singers and musicians who meshed and knew how to put on a show. They didn't mind looking silly if it made the show go over. They'd even dressed up in diapers to look like Cupid on Valentine's Day and shot paper arrows out into the crowd. When the song "Elvira" started playing on the radio, Jerry slapped on a wig and a dress to get the audience laughing and having fun. The jazz band could have pulled some of the same type of stunts if they'd wanted to.

Mr. Cleveland and Mr. Brodson took the Rebel Band on the road the end of April to another prison to put on a show. It was great being outside the prison walls even if it was just long enough to drive to a different prison. Mr. Brodson promised there would be other trips. But in prison things had a way of happening that kept men from keeping promises.

Jerry's mother came down the end of May. It was his dad's turn to stay home to milk the cows. They laughed and talked while Jerry gorged on the food she brought him. Sometimes it was as if they'd both just shut the door on the bad times they'd had when Jerry was a kid. His mother didn't talk about things he could do better. Instead she talked about what they'd do when he came home as if that might be next month or maybe tomorrow. She caught him up on the news about the people at church and the family. She talked about the crops and the cows and how the hay was almost ready to cut. If she noticed him getting the least bit upset, she backed away from whatever she'd said. It was as if the mother he'd had when he was six and sixteen had disappeared when he went to jail and in her place, was this new, more loving and sympathetic model.

At the same time, on his side, he did his best to keep from upsetting her by not saying anything about the guy in his dorm who'd gotten beat up because he'd dealt himself a winning hand in a poker game or the checkpoint guard who took pleasure in making Jerry feel lower than a bug smashed on a rock by strip searching him in front of everybody. And of course he never said the first word about Joletta coming to visit or writing him.

So instead of telling her things that were eating right through him, he talked about how the band had been doing and sang her bits of the songs they'd sung at their last show or asked her advice about a crazy skit they were trying to work up. He talked a lot about the Guides to Better Living course, because self-motivation, positive attitude type things were high on his mother's list. She thought anybody could think and pray things better.

She listened intently to everything he had to say, and then bragged on him. "I'm so proud of you, Jerry. Not many young men your age could handle what you've had to handle. And you're not only handling it, you're learning and growing stronger in every way. Your dad and I are both so proud of you." She laid her hand on his cheek and smiled at him. Tears popped into her eyes but didn't overflow. "I'd do anything to get you out of here. Anything. You know that, don't you?"

"I know, Mom, but if it's not to be, then I just have to make the best of it till I can go before the Parole Board five years from now."

"No, five years is too long." She shook her head, and her tears disappeared, burned away by her sheer determination. "We'll get them to review your case before that. I've been in touch with Judge Rutherford again. I won't let him or the Parole Board forget about you."

"It would be great if they'd look at my case and decide I was ready for release, but even if they don't, I'm doing okay in here. Did I tell you I've been picked as corresponding secretary for our Tatnall AA Group?"

"You did. I know you'll do a great job," his mother said. "You've always been good at writing. Your letters home mean so much to us."

"I know I should write more, Mom, but sometimes I just get so busy with everything."

"It's okay. We understand. You've always been a hard worker," his mother said.

"On the farm maybe. This kind of work is different, but I love it. I get to correspond with people all over the country. Just the other day, I got a letter from this couple out in Wisconsin. The man used to be an alcoholic, but he's been dry now for twenty years and he runs this great big farm out there."

"Wisconsin," his mother said as if Jerry had said he knew somebody from Mars. "They have a lot of dairy farms out there, don't they? You'll have friends all over before long."

"Nobody can have too many friends." He reached over and touched her hand that she'd let fall back to the table while he was talking. "So even if we don't find a way for me to get out right away, I'll be okay. Guides is teaching me to keep the right kind of mental attitude so I don't let every little old thing push me down into a deep black hole the way it did before. I still have to live with what I did, but I don't have to let it paint everything in my life black. I have to go forward, so that when I do finally get back out into the free world, I can be successful in whatever I do with the rest of my life."

"You'll do great things, Jerry. I've always known that," his mother said. "But I can't help worrying about you in here and wanting you home now."

"You'd better believe I'd like to walk out of here with you today, Mom, but things aren't always that easy. I can't always expect everything to go smooth. I just have to make sure I can handle it when it doesn't."

"I pray every day, every hour, that the Lord will keep you under his wings, Jerry." Her eyes on him were intense. "And never, never underestimate the power of a mother's prayers."

He didn't. But it wasn't something he thought about all that much either. His folks prayed for him. He prayed for them, and it just went in a neat little circle. It was like getting up in the morning and stripping down to take a shower. It was just something he did hardly without thinking any more in spite of there being not the least bit of privacy in the open shower areas.

Time passed. He didn't exactly feel the Lord's wings hovering over him, but at the same time he was staying alive in the jungle. Their Rebel Band was gathering strength and more and more people were banging him on the back telling him how great he could sing. He graduated from the Guides for Better Living and became an instructor for the program. That along with the secretary work for the AA group and his band practices kept him on the run so that he barely had time to eat. And he was happier than he could ever remember being.

That seemed a strange way to feel locked up in prison with more long years of confinement stretching out in front of him. But it was as if he'd taken life by the horns and was guiding it the way he wanted to go instead of just letting it pitch him around willy-nilly wherever. He tried to explain it to his parents in a letter.

Guess what??? I feel Healthy! I feel Happy! I feel Terrific! People here cannot understand why I'm full of happiness. Well, they just don't know what it is, but

I do!! We can find happiness in what we are, not in what we have. I used to confuse happiness with pleasure. Pleasure is an agreeable sensation or emotion, while happiness is the basic quality of life. Right???

One of the reasons it is sometimes hard for people to have happiness is that they chase it too aggressively. I believe happiness comes when we least expect it. I might say to myself, I'm going to be happy, but it does not respond to this kind of treatment.

Happiness lies within. In a way happiness can be a habit. If we want to form the habit of happiness, we must develop certain things like: hopefulness, patience, love, good cheer, and a forgiving spirit. To be happy, make others happy! Right on!!! To have a good habit, have a happy habit!

Your Loving Son, Jerry

Two weeks after he wrote that letter, life tossed its horns high and almost threw Jerry off. It was Sunday. Their band put on an outstanding show. One whole section was filled with free world people and inmates filled the rest of the seats until the place was packed. The jazz band hadn't played. Mr. Brodson said several of them were down with the flu and hadn't even come out for the entertainment.

The free world part of the entertainment had taken the stage first. The crowd had been restive while the up and coming country band sang and played. The energy in the place was ready to explode as the free world band cleared the stage and Mr. Brodson began introducing the Rebel Band. When Jerry and the other guys ran on stage, cheers bounced off the walls.

They put on one of their best shows. The crowd stayed on their feet, clapping and singing along. The electricity in the air was so potent Jerry almost expected to see crackles of lightning flashing over the men's heads out in the audience. It made his skin tingle as he sang the encore the crowd demanded.

After Mr. Brodson finally made them end the show and the band had their few minutes of socializing with the free world band while they helped them pack up their equipment to leave, Rusty, the drummer, grabbed Jerry's arm. He was still clicking his sticks in rhythm. Rusty was always clicking something. If he didn't have sticks, he used his fingers, toes, spoons, whatever he could find. "Hey, come on, Shep, let's go out in the yard and let the men tell us how great we were some more. I know you can't ever get enough of that."

"Man, it was something today, wasn't it? It was like there was some kind of electric charge in the air. You sure B.J.'s guitar didn't have some kind of short in it?" Jerry said. His ears were still ringing from the noise of the band and the cheers.

"Don't blame me, Shep," B.J. said. He ran his hands through his mop of blonde hair to put it back in some order before one of guards could order him to find a comb or worse, a barber. B.J. liked to keep his hair as long as the prison officials would let him so he could whip his head back and forth and make his hair bang against his face while he was playing. "It was all them high notes you were bouncing off the ceiling that were coming back down and frying their ears."

"I don't think we're going to be able to top this one, guys," Walt said. "I wish Jesse had been here to hear this." Walt had moved up to one of the main singers' spots after Jesse left. He was still always after Mr. Brodson to let them sing some of Jesse's songs.

"Jesse's out with a new audience now," Jerry said.

"Yeah, where we all want to be." Rusty tapped his sticks fast on the stage floor to make running footstep sounds.

"Don't be trying to put no damper on our spirits, Rusty. We may be locked up, but we can still sing and play," B.J. said. "So come on, we can clean up this place in the morning. Mr. Brodson won't care. Let's go take a walk around the yard and hear what the guys really thought."

Jerry started down the hall toward the yard with the other guys, but as he passed by the corridor that led down to the AA office he remembered seeing Arthur, the head of their AA group that morning at church. He'd promised Arthur he'd work on getting some letters out to other groups that afternoon. Jerry stopped. "I'd better not go out. I'm way behind with the AA stuff and all."

"Oh come on, Shep. You can do it tomorrow. Don't always be so responsible," Rusty said. "We're convicts, remember? Bad guys. The only thing we're responsible for is trouble."

"Can't argue with that," Jerry said. "But I gotta do them today. I promised I'd get a bunch of letters out this week and I'm not exactly Speedy Gonzalez when it comes to typing. You guys go ahead. You can tell me all about it tomorrow."

"Yeah, I don't blame you," B.J. said over his shoulder as they went on up the corridor. "I wouldn't want to go out amongst all those crazy for women men either if I sang like a girl."

"Stick a sock in it," Jerry called after him with a grin.

He never saw any of the guys again.

CHAPTER 33

Jerry was typing away when Stevie, one of the guards, yelled down the hall back into the AA office. "You in there, Gerald?" He sounded out of breath as if he'd been running laps out in the yard or chasing somebody.

"I'm right here," Jerry called back. "Trying to get some letters out. Something wrong?"

"Man, am I ever glad to hear your voice." Stevie came down the hall close enough to see Jerry, but not all the way into the room. He was still panting a little. "I got to be quick. Bad things are going down. They put out a hit on your Rebel Band."

"A hit? On us? Who would do that?"

"Can't say. I done said more than I should, but I know you won't be telling and getting me in trouble. And you gotta know what's going on if you want to stay alive. They told me to make sure you were alive." Stevie pulled a handkerchief out of his pocket and wiped his forehead. He was on the heavy side, but as strong as ten men. Nobody would have messed with Stevie even if he hadn't been carrying a gun and a billy bat.

Jerry stood up and took a couple of steps toward Stevie.

Stevie held his hand up to stop him. "Stay put. I'm locking you down in here. Nobody will be able to get to you in here so just sit tight till we get things settled down."

Jerry stayed where he was. "The guys okay?"

Stevie mashed his mouth together and shook his head a little. "The story I'm hearing said the black goons that jumped them had eight inch prison honed specials and baseball bats. Your guys didn't have a chance. Fists against knives don't even up too good."

Jerry had to swallow twice before he could ask, "They dead?"

"I wasn't out in the yard, so I can't say for sure yet, but I wouldn't be surprised. The whole place is on lock down, but since your name was on the list, you're better off here than in the dorm. Look, I can't talk no more. I gotta go bash heads to keep the place from blowing up. The big boss just wanted me to come find you to be sure you were in a safe place. Besides, come tomorrow, you'll know more about what happened than I will anyhow. If you're alive, and we aim to keep you alive."

After Jerry heard the doors crashing shut behind Stevie and the locks being set, he sat back down in front of his typewriter. He was about halfway through a letter to the secretary of an AA group up in Indiana. He'd been writing about their group there in prison and how they'd added a new member just last week. That member had been Walt. And now Walt might be gone. Not just out of prison or transferred to another prison, but gone.

He could have been gone with him if the Lord hadn't sent an angel to stand in his path and keep him out of the yard. Maybe the angel had been motioning him down the corridor to the AA office. Maybe Arthur had been the angel that morning in church when he'd made Jerry promise to get the letters out by tomorrow. Maybe his mother was the angel with her constant prayers to the Lord to keep him safe inside.

"Thank you, Lord, for keeping me inside. For keeping me safe," Jerry whispered. Then he felt guilty thanking God for letting him live when the others may not have. Walt, B.J., Rusty, Jake, Pewee, Shorty. They could all be dead. Jerry felt weird as if he should be with them. He could almost feel the blades ripping into his body and the bats bashing out his brain. The muffled sound of alarm signals and running feet came through the locked doors, but in the AA office the silence banged against his ears. Just a few hours ago cheers had been echoing in his ears. They'd thought everybody loved them. They were going to get out and go right to the top of the charts. And now they might not be going anywhere except to meet their maker.

Maybe that's where he was, too. Maybe he just thought an angel had pushed him toward the AA office. Maybe instead he was in a big waiting room for heaven. Jerry shook his head and told himself to stop being idiotic. He was sitting at his desk in the AA office. His heart was still beating. His blood was still swooshing around his body. His lungs were still taking in air. His fingers could still push the typewriter keys under them. Jerry typed the word *the*. The little ball on the electric typewriter spun around and clattered up against the paper. His ears welcomed the noise as his eyes went to the pile of still unanswered letters.

He was locked in the office. He couldn't do anything about whatever had happened. He could sit there and let fear make his fingers tremble. Stevie had been clear about Jerry's name being on the hit list. Or he could shut his eyes and work on pulling up that positive mental attitude he was always harping on in his Guides classes. Nobody could get to him in here. He was safe at least until they unlocked the door. He had no idea how long he would be locked down inside here, but it could be hours. He might as well use the time productively and finish off the stack of letters. Then whatever happened after they let him go back to the dorm, he'd at least be caught up on his AA work.

Besides he didn't know for sure that any of the guys were dead. Even Stevie hadn't known that for sure. He'd just heard about what had happened, and rumors had a way of flashing like wild fire through the prison when anything went down. Sometimes the fire flared up bigger than ever from the wind in the mouths repeating the story each time until what had really happened and what was being told weren't a thing alike. Maybe the guys were up in the hospital getting stitched up. There were guards out in the yard. They wouldn't have just stood around and let bad stuff go down without breaking it up even if they had to break some heads to do it. They would have been happy to break heads.

So Jerry locked out the fear and worry and read over the half finished letter in his typewriter. He had to erase the first letter of the word *the* he'd typed a few minutes earlier so he could capitalize it for the beginning of his next sentence. He kept typing about what had happened at their last meeting and their plans for the summer meeting with one of the free world groups.

Every once in a while Rusty's face would sneak into his thoughts or B.J. would be laughing in Jerry's head about something stupid one of the guys in the band had done. Jerry pushed it away. He had to concentrate on what he was doing or he'd hit a wrong key. It was a pain to correct typos since he had to stick a piece of paper between the top page and the carbon copy before he could erase whatever letter he'd hit wrong and then pull the paper back and erase the error on the carbon copy.

He had all the letters done by the time a guard remembered to come get him. It was late. There would be no supper. When Jerry tried to ask about what had happened, the guard told him to shut his mouth and just keep walking till they got to the dorm.

The prison seemed extra quiet. It was as if the inmates' mouths had been locked down along with the doors. When the guard opened up the door to put him back in the dorm, every eye fastened on Jerry. Even the men who pretended not to be looking were watching him as he crossed the floor to his bunk.

Old Oscar wasn't in his bunk below Jerry's. A big white guy with dirty blonde hair raised up a little off his pillow and grinned at Jerry. He kept his voice low as he said, "You must have had a lucky star shining on you, boy."

"Where's Old Oscar?" Jerry asked.

"They done moved him over to the west side. He'd sure enough be dead if he was still over here. Ain't a one of us in here would let one of them live after what they done to the band."

"Old Oscar didn't do nothing, did he?" Jerry asked.

"He did enough. He was born black." The man narrowed his eyes on Jerry. "It's them against us. If you didn't know that before now, you better be knowing it now. That is, if you want to keep breathing tomorrow. There's some that ain't and some more that ain't gonna be once we get to them. We've got long memories."

"Pipe down in there," the guard out in the corridor yelled. "This ain't social hour. Go to sleep. You be good little boys, you might even get breakfast in the morning."

"I'd like to put his name on a list," the big white guy muttered.

"We'd just get somebody worse," Jerry said.

"Yeah, maybe, but he'd be gone," the white guy said.

Jerry climbed up in his bunk and turned on his lamp. Moths and all their friends would be flying around his head in no time flat, but he needed to see the light. He kept his voice barely above a whisper and talked toward the ceiling as he began introducing himself, "My name's Jerry."

"I know who you are." The other man's voice came through the cot up to him. "You sing in the Rebels, or you used to sing in the Rebel Band. I don't think there is a Rebel Band any more. You might be the only one standing now."

"No way," Jerry said.

"They went down. A gang of coons was waiting to jump them over around the basketball courts."

Jerry turned off his light and didn't say anything else. He didn't want to know any more. He didn't want any more of the man's words to crawl up the wall to his ears. He wanted Old Oscar to be down there snoring and daring Jerry to do anything to wake him up. He wanted to go back to this morning and live the day over, only this time the whole bunch of them would stay in the theater and work on a new show.

That might have kept it from happening on this day, but that didn't mean it wouldn't have happened. They'd have been waiting somewhere else, and then he might have been in the middle of it. Not that he was safe just because he hadn't been out in the yard when it had gone down. The beasts in the jungle wouldn't forget about his name being on the list. He'd have to watch his back every minute of every day.

Maybe they'd transfer him out of here. He'd actually been approved for a transfer to another prison months ago, but what with the band going so well and with him getting so involved in AA and teaching the Guides for Living courses, they'd sort of filed the idea away. Why move him when everything was going good here at Reidsville? He was almost up to trusty status, his major goal when he first came into the prison. And there were rumors that Mr. Cleveland was going to get a job at a new facility being built as a model prison down in Montgomery. There was some talk of getting Jerry transferred there when it opened. But would it open soon enough to help him now?

He lay in his bunk and listened to the men settling in to sleep around him. The man below him quit talking. Jerry would have to find out his name come morning. But for now he was just glad to pull in air to fill his lungs and then let it out.

The next morning an old inmate named Harry sat with Jerry at breakfast and filled him in on what had happened. Harry had been at Reidsville for over ten years. Jerry had never been exactly sure what the old man had done to get locked up. He couldn't imagine Harry killing anybody, but then when he thought about it, he couldn't imagine killing anybody himself and he had.

Harry was a short little guy with a bald head that reminded Jerry of his own dad. Harry's blue eyes were sort of faded and tired looking as they stared out of his wrinkled face that stayed brown year around. Harry had been on the ditch digging detail in the hot Georgia sun so long that his face had dried up and cracked like an old piece of leather. Now because of the way his fingers were twisted with arthritis, Harry worked in the barbershops sweeping up hair clippings. It was rumored he sometimes put a snippet or two of the hair in his pocket and played at voodoo, but Jerry didn't believe it even if Harry did admit to being born in Cajun country down in Louisiana. Jerry liked Harry, and while the wrinkled old man didn't talk much, when he did, Jerry knew he could believe what he said.

"Were you out there where it happened, Harry?" Jerry asked him.

"I was," Harry said. "Lucky you weren't."

"Are they all dead?"

"Not all of them. Two at least. I don't know which ones. It was crazy like those pictures you see on television of them fish down in South America or wherever that strip the flesh off a man in nothing flat."

"You mean piranhas?" Jerry said.

"Yeah, whatever they're called," Harry said. "That's the way they jumped on those white boys. The poor suckers didn't have a chance. There must have been about two dozen of them, maybe more, and only five or six of your boys."

"Where were the guards?"

"Not where they needed to be, same as always." Harry slurped some coffee out of his cup. He made a face and wallowed the liquid around his mouth a minute before he swallowed. "They came running and did some shooting and bashing, but it was already too late for some of the boys."

"Which ones?"

"Can't say. Like I said, I wasn't that close. I was backing off at the first flash of a knife. I ain't got no fight with nobody. But I think I saw them carrying B.J. out to the hospital. The way his head was bashed in and with blood everywhere, it was hard to tell if it was him or not, but it was a big guy and B.J.'s the biggest of you boys. One thing sure, whoever it was looked more dead than alive, but I reckon he must have still been breathing or they'd have just pulled the sheet up over him before they carried him in. Then again maybe the guards just wanted us to think he was breathing."

"Why would they do that?"

"So the white boys would back off and give them a chance to herd them that did it inside before the whole place exploded. It wasn't far from it. I'm surprised it didn't."

"Why'd they do it?" Jerry asked.

"Rumor going around says the Jazz Band got sick of you guys getting all the candy and decided to put you out of the singing business. Permanently."

"Not Adrien and Joel surely. Or Burton." Jerry couldn't imagine any of them wanting him dead. They had been sharing practice times for months.

"I ain't saying names. I'm just telling you what's going around, but if I was you, I wouldn't go anywhere near the west side of this place for a long, long time. In fact, it could be you should just go beg them that pull the strings to let you go somewheres else." Harry looked at him over his coffee cup. "You ain't never gonna be safe in here again."

"We weren't doing them any harm. We were just singing."

"Not no more. They seen to that."

CHAPTER 34

With the blacks all on the West Side and the whites all on the East Side, things began to settle back into a routine. Jerry went about his day-to-day activities, getting up, going to eat, doing his jobs without ever seeing a black face. Both bands were disbanded. All entertainment programs were canceled indefinitely. Mr. Brodson transferred to another prison. Jerry quit even singing when he took a shower. It seemed wrong somehow to still sing when all the others were gone.

He never found out for sure what had happened to them, but the prison rumor mill had Rusty and Walt dead and B.J. and Shorty the next thing to it. The others had been shipped out to other prisons. Every day when he got up, Jerry expected to hear they were moving him out, but the days passed and he was still there.

That's what he told his folks each time he wrote them. *I'm still here.* It was sort of a silly thing to write since he was locked up and had no choice about where he was going, but at least it told them he was still breathing. Of course they didn't know how close he'd come to not breathing any more. He had written them that the place was in an uproar because of trouble between the blacks and whites and the prison had been segregated, but as for him being one of the prime targets, some things were better left untold. He did tell his dad enough of the story when he came down to visit in June to explain why the band had been shut down.

Jerry was careful not to tell too much and start up the worry machine on the home front. What had happened had happened. It was over now, and there wasn't the first thing any of them could do about it. His folks didn't need to know about the shivers that ran up and down his back when he was walking to his job at the AA office or how he had to keep checking over his shoulder to make sure nobody was getting ready to jump out of the shadows and take him down.

He had been glad it was his dad's turn to visit while his mother stayed home to do the milking. His father never seemed to want to know too much about anything bad going on at the prison anyway. It was as if what they didn't talk about didn't really happen.

So Jerry didn't have to explain it all in living color detail to his dad the way he would have had to if it had been his mother there. In fact, when his dad came down to visit, sometimes they just broke out in silence once they'd covered how much milk the cows were giving and how the crops were growing and what was going on at church. That never happened when his mother visited. His dad said that was because women didn't appreciate a few minutes of silence every once in a while to gather one's thoughts the way men did.

A week after his father was there, Miss Atwood came to see Jerry. She'd heard about what had gone down in the prison and wanted to help. She looked the same—short, sturdy, in control, with her brown hair chopped off just below her ears. She kept pushing her glasses up on her nose while she talked the same way she had when she'd counseled him at that chamber of horrors, the State Hospital.

"I've changed positions," she told him. "I'm a counselor at the Richmond County Correctional Institution in Augusta now. It's a road camp, nothing like here, and I think if I can get you transferred there, it will be good for you. You've done well here at Reidsville, but it's time for a change. Especially now with all the tension here. It could still boil over at any time, and you'd be safer out of here if that happens."

"Yes, ma'am." Jerry had no argument with that. He was tired of listening for footsteps behind him in this jungle.

"I've kept up with what you've been doing ever since you were at Milledgeville, Jerry, and your mother writes me off and on as well. In spite of the trouble the two of you had in the past, she cares deeply for you, and I don't believe there's anything she wouldn't try if she thought it would get you out of here."

"I know. She says you don't know what might work until you try it. But so far, the Parole Board just keeps telling her they won't consider my case until my regular parole date comes up. April 1976."

"I know. That must seem like forever to you," Miss Atwood said.

"Almost four years from now. And most of the men in here say I can't count on getting out even then, that hardly anybody gets paroled at their first hearing." Jerry felt half depressed even talking about it. He didn't usually think about the date so far in the future.

His Guides to Better Living course and his AA literature said it was useless dwelling on things a person couldn't change. It was better to take some positive action like writing a letter to someone who might help him or researching what the Parole Board needed to consider an early release. It was better to plan how to make something different happen than to just sit and worry about what was happening.

That's what he told Miss Atwood. She looked at him as if she was a teacher and he was her prize student. "It's good to hear how you can think things out now. You're really doing well, Jerry. Another reason to get you out of here to a better place. I don't want to see your progress falling back. So if it's okay with you, I'll contact your parents and we'll work on getting you transferred to Augusta. Trust me. It will be better for you there."

She called his parents, and they were willing to do anything to get him out of Reidsville. Maybe he'd told his dad too much about what had happened at the prison after all.

Two weeks later, a guard caught him before he went to breakfast and told him to pack his things, that he was moving out. He didn't have much to pack. His fan, his music books, a few letters and pictures from the folks at home, his underwear, his ink pens and his radio. Maybe reception would be better in the new prison. His trumpet was locked in the band room, so he lost that.

He couldn't tell anybody goodbye. There wasn't time. He scribbled out a couple of lines to Harry. *I'm being transferred out. Not free, but maybe someday. Stay as mean as ever. J,* He really didn't care about telling anybody else goodbye except the guys he worked with in the AA office, and he could write to them after he got to Augusta. The only other man he wanted to tell goodbye was on the West Side. He would have liked to tell Old Oscar he was leaving and that he appreciated Oscar not killing him when Jerry disturbed his sleep. He even thought about telling Oscar that he'd once wondered if Oscar might be an angel the Lord had dropped down in Jerry's path. Old Oscar would laugh at that for sure. At least as much as Old Oscar ever laughed which was just a sort of heavy heave of breath.

At Richmond County, the buildings looked more like a school than a prison. Nothing like Reidsville. They drove through a gate in a fence but it was just a regular wrought iron fence without any barbed wire or spikes at the top. Even the air inside felt different.

Maybe that was because he went in as a trusty from day one, or maybe it was because he could breathe in and out without wondering if he'd better enjoy the privilege while he had it. He saw plenty of black faces in the dorm he was assigned to and everywhere he went since there was no segregation of races at Richmond, but he didn't feel the first hint of tension between the blacks and whites.

They were all the same—men serving out their terms. Jerry had been lifted up out of the jungle of Reidsville and taken to one of those modern zoos that didn't believe in cages. The inmates at Richmond did their assigned jobs and came back in at night to be fed and locked in. Nobody was out to devour anybody else.

Nobody had to wander around in the hopeless fog of life with no parole the way some of the men had done at Reidsville. Here everybody had hopes of getting out. Even Jerry. Maybe not soon, but someday.

Jerry was assigned to the chapel as assistant music director and chaplain counselor. Miss Atwood had seen to it that the people at Richmond knew about Jerry's musical talents. The chaplain, Elton Foster, was a great lead singer, and luckily enough the two other chaplain assistants sang bass and baritone. Or as Chaplain Foster said, luck had nothing to do with it. It was God's plan for Jerry to join them with his tenor voice and complete their quartet.

Jerry was back in the singing business big time, and he loved it. He had great voices in the choir, most of them coming out of black faces. But these faces were smiling at him, laughing with him, paying attention when he told them how to make the choir sound better and better. Jerry got what his mother called holy goose bumps every time the choir sang.

Chaplain Foster had heard the call to preach when he was still a teenager, but it had taken him years to discover his true calling was working with men who needed to transform every aspect of their lives in order to be the men the Lord wanted them to be.

"Every man has a calling," he told Jerry. His dark blue eyes were intense and the lines on his face deep and serious. His black hair fuzzed up at the ends and sprang away from his head with no respect for a comb. Chaplain Foster never worried much about how he looked. He said the Lord looked on the inside, and he had too much work to do on that part to worry about how the outside part looked. "It's our duty to seek out and find that calling, to see what the Lord has in mind for us. We're not to think about what we want to do and see if we can fit it into the Lord's plans. We just need to jump right into the circle of God's purpose for us."

"My mother's always saying something the same about how the Lord has a purpose for me, but what if I never figure out what that purpose is?" Jerry asked.

Chaplain Foster's eyes got even more intense on Jerry as he looked at him a long moment before he answered, "It's a blessing to have Christian parents, but a man can't hold onto their shirt tails all his life. You can't find out what the Lord wants from you by way of your mother, Gerald. You have to go directly to the Lord. Go right up to the throne and ask what cross he wants you to carry because all men, all people, have their own cross. And we can't pick up somebody else's or the one that looks best to us. The Lord picks it and hands it right to us. But, praise the Lord, if it's heavy, he's right there beside us, helping us carry it on down the road of our life. That's what our drama tries to get people to see."

Chaplain Foster liked showing people the messages the Lord laid on his heart instead of just telling them about it. With all inmate actors, he took one of those messages to the churches on the outside through a drama called *The Challenge of the Cross*. Chaplain Foster said if he could reach people for Christ using men who were paying their debt to society then he was surely changing all their lives for the better.

It was great going out the prison gates and into the free world churches. They wore their prison stripes, but nobody at the churches seemed to mind. In the drama some of the inmates would sit out in the church among the congregation. The inmate who was acting as the evangelist would throw out a challenge for someone to come up and accept one of the crosses in the container at the front. One of the inmates out in the congregation would jump up and say, "I accept the challenge." He'd go forward and pick one of the crosses, usually a small one.

Then the evangelist would say, "No, brother, that's not the right cross for you. That's not the cross the Lord has chosen for you to carry. You can't just come up here and pick up some easy cross you think you can get by carrying. The Lord is talking to you here. You can't be listening to what you want. You listen to what he's telling you. He'll show you which cross to pick up." He'd pick up one of the bigger crosses and hold it out toward the man.

"But that one looks too heavy," the man who'd come forward would say. "I can't carry that."

"And who made your back?" the evangelist would say. "The Lord, that's who. If he doesn't know what you can carry, who does?"

Everywhere they went, the powerful message of the drama inspired people to make decisions for Christ. Jerry and the others in the quartet stood in the background and sang songs about the cross. They had no music other than the sound of their voices. Singing a cappella seemed to give the words of old hymns like "The Old Rugged Cross," "Near the Cross," and "Wherever He Leads, I'll Go" extra power. It was just like old times when he was a teenager singing in the churches and seeing the people out in the pews lift handkerchiefs to their eyes as the message of the songs touched them.

And sometimes in between the songs, Jerry felt a tug or two on his own heart-strings as he listened to the actors arguing about which cross to take. He'd watch the people of the church come forward to rededicate their lives and their faces would almost be glowing. He sometimes felt that kind of glow while he was singing, but when the song was over, the glow seemed to seep right out of him and leave an empty place in his heart.

He told himself that was okay. His heart wasn't really empty. He was doing plenty for the Lord. His whole life was revolving around singing for the Lord. His songs made people feel spiritual. He could see it on their faces as he sang. And he said his prayers. He prayed for his family. He prayed for the other men in prison. He thanked God for keeping him alive and helping him keep his positive mental attitude. He read the Bible when he had time and wasn't too tired at night after all his other duties.

That surely was purpose enough. Maybe he wasn't supposed to feel anything more than he already felt. Maybe he was just imagining that others had something he didn't have. After all, hadn't the Lord been setting down angels in the crossroads of his life? Pete and Mama Harmon, Miss Atwood, Mr. Cleveland, even Old Oscar. While Jerry hadn't always gone the right direction down the right roads, he'd recognized the Lord's hand in his life. Why was he always expecting something more?

He talked to Chaplain Foster about it. He told him how he'd walked the aisle to accept Christ when he was just twelve. "Everybody kept telling me it was time to go forward, and I felt like I should. I mean they knew more about what Jesus wanted and all than I did."

"Jesus just wanted your heart, Gerald. Did you give him your heart?"

"I think so. I meant to," Jerry said.

Chaplain Foster smiled at him. "If you truly did, you'll know it. And if you didn't, there will come a day or night when the time will be right." The chaplain put his hand on his shoulder. "I'm praying for you. The Lord will show you which cross he has for you to carry. And when he does, you'll know it. And I'm praying you'll be ready to pick it up."

CHAPTER 35

On a sizzling hot day in August, they took *The Challenge of the Cross* to a church youth camp about forty miles from the prison. As they unloaded their sound equipment and set up the props for the drama, the heat was rising up off the ground in waves. Some of the men started wishing for an air-conditioned church.

"Now which one of you has ever read the first thing about an air-conditioned church in the Bible?" Chaplain Foster asked when he heard them grumbling.

"I'll wager there wasn't no Georgia summers either," Sam said as he pulled his sweaty shirt away from his chest to get a little air. Sam was a big black man with a deep bass voice. "I mean I would wager if it weren't a sin to go around betting on stuff."

Chaplain Foster laughed. "There's plenty of hot desert country in the Holy Land."

"Desert heat ain't the same as Georgia heat," Sam said. "Desert heat is just hot, dry baking type heat, but Georgia heat makes a body feel like a dishrag that's done been dipped in boiling water on top of a woodstove and then rung out and left to steam on the back of the stove."

"Man, would you hush up?" Jerry told him. "Talk about ice boxes or snow. Not hot stoves and steam."

"I can't talk about snow," Sam said. "I ain't never seen no snow."

"You're kidding," Jerry said.

"Nope. Not the first flake. You ain't in the north no more, boy. You in the south now."

"Well, let me tell you about it." Jerry looked up and held out his hands as if he could wish down some snowflakes to catch. "Snow can come down soft and fluffy and pile up deep as your knees in no time flat, or it can come down hard and mean with the wind whipping it in your face and drifting it up over the fence posts. You can do a back flop in a nice smooth patch of the white stuff and wave your arms to make a beautiful snow angel. And then when you get up you're covered with snow and got snow down your collar and in your hair. Snow down your collar can cool you right down."

"Well, I ain't got no snow down my collar and I ain't a bit cooler," Sam said, flapping his shirttail to make a breeze.

"Jerry isn't either on the outside, but his brain's done froze," Dave said.

Dave, the baritone in their quartet, and Jerry had hit it off from the first day. Dave had a wife and kids on the outside. He'd told Jerry he'd let alcohol and drugs mess him up big time until he got locked away. He was off the stuff now and had Jesus in his heart, but he still had to pay for what he'd done. Part of that payment was not being home with his kids where he wanted to be. He said he told his boys to listen to their mamma, go to school, and do the right things, but what kind of daddy had to just see his kids on prison visiting days?

The hardest thing he had to live with was his oldest boy being diagnosed with leukemia a few months after Dave got sent up. It just tore Dave's heart out to get a letter where little Davey had been to a doctor for a new treatment, and Dave couldn't be there to hold the boy in his lap, to kiss the tears off his cheek, to tell him about his best friend, Jesus. Dave told Jerry the Lord had laid it on his heart to do everything he could to keep other men from making the same mistakes he'd made and having to endure this punishment of being locked away from his family.

Now Dave spoke up. "And we shouldn't none of us be complaining about a little hot weather. The Lord is giving us an opportunity here to tell these kids about Jesus. If we have to sweat a little in the process, then the Lord will put some more sweat in us to take its place."

"Oh, quit preaching and find a power outlet," Jerry told him as he pitched him the end of an extension cord.

"I've already found my power outlet." Dave pointed up at the sky.

"We may all get a little extra shot of power from the looks of those clouds piling up in the west," Sam said.

"We'll just pray the rain holds off till after our program," Chaplain Foster said. "Remind me to mention that when we do our prayer before we start the drama."

As the young people filed in to fill the rows of wooden chairs under the big shelter, thunder began playing an accompaniment for them in the distance and lightning ran jagged streaks along the horizon.

Heat gathered with them under the flat roof of the shelter and sweat was pouring off them even before they ran through one verse of "The Old Rugged Cross" for a sound check. Moths and hard shell bugs were banging into the floodlights on the corners of the shelter.

Dave leaned over to Jerry before they started, "You might choke on one of those high notes you keep trying to hit if one of those brown bugs flies in your mouth."

"Won't be no problem," Jerry said. "I'll just crunch down on him and keep on singing. I've eaten worse."

"Yeah, every day in the cafeteria back at the prison. Your mama coming to see you again any time soon? That was some fine food she brought us the last time she came down."

"Keep a lid on it, guys," Chaplain Foster said. "How do you expect the kids out there to settle down and start listening if you're blabbing up here instead of concentrating on getting the message across to them?"

"Sorry," Jerry said.

The chaplain gathered them for a quick prayer before they started. "Here we are, Lord. Use us. Lend us your power and open hearts to receive your word. Hold off the storm and help us sing and act out the message you want these people to hear as we've never sung and acted before. In your precious holy name we pray. Amen."

Jerry didn't know whether it was the storm sweeping closer or the dozens of fresh young faces looking up at them expectantly waiting for some revelation from God, but the air fairly crackled with electricity. The wind and lightning licked at them from the edges of the campground, but it was as if some unseen force was holding the storm back until they could finish their program. The shelter was a safe harbor in the midst of the storm all around them.

The men had to push their voices to the limit to be heard over the thunder, but nobody missed a note. None of the men in the drama flubbed their lines. They forgot about the sweat rolling down their faces and their shirts sticking to their backs. They forgot about the lightning flashing around them. They forgot about the bugs dive-bombing their heads. They forgot everything but the message the Lord was channeling through them out to these young people.

And the young people were the same. They didn't giggle or hold hands with their girlfriends and boyfriends. Every eye was fastened on the players of the drama. Every ear was straining to hear the message. Every heart was searching for God.

Even before they started singing, "Take up thy cross and follow me," Jerry knew something special was happening. They'd hardly gotten five words into the song before kids started leaping out of their seats. Practically every person in the crowd came forward to make decisions for Christ, and the men stopped singing and got down on their knees to pray with the young people.

Tears mixed with the sweat as they knelt in groups. Jerry put his hands on the young boy's shoulders next to him and someone else put his hands on Jerry's shoulders and all at once Jerry felt the spirit slam into him. The door to his heart was knocked wide open, and he felt Jesus inside, but not just in his heart. He felt Jesus in every inch of his soul and being. He knew now what everybody had been telling him was true. He did know. This was what the Lord wanted from him. Not just lip service and prayers thrown out into the dark of the night. Not just his songs, but his heart and soul, his whole being.

Jerry surrendered it all to the Lord with joy. He finally knew what it meant to accept Jesus as his Savior, his Lord, and his God. And he finally believed the Lord loved him in spite of the bad things he'd done and not just with his head because people told him it was true, but with his heart because he knew it was true. He finally believed the Lord could forgive those bad things and use him in spite of what he'd done in the past. He finally knew that the rest of his life he would be a witness to the love and forgiveness of the Lord.

The words Jerry prayed weren't as important as the sure feeling inside him that the Lord was shaping those words, revealing his purpose for Jerry's life. "Dear Lord, I'm yours. Use me to demonstrate thy love and mercy." Jerry prayed. "Help me grow in the spirit as I dedicate my life to thee forever and ever. Amen."

A rush of raindrops spattered down on the shelter's roof and then the storm turned and eased off into the distance leaving behind a cooling wind to sweep through the crowd of kids still on their knees. Chaplain Foster was moving from group to group blessing the young people and encouraging them to go back to their home churches and share their decisions with their pastors.

When at last every prayer had been prayed over every young person there and Jerry rose up off his knees, he was a different person. He'd come into the shelter as a man unsure of his path or what was in his heart, but now he knew. The Lord was there in his heart. Jerry had placed his hand into the Lord's hand. He was ready to go wherever the Lord led him.

Chaplain Foster put his hand on Jerry's shoulder. He'd been crying and his voice was hoarse as he said, "I've never seen a night like this."

"Me either," Jerry said.

Chaplain Foster gave Jerry a closer look as if Jerry's very voice sounded as different as he felt. Then the chaplain smiled and gripped his shoulder harder. "Didn't I tell you you'd know?"

"Praise be the Lord." Jerry more sang than spoke.

"I couldn't sing a lick if I had to. See if you can lead us in a couple of verses of 'Amazing Grace' to close out the night."

Jerry started out and the voices in the shelter began joining in, and just as the words of the song said, there couldn't have been a sweeter sound. It was such a beautiful sound that Jerry was sure angels had come down to sing along with them.

CHAPTER 36

Back at the prison, Jerry looked the same in the mirror when he shaved in the mornings before going to read a scripture passage over the intercom to get the prison day started, but he wasn't the same. Everything was different. As he read the scripture and prayed, it was as if each word had been written for him. He wanted to not only hear it, but to understand what it meant. Before he'd read the Bible dutifully for comfort, for curiosity, as a way to pass the time, but now it wasn't just words any more. It was a message to him, and he wanted to know what that message was. So he enrolled in a Bible study correspondence course.

Now when he went out with the quartet to sing and give his testimony to churches on Sundays, it wasn't just a performance. It wasn't just a way to escape the reality of prison for a few hours. Now when he talked about what the Lord had done for him, how the Lord had protected him and watched out for him even when he was straying—no, more than straying—running down the wrong paths away from God, his words had conviction because now he personally knew the Savior he was talking about. And he wanted everybody else to know him, too.

While he was talking and singing, Jerry would watch the people in the congregations. Sometimes he saw himself in the fresh young faces of the teenage boys in the pews. He recognized the desire for God warring against the temptations they were facing out in the world away from their families and churches. From the way some of them turned their eyes away from him when he talked about how alcohol and drugs had stolen his youth, he figured they had already started down the wrong paths. After all, he'd sat in a lot of church pews on Sunday mornings after he'd drunk himself unconscious on Friday or Saturday nights.

Jerry wanted to go down the aisles and grab hold of the young people and make them look at him, make them really see the prison stripes he was wearing and what could happen to a man if he let alcohol and drugs take him over. Jerry wanted to be the angel in their crossroads who stopped them from going down the wrong roads the way he had.

But he couldn't go yank them out of their seats and demand they listen. He could only point the way. He could only tell them what had happened to him. He could only tell them what Jesus had done for him and what Jesus could do for them. Some of them listened and came forward with tears in their eyes and a new life in their hearts. Others stayed stuck to their pews, but sought out Jerry or one of the other quartet members after the service.

Sometimes a boy would look at Jerry and say, "Man, I might do a little partying now and then, but I could never do what you've done. I could never kill somebody."

"I pray you're right," Jerry would tell him. "That's what I would have said when I was your age. I didn't care about my own life, but I would have never dreamed that I might take another man's life. But when you start down the road with the devil, things can happen that you can't even imagine happening."

The boy would shake his head. "I wouldn't never have no truck with the devil."

Jerry would look straight in his eyes and ask him, "Who do you think is putting that beer in your hands or slipping you that pill and telling you how good you'll feel if you'll just swallow it? Who do think is laughing the next morning when you wake up sick as a dog or when you get in trouble at school?"

Sometimes the young people would listen. Sometimes they wouldn't. As Chaplain Foster told the men as they drove back to the prison, all they could do was tell their story and leave it up to the Lord to use their witness however he saw best. The Bible said to sow the seed, broadcast it far and wide, and pray that it would find good ground to take root and grow.

Chaplain Foster was tireless in seeking new places for them to take their stories and the drama. Somehow he got them in Bell Auditorium in Atlanta in front of fifteen hundred people to put on the drama. Jerry had never sung in front of so many free world people, and when they gave the invitation, more than a hundred people came forward. It was the same everywhere they went. People were making decisions for Christ. Sometimes Jerry felt as if the Lord had turned a spotlight on over his head and that people could look at him and see what a difference the Lord could make in one man's life, and that the Lord was using that to make them see the need to move away from the darkness of sin into the light of life.

In August his folks hired somebody to do the milking so they could come down together to attend one of the church services where the quartet was singing. It was the best visit Jerry could ever remember having with his mother and father. He was in prison, but his parents were proud of him. His mother even told him out loud in person that she loved him. She'd written it in her letters, but he couldn't remember her ever saying those three words to his face before. Even more amazing, he was able to say "I love you" right back without the words tripping over his tongue and getting stuck on his lips.

They were a family. Maybe not the usual Mom and Pop family since Joletta was still lurking in the background even if he hadn't heard from her or seen her since she and her husband had moved to California months ago, but more of a family than they'd ever been. He told his parents that in the letter he wrote them after they went back home.

Words cannot express the feeling I had being with you Sunday. This move here has got us all on cloud nine. And Sunday night, it's still hard to believe the change. It would never have been like that at Reidsville. I know Sunday night we were brought closer together as one family. I love you both very much and thank God that I've got two wonderful parents like you!

Who would have ever thought that he'd have to go to prison to feel as if he belonged with his parents? That strange lost feeling he'd had as a kid had vanished. He knew who he was now. He knew his parents loved him. Best of all, he knew Jesus loved him.

The quartet went to South Carolina to sing at Chaplain Foster's home church and then Warden Talbout's church. They recorded a television program. Jerry was completing his Bible study lessons and getting A pluses. He had even written his mother to send him some math books, so he could tackle that roadblock in his mind.

He could do math. With the help of Jesus, he could do anything. He checked into taking some college correspondence courses, and he even won a silver medal in ping-pong at the prison Olympics. He might never get out of prison, but at least he was growing and serving the Lord and keeping his mind and body strong and positive.

Then things changed at the prison. Warden Talbout had a heart attack. They quit letting Jerry have counseling sessions with Miss Atwood. She sent him a message that all was well and for him not to worry, but two weeks later she was gone, her position eliminated at the prison. Chaplain Foster said the prison was losing funds for the social programs. Warden Talbout had another more serious heart attack, and Mr. Marley, the assistant warden, took over. Mr. Marley decided they had too many chaplain assistants. Since Jerry could type, Mr. Marley moved him to the newspaper office.

Jerry didn't mind the newspaper work, and he was still allowed to work in the chaplain's office after six in the evenings and on weekends. They were still busy spreading the word. Mr. Marley hadn't stopped the quartet from going out to sing, and the church choir was as strong as ever in spite of some of Jerry's best singers being released. New singers came in to take their places. They were working on a new drama to present the Christmas story in scenes while someone narrated the Bible story.

Jerry did his best to hang onto a positive mental outlook. As Chaplain Foster told him, sometimes a person just had to bloom wherever he was planted even if that meant he had to squeeze out between the rocks of all the restrictions of prison to reach up toward the sun.

Dave's son died a few days before Christmas. A guard accompanied Dave home for the funeral. He came back on Christmas Eve, and so Jerry spent his fourth Christmas in prison comforting his friend. They sat in the chapel and read Bible verses to one another and cried.

"Why didn't the Lord take me instead of Davey?" Dave asked. "He was just five years old. He had his whole life ahead of him, and he was such a good little boy. Marlene said he was smiling at her right to the end and telling her about the angels he was going to play with up in heaven. And me, what was I doing while my boy was dying? I was stuck here, not doing anybody any good."

"That's not true," Jerry tried to counter. "You've been a blessing to me and you've brought people to Christ with your singing."

Dave put his arms on his legs and dropped his head forward. Tears dripped off his face and made wet splotches on the wooden floor. After a minute he said, "But I wanted to be home. I wanted to be my son's father at home, not my son's father who had to have a prison guard with him even to attend my little boy's funeral. Why did we ever let the devil get such a hold on us that we ended up here, Jerry?"

"I don't know, Dave. But I guess that's why the Lord wants us to keep telling our story so that we can keep others away from places like this."

Dave looked over at him with anguish on his face. "But do you think we do? Do you think anybody listens? Did you listen when you were a kid?"

"Not to my folks. Not to the preacher," Jerry admitted. "But I might have listened to somebody like me. I might have. And, you know, if even one kid listens, don't you think we've done something worthwhile?"

"Right now I can't think about other kids. Only Davey," Dave said.

"That's okay. The Lord understands. He's sitting here right beside us crying with us."

"Do you think so?"

"I know so," Jerry said.

"Read Psalm 23 to me again, Jerry."

"The Lord is my shepherd; I shall not want." Jerry kept reading out of his Bible and somehow they got through the long Christmas Day.

Three days later, one of the guards called Jerry out of the newspaper office. "Pack your bags, Shepherd. You're being transferred out of here."

CHAPTER 37

The move took Jerry totally by surprise, but when he heard Millard Cleveland was an assistant warden at the institution he was being transferred to, he was happy enough to go. At Reidsville, Mr. Cleveland had taken a personal interest in Jerry, and now he was dipping him out of the pool at Richmond just as the water there began to stagnate with the acting warden cutting out some of the chapel programs.

"It's the Lord's doing, Jerry," Chaplain Foster told him. "The good Lord's been right beside you all the way and now he's moving you to a place where there will surely be even more opportunities for you to shine like a beacon to lead others to him."

"Don't forget me, buddy," Dave said as he hugged Jerry and fought back tears.

"Never, brother," Jerry told him. "You can't forget somebody when you're praying for them every day."

"Do you think I could hide in your duffel bag and you could carry me on down there with you?" Dave said.

"I'd carry you with me if I could, but the guards don't allow no passengers."

"I know. It's not like we can pick and choose which five star hotel they put us up in," Dave said.

"That's true enough. And somebody has to keep up the good work here with Chaplain Foster. I'll pray for the Lord to send you a tenor."

"Now are you saying you're going to pray some nut who sings like a girl will do something he ought not to do so the State of Georgia will lock him up in here with us so we can keep our quartet going? You think that's something you ought to pray?" Dave smiled.

"Not when you put it that way. How about I pray that one of those nut cases already locked up will see the light and start singing like a girl for the Lord, and that's the one the good Lord will transfer down here to help you guys sound halfway decent?"

Jerry hated leaving Dave, but at the same time, he was excited about the move. Chaplain Foster said if a man had to be behind bars, then the new state of the art facility in Montgomery County, Georgia was the place to be. The staff had been hand picked and maybe the inmate population as well to make sure the prison was successful in its mission of not simply punishing the inmates but giving men who'd made mistakes a second chance to succeed. Besides, as Dave had said, it wasn't as if Jerry had a choice of where he was locked up. He was still a prisoner. He had to go where the authorities told him to go.

The Montgomery County Correctional Institution still had a new, just built smell when Jerry was brought past the front gates into a huge rotunda. The place looked more like a convention center for convicts than a prison. Jerry's and the guard's footsteps echoed in the huge open area as they passed by entrances to the cafeteria, a barbershop, and the chapel on the way to the dorm where Jerry would be sleeping. Light exploded down from the windows at the top of the rotunda. Jerry glanced over his shoulder, but he didn't catch any shadows in the corridors. Were there no shadows here like at Reidsville or now that he was walking more fully in the light of the Lord, did he just not see shadows the same way anymore?

The dorm reminded him of Reidsville with the same double bunks and storage cabinet size lockers, but that's where the comparison ended. This place sparkled it was so clean. Even better, it was air-conditioned. Sweat soaked, mosquito swatting summer nights would be a thing of the past.

Jerry was assigned as a server in the officers' dining area. He carried the food to the tables and kept the coffee flowing. The first day he was there, he met the chaplain, Ben Kelley, who was always wagging his coffee cup up in the air for a refill. Chaplain Kelley had a full head of silver hair, but his eyes were young and alive. He told Jerry people in his family just turned gray way before their time but he preferred turning gray to his hair turning loose.

Jerry laughed as he filled the chaplain's coffee cup. "That's the problem men in my family have. Their hair turns loose. I have an uncle who was bald by the time he was twenty-five." Jerry finished pouring the coffee and put his hand on top of his head as if he could make the roots of his hair hold tight.

Chaplain Kelley looked directly into Jerry's eyes and smiled. "Well, you look like you've still got plenty up there for the time being. And they always sell fuzzy rugs you can smack on top of your head if your hair does fall out."

"They sell dye, too," Jerry said.

"Yeah, but I like gray. Makes me look wiser than I am." He kept looking directly at Jerry. Some of the other prison officials Jerry served looked over the top of Jerry or right through him as if he wasn't even there, but Chaplain Kelley looked straight at Jerry as if he wanted to know the real Jerry and not just see him as another inmate whose job it was to pour coffee. "Mr. Cleveland tells me you're a great singer. We want you in the choir on Sunday."

"Sure thing." As Jerry hustled on to the next table to refill more coffee cups and clear plates off the tables, he just had a feeling about Chaplain Kelley. He was going to be one of those angels the Lord kept dropping into Jerry's path. Jerry certainly didn't plan to ever take the wrong fork at a crossroads again, but everybody needed guidance from time to time to make sure they were stepping out on the right roads. With both Mr. Cleveland and Chaplain Kelley pointing the way, Jerry surely wouldn't take a wrong turn.

He hardly noticed his twenty-third birthday passing on January 3, 1973. It was his fourth prison birthday and his first birthday as a truly committed Christian. He remembered standing before Judge Rutherford when he was sentenced and hearing the years count off in his head before he'd be eligible for parole. At the time, he couldn't even imagine that many years passing, and now he was more than halfway through. He still didn't like to think about being incarcerated three or more years longer, but he knew whatever happened, he could survive it now. No, not just survive, he could flourish and bloom. The Lord was going to use him wherever he was—inside prison or out in the world.

And he was ready to be used. Here at this new institution designed as a showcase of prisoner rehabilitation in Georgia, Jerry felt like a blank notebook just waiting for his pages to be filled up with work for the Lord.

Mr. Cleveland began filling his pages before the week was out. He started organizing a Guides for Better Living class for Jerry to teach in the evenings. He pointed Jerry toward the AA Group in this prison, and at the first meeting, the group elected Jerry secretary the same as he'd been at Reidsville. Mr. Cleveland took him and a couple of the other inmates out to tell their stories at high schools, junior highs, and colleges in a program called Operation Get Smart. They took turns at the podiums telling the students about the mistakes they'd each made and what it was like to live in institutions and prisons and how with the wrong steps the students could end up in trouble themselves.

Some of the kids listened. A lot of them didn't, but Jerry didn't get discouraged. If even one kid heard what they said and moved down the right road in life instead of taking the wrong turn, then they'd done something good.

But Mr. Cleveland didn't just get Jerry busy in the prison activities. He tried to set up a meeting with Judge Rutherford for Jerry in hopes the judge might recommend an early release date to the Parole Board. The judge didn't agree to a meeting, but he did ask Jerry to write him a letter detailing everything Jerry had done in prison.

Jerry spent hours on the letter, filling page after page with not only what he'd done in prison but also what he'd learned about himself. He didn't want to leave out anything that might make the right impression on the judge.

It was at Reidsville in Chaplain Chatham's therapy group that I started finding myself. One of my problems was self-acceptance. I would have no satisfaction in life until I gave up the shams and pretenses and was willing to be myself. This was when I found out I had another problem. I was using alcohol to drown all my mistakes, failures, and fears of being humiliated. So I started to solve this problem by joining the AA Group in the institution.

When Jerry read over what he'd written, he could hardly believe that once he'd thought so little of his life that he'd tried to throw it away so many times. It had taken prison for Jerry to look in a mirror and decide he was a person with worth, someone the Lord could love and use. That's what he wanted the judge to see in his letter. He kept writing about what he'd done, being secretary for the AA group at Reidsville, teaching the Guides for Better Living classes, singing in the choir and band, putting on the dramas at Richmond. He wrote about how he'd sung and given his testimony at churches all over and how much he appreciated the opportunity to witness to young people through the Operation Get Smart program there at Montgomery. The more he wrote, the more he saw the hand of the Lord in his life. All of these things couldn't have just fallen into place without divine intervention.

He chewed on the end of his pencil and thought a while before he wrote the final paragraphs in the letter.

To me, the four years I've spent in prison have not been wasted. In fact, they have been the best years of my life. My parents and I are closer together than we have ever been. I have also become closer to God and able to understand His way for my life. I now have a better outlook on facing everyday life, and more encouraging ways of facing problems. To rid my mind of cobwebs, think clearly, and explore my subconscious for new ideas. To set my sights on a goal and attain it, through persistent thinking and positive action. All this could not have been possible if I had not at first wanted to help myself, and then gotten help from people like yourself who are concerned and wanted to lend their helping hand. And most important was the help of God, because I put all my faith and trust in Him to help me climb up the steps these past four years.

My "self" right now is what has always been, and all that it can ever be. I did not create it. I cannot change it. I can, however, realize it, and make the most of *it. I know now there is no use straining to be <u>somebody</u>. I am somebody, not because I've made a million dollars or can sing high notes, but because God created me in his own image.*

Whenever I am able to leave prison, I will be a better, wiser, stronger man and not a mixed up nineteen-year-old kid. I hope from this letter, you have gotten to know me as I am now and not what I was. I know now that I have the ability to "take it" no matter how rough the going may be. Why? Because I believe and I have faith. I will always be striving to do my best.

Respectfully Yours, Gerald Warren Shepherd

He reread the letter a dozen times and let Mr. Cleveland check it over as well. He wrote his parents and told them the letter was nineteen pages of the truth, the whole truth and nothing but the truth.

Two weeks after he mailed his letter, Judge Rutherford sent him a copy of the letter he'd sent to the State Board of Paroles and Pardons. The judge said he did not usually make recommendations, but that he felt Jerry had been rehabilitated and was ready to face life. He recommended that Jerry be released on parole as soon as the rules permitted.

Jerry wanted to frame the letter. It was that good. He wanted to frame it and hang it on a wall somewhere, preferably at his house in Kentucky. Even Mr. Cleveland said he'd never seen a letter from a judge quite like it and that Jerry couldn't have asked for a better letter. Jerry could almost hear the prison doors unlocking. He could almost feel his feet walking in the fields back home on the farm. The Parole Board would have to take notice of such a good letter from a judge.

They didn't, or maybe they did. Maybe the rules didn't permit them to consider Jerry for early release. That's what Mr. Cleveland told him after a couple of weeks. What they'd really needed the judge to do was give Jerry a time cut on his sentence. Then the Parole Board could have taken action. But he hadn't done that. He'd written a great letter, an encouraging letter, but nothing was going to change. Jerry was still going to have to serve out his time until he could go before the Parole Board in 1976. Three more years.

Jerry was disappointed, but he didn't dwell on it. He was too busy. He had AA meetings to attend and AA letters to write. He had Guides classes to teach. He had songs to practice for the choir. He had speeches to give for Operation Get Smart. He had his Bible study courses to do and college classes to enroll in. He had coffee cups to fill.

CHAPTER 38

The person Jerry most liked pouring coffee for was Chaplain Kelley. They kept a running conversation going and never had any problem picking right up where they'd left off whenever Jerry had a few minutes break in his serving duties.

"I heard about that drama you and some of the other inmates put on over at Richmond. You think you could do that here?" Chaplain Kelley asked him one day.

"I don't see why not," Jerry said. "You'd have to recruit the men to act the parts and for the quartet."

"I don't think we would necessarily need a quartet. You can do the singing," Chaplain Kelley said. "And you could probably pick the actors. You know more about what kind of men the drama needs than I do."

"Can I pick anybody? I mean if they fit the part. They wouldn't have to be Christians already?" The idea was intriguing.

"You got somebody in mind?" Chaplain Kelley asked.

"A couple." Just two days ago, Jerry had been talking to a new inmate in the dorm and thought how much his life had mirrored one of the parts in the drama. Then there was Big Jake, a big, tall white inmate with vivid blue eyes that seemed to almost pierce through your skin when he talked to you. One of his hands made two of Jerry's and was perfect for pounding on a pulpit to get a congregation's attention. Best of all, Big Jake knew about church. His grandfather had been an old time fire and brimstone preacher, and Big Jake had spent every Sunday of his growing up years hearing the gospel shouted out. Big Jake said it never did take with him, and he guessed that was why he'd ended up in the slammer.

Chaplain Kelley said, "If you can get them to agree to do it, I'll get it cleared with the warden for them to come to practice. How soon do you think we can get the show on the road? I'll need to line up some churches."

That was the way it was with Chaplain Kelley. He expected things to get done. He didn't make excuses for himself, and he didn't let the people around him make excuses. A man was responsible for what he'd done and responsible for what he could do, and Chaplain Kelley thought Jerry could do a lot.

"The Lord's loaded you down with talents you can use for him," Chaplain Kelley had told Jerry in one of their early on conversations. "You wore blinders for a while and tried to run your own race without paying attention to the course the Lord was urging you to run. You kept trying to knock him out of the way, but that's the great thing about our Lord, he doesn't give up on us. He knows our hearts and he just keeps right on running there beside us nudging us back toward the right track and sometimes he just picks us up and carries us through the roughest times."

"That's what he must have done for me at Reidsville. That's the only way I could have stayed alive in there."

"And your rough times might not be over," Chaplain Kelley said. "Can't any of us know the future. All we can know is that Jesus is the same yesterday, today, and forever. And he promises to be with us through whatever happens. That's how Stephen could ask forgiveness for the men who were stoning him. That's how the old first century preacher Polycarp could help gather the wood to lay around the stake where they burned him to death. That's how your friend, Dave, back at Richmond can bear the loss of his little boy. With the help of Jesus. And that's how you can do whatever you're called to do now that you've quit trying to run away from that calling."

Jerry settled into the routine at Montgomery. Up every other day at three a.m. to serve in the dining room. In the chapel or teaching Guides or doing AA correspondence on the other days and at night when Mr. Cleveland wasn't taking him out to present his testimony. It was better running the course the Lord laid out for him. Sometimes he felt as if his feet were just barely skimming the ground.

In the middle of February, his feet could have been slipping out from under him. A weird cold front came dipping down from the north deep into Georgia to dump several inches of snow on the prison. A lot of the inmates and prison workers had never seen a snowflake much less a blanket of the white stuff on the ground covering up the harshness of the prison fences and concrete barriers. Out in the exercise yard, the inmates acted like kids as they built snowmen, pummeled one another with snowballs, and stuck out their tongues to catch snowflakes. Jerry thought of Sam back in Richmond who had never seen snow, and he hoped he was lying on the ground making an extra large snow angel and getting lots of snow down his collar.

When the snow stuck around through the night and into the next day, the state of Georgia practically shut down. The guards on night duty were afraid to drive home, and the guards on day duty called in afraid to drive to work.

A short sturdy guard named Marvin came and got Jerry out of the dining room. "Hey, Shepherd, you're from up north, aren't you?"

"If you call Kentucky north," Jerry said.

"It snows in Kentucky. It's north," Marvin said. "Look, I know this is going to sound crazy and all, but Warden Powers says you and a couple of other inmates from up north have to go out and bring the day guards in."

Jerry stopped sorting silverware and looked straight at Marvin to see if he was joking. "You're saying you're sending us out to get our own guards?"

"Yeah, that's a rip, ain't it? You do know how to drive in the snow, don't you?"

"Well, yeah. If I can remember how to drive at all," Jerry said. "It's been a while."

"It's like riding a bike. You don't forget how. Here's the keys, a map, and directions. You're to go get the guards listed up on top there first and then Warden Powers. You'll have to make several trips."

Jerry took off his serving apron and reached for the keys. He'd forgotten the good feel of a set of keys in his hand. Marvin must have noticed his smile, because he said, "Now don't you go forgetting the way back. We'd catch you and you'd have to start all over getting to where you are now."

"I'm not that dumb," Jerry told him.

But it was a thought. A thought that lay there and tickled his brain all the time he was driving around hunting for the right streets. Gripping the wheel and hearing the tires against the road felt almost too good. He wanted to mash down on the gas and see if he could do donuts on the slick roads. He wanted to go crazy and drive to Atlanta or Florida. It might be years before he got to drive anything again, but even while all those reckless thoughts flashed through his mind, his foot was steady on the gas pedal as he kept the wheels turning slow and easy in the snow.

The roads were practically empty except for all the cars abandoned in the snowy ditches. The highway didn't seem all that slick to Jerry, but then Southerners were always too ready to slam on their brakes at the first slip. Jerry's heart gave a little lurch when a police car with lights flashing came up behind him, but the policeman just waved as he went on by as if Jerry was a fellow officer.

It took Jerry a while, driving slow and trying to read the map and the road signs, but he finally pulled up in front of the first house where he was supposed to pick up a guard. He tooted the horn.

Petey came to the door and did a double take when he saw Jerry behind the wheel. He backed away out of sight and then peeked back outside as if to be sure he wasn't seeing things. Jerry tooted the horn again, and Petey leaned out the door to yell, "Hold onto your horses. I gotta get my coat."

A few minutes later he was climbing in the car. "Man, I can't believe this. I thought I was gonna get the day off, but no, they send a convict out to pick me up before they'd let that happen."

"What can I say?" Jerry grinned at him. "We missed you back at the Georgia State Hotel."

It was easier finding the other guards' houses with Petey directing him down the right streets instead of having to read the map. Jerry had never been all that good at reading maps. When he'd been on the run, he hadn't worried about maps. He'd just found a road and taken it till it ran out and then found another one. But then all the roads had run out, and he'd ended up behind bars.

Now he had to use maps. He had to stay on the right road no matter how enticing the open road looked out there beyond the intersection to the interstate. Warden Powers trusted him. Chaplain Kelley depended on him to keep his coffee cup full and make him laugh with some crazy story about Jerry's days back on the farm. Chaplain Kelley had even been talking about getting Jerry assigned as his assistant. The chaplain had never had an assistant before, but he thought now would be a good time to start since his desk was piled high with unanswered correspondence and overdue paperwork. Just the week before he'd asked if Jerry could type and take shorthand, and then had said one out of two wasn't bad. He'd said he could always talk slow when he was dictating a letter, that he'd need time to think about what he wanted to say anyhow and just how fast could Jerry scribble?

As it turned out, fast enough. In April, Jerry was assigned to the chaplain's office. Now he and Chaplain Kelley spent all day working together and the more they talked, the closer they got until Jerry felt as if he'd found a second father. He didn't know why he'd been so blessed. His own father was a strong man confident in his belief in the Lord and his purpose in life to serve and be faithful. His eyes gleamed with the joy of living.

Br. Ben was the same way. He was always ready to share that joy with anybody he was around. He not only truly believed that with the help of the Lord any man could succeed in life, he had a way of making the inmates he counseled believe it as well. They could stay off the drugs. They could go back out into the world and be good citizens. They could hold down jobs and support families. They could be forgiven for the bad things they'd done. They could feel the love of God. They could believe anything was possible.

Between Br. Ben and Mr. Cleveland, Jerry was on the road a lot with his testimony. He didn't try to come up with anything fancy. He just stood up in front of the churches or the schools and told them the truth of what had happened to him, where he'd gone wrong and how the Lord had helped him put his life back together. In nearly every church, young people came forward to surrender their lives to the Lord.

Sometimes Jerry didn't plan what he was going to say at all. He just stood behind the podiums and opened himself up to be that beacon Chaplain Foster back at Richmond had encouraged him to be. He simply wanted everything he said or sang to say, "Here I am. Look at me. See what the Lord has done for me."

Summer came and he finally rounded up enough actors for the drama, *The Challenge of the Cross*. Some of the men just agreed to take part to get out of their work duties for practice and to have the opportunity to be outside the prison walls for a few hours while they were presenting the drama.

When Jerry went up to them, they'd be like Big Jake. "Now I don't have to believe all this stuff, do I?" Big Jake had said when Jerry asked him about being the evangelist in the drama. "I mean when I was a kid, my folks shoved enough religion down my throat to choke a horse, and it never did me the first bit of good."

"Nope," Jerry told him. "I'm picking you because you look right for the part. I'll leave the rest of whatever the Lord wants from you up to him. I just want you to play the part."

"I reckon I can do that. I've seen plenty of pulpit pounders in my day, but none of them ever said a thing I thought made sense," Big Jake said.

"What about Chaplain Kelley?" Jerry asked.

"He's a good man, and he can spout off a fine line of Bible verses, but then so can I. And it's yet to make me any better."

"You come on out to practice next Sunday afternoon. I've got a feeling that you're going to make the best evangelist this drama's ever had, Big Jake." Jerry didn't try to convert the men he picked for the drama. He just waited and let the drama do that. After all, he knew himself the power of the words and songs. He knew what had happened to him on that stormy night at the youth camp.

The first night out, Big Jake ended up in tears as he finished his part of the drama. He looked around at Jerry while Jerry was singing "Take Up Thy Cross and Follow Me" at the end of the service and nodded a little before he raised his hands and shouted "Praise the Lord." The people in the church thought it was part of the drama, but Jerry knew the Lord had written a new ending to their drama that night. Or maybe a new beginning for Big Jake. Two of the other actors also ended up on their knees with new commitment in their hearts.

By the middle of August they had taken the drama out to six churches and one hundred and sixty-seven people had come forward to make decisions. As Br. Ben told Jerry, "Sometimes the best thing a man can do is just get out of the Lord's way and let him work."

CHAPTER 39

It was amazing the churches the Lord opened up to them. One Sunday night Jerry looked out into the congregation and saw Judge Rutherford's eyes fastened on him. At the end of the service as Jerry was singing the invitation, he got his mother's holy goose bumps when the judge came forward to accept the challenge of the cross. It was almost more than Jerry could believe that he was part of something that could move and inspire the judge who had sentenced him to prison. Br. Ben was right. The Lord could use anybody as long as that person was willing to lay his life down at the Lord's feet.

A few weeks later, Jerry was in the chaplain's office pounding out letters on Br. Ben's old typewriter when four state troopers burst through the doors of the office followed by a blond man about Jerry's size and a slim, dark haired woman. Jerry's fingers sprang out and hit a few wrong keys before he stood up to meet the onslaught of policemen. He didn't know who the couple with them was, but they had to be important to need so many escorts.

Both the man and woman were showing a lot of teeth in big smiles as the man moved past the state troopers toward Jerry's desk with his hand out. "Hello, I'm Governor Jimmy Carter, and this is my wife, Rosalynn."

Jerry's knees turned to gelatin, but somehow he managed to stay upright and keep an answering smile on his face. This was the man who had the power to pardon Jerry. Jerry's mother had already appealed to the governor at least once for an early release and been turned down. Now the governor of the State of Georgia was standing right in front of Jerry, smiling and talking to him.

"We're making the rounds of all the state's correctional institutions, and we've been told this one is a model first class institution. So we came out to see for ourselves," the governor said in a soft southern drawl. "Sit down with us and tell us what you know about the way things are going here. We didn't come here for some practiced speeches. We came here to hear it straight, and you look like the man who can tell us. Don't you agree, Rosalynn?"

"I do, Jimmy." She smiled at Jerry as he hustled to pull a chair forward for her. "But first, please tell us your name."

"Jerry, I mean Gerald Shepherd."

The governor sat down in a chair beside his wife. He ignored the state troopers taking up posts around him and said, "Well, Gerald, tell us about the institution here. How is it helping the men who are here?"

So Jerry went through the programs and activities available to the inmates at Montgomery and how so many of the men were going back out into the world and being successful and not returning through the revolving doors of the prison system.

"That sounds great, Gerald. That's what we want to do with our institutions here in Georgia. Rehabilitate men and see them become good citizens of our state once they've paid their debt to society," Governor Carter said. "But tell me, what are you doing? I mean you personally, Gerald. You mentioned this Operation Get Smart program. Do you go out and tell your story at schools? And what about churches? It seems you might have the kind of testimony church people need to hear."

Jerry didn't feel so nervous now. The words were flowing out the same as they did when he went into a church or school to give his testimony. It wasn't Jerry. It was the Lord working through him. "Yes, sir. A couple of other inmates and myself go to whatever schools Mr. Cleveland or Warden Powers lines up to present our witness to the students, and we're also ready to go out and give testimonies at any church interested. Lately we've been having a lot of success with a drama we put on called *The Challenge of the Cross*. I took part in this drama when I was at the Richmond County Correctional Institution and Chaplain Kelley has helped me get it started here at Montgomery."

Both the governor and his wife were completely focused on what he was saying. Governor Carter nodded when he mentioned the drama and said, "I've heard something about that. This *Challenge of the Cross*. It must be powerful."

"Literally every time I've been part of putting on the drama, people have come forward to make decisions for the Lord," Jerry said. "And the drama doesn't just change the lives of those out in the audiences listening. It changed my life. I always tried to serve the Lord in church activities and things, but I was doing it on my own strength because that was what everybody always told me I should do, but then one night after we'd put on the drama at a youth camp, I opened up my heart and let the Lord take over. After that night, everything about me changed."

"For the better, I'm sure," Governor Carter said.

"Yes, sir." Jerry said. "The drama just has a way of reaching out to a person wherever they are and showing them where they should be and how they can get there. I've been a front row witness to the changes it's made in the lives of most of the men who've taken part in the drama and that's been quite a few men, because you see, a lot of the men I pick for the parts are short-timers, not in for very long. They do a few performances and then they get released from prison. So I'm always having to recruit new men for the parts."

"And how do you do that?" Mrs. Carter asked, leaning forward a bit as if she didn't want to miss a word Jerry said.

"First I pray about it, and then I watch the men when they come in. When I see a man who seems to have the same life story as one of the characters in the drama, then I ask him to take part. That way it's not so much acting a part as doing a part they've already lived. So far, it's worked really well. Once the men get involved in the drama they just seem to turn into sponges absorbing everything spiritual. They start wanting to learn more and more about the Christian life, and you can almost see them growing stronger in the faith with every performance."

"I'd like to see it," Mrs. Carter said, leaning back in her chair.

So that's how they got invited to the church Governor Carter attended in Atlanta, Georgia. When Chaplain Kelley pulled up in front of the big church and stopped, the men inside the vehicle stared out at the impressive building rising up in the air in front of them. After a couple of minutes, Big Jake said, "I've never known you to lead us wrong, Chaplain Kelley, but are you real sure we're at the right church?"

Br. Ben peered out the window at the sign in front of the church. "Northside Drive Baptist Church of Atlanta, Georgia. This is it."

"The same place the governor goes to church? They're wanting us in there?" Big Jake said.

"You did tell them that some of us are a shade on the dark side? I'm not sure those doors will open up to let me walk through," Jerome, one of the black actors, spoke up from the front seat beside the chaplain. "I doubt there's ever been a man with my particular skin tones inside there unless it was for cleaning the johns on Monday morning."

"There's a first time for everything," Jerry said. He pulled up on his door handle and pushed the car door open. "They asked us and here we are, ready or not."

"Who are you talking about being ready or not?" Big Jake asked. "Them or us?"

"Them, of course," Jerry said as he got out. "We're always ready, right, guys?"

"Right. If you say so," the men echoed weakly as they climbed out and followed Jerry and Chaplain Kelley up the steps and into the church.

But once they set up their props and began presenting the drama, as always the Lord took over and they forgot the vaulted ceiling of the church and the rows of pews filled with well-dressed Atlantians spilling away from them. They forgot about the governor and his wife sitting in the fifth row with policemen on all sides of them. They just let the Lord's words roll through them, and at the end of the service, people began stepping out into the aisles to come forward and make decisions for the Lord the same as at every other church where they'd presented the drama. Even the governor and his wife came to the front to recommit their lives.

The service couldn't have gone any better. Jerry had a great group of actors who might not have been committed to the Lord when they began performing the drama but who now thirsted after spiritual things and wanted to be the same kind of beacon to others that Jerry wanted to be.

As Br. Ben was always telling them, the Lord didn't need perfect men. He needed willing men.

That's what Jerry told his mother when she came to visit. He was still so excited about how successful the drama had been not only in the governor's church but also in all the churches that he couldn't quit talking about it. His mother was happy to listen.

"I've always known the Lord was going to use you in a powerful way, Jerry," she said, her eyes glistening with pride. "And this is just a beginning, a warming up for what the Lord has in store for you once we get you out of here."

"I'm ready," Jerry said.

His mother had her own news. She and his dad had just bought a farm in Mercer County. "I know you've been looking forward to coming back to the farm there in Shelby County," she said, looking a bit worried for a moment, but then the worry was pushed aside by her excitement. "But this farm will be even better. It's bigger. We can have more cows and just wait till you see how the rich green fields roll away from your eyes. It's not too flat like in Indiana or too hilly like Eastern Kentucky. It's perfect."

"You sound practically poetic, Mom. I mean I know you like farming, but what's so much better about this farm than whatever was for sale in Shelby County?"

His mother dropped her eyes to the table and a little blush bloomed in her cheeks. She smiled almost shyly as she looked up and said, "You'll probably laugh at me, but when I was younger than you, just out of high school and going to business school in Lexington, we always drove past that farm there in McAfee every week when my father took me to school. I practically held my breath from the time we crossed into Mercer County until I saw the first fence post around it. I told my father that someday I'd marry a man who'd buy me that farm."

"And you did." Jerry tried to picture his mother so young and already so sure of what she wanted. He'd seen that kind of determination in her eyes often enough and had fought against a lot of the things she'd determined he should be, but now they'd gotten past those stormy childhood and adolescent years. Now they could look at one another and feel love and acceptance. They could enjoy being together.

"I did. I was so young then. It was just a dream, but I've never seen another piece of land I'd rather live on. It'll be a beautiful place for you to come home to and make a new start as soon as we get the Parole Board to hear your case."

"We may have to wait a few years for that," Jerry said. "At least 1976."

"No. That's too long," his mother said. The same determination filled her eyes that had claimed that piece of land in Mercer County long before she actually had any way of owning it. She glanced at her watch and with a sigh, stood up and began gathering up the leftover food that Jerry hadn't been able to stuff into his mouth. "You can give the rest of this food to that nice guard I was talking to before you came. I think he said his name was Perry or Larry maybe. Anyway, he said he especially likes my brownies."

"You spoil them, Mom."

"It's nothing. Just a few brownies," she said. "I'd bake a million brownies if that would guarantee your safety in here."

"It's not like Reidsville here, Mom. I'm okay."

She stopped and laid her hand on his cheek. "You're better than okay. You're wonderful, Jerry, and I'm so proud of you. Always remember that. No matter what happens."

"I know, Mom. I couldn't have better parents than you and Dad."

"Well, that's true of your father, but there are plenty of things I could have done better."

"That's all in the past, Mom."

The moment she had to leave after their visiting time was up was always hard for both of them. They wanted to cling to the moment as if they could stretch it out and make it last since they both knew it would be at least a couple of months before they'd see one another again. "You will write, won't you, Jerry?"

"You know I will or you can call Br. Ben's office. He doesn't mind if you call me to see how things are going. You know my hours there."

She hugged him and kissed his cheek. "Take care of yourself and keep depending on the Lord, Jerry."

"I will, Mom." He walked with her to the door that led back out into the free world, a door he couldn't follow her through.

She stopped before she went through the door and turned back to hug him one more time. Then she put both hands on his cheeks and looked straight into his eyes. "Jerry, if it took my life to get you out of prison, it would be worth it."

CHAPTER 40

On September 13th, Jerry got up and prayed his morning prayer the same as every other morning. "Good morning, Lord! Thank you for this new day you've given me. Grant me the courage and strength to do whatever it is you have on the agenda for me on this day. I'm ready, Lord, to serve you. Whatever you give me to do, I'm ready to grab it by the horns and get it done. With your help, Lord. You know, Lord, I can do nothing without your hand to guide and help me. Thank you for the blessings of yesterday and for the blessings you will be sending my way today."

Jerry was busy. He was happy. He had confidence in his ability to handle whatever came his way. He liked feeling useful. He liked feeling as if the Lord was watching over him and guiding him. He liked going top speed to fit everything in. The Lord was opening the doors for him. The Lord would help him run fast enough to go through all of them.

He was in the dining area wolfing down his evening meal so he could go back to the dorm and catch up on his Bible study homework, when a guard came over to tell him to report to the chapel.

"Why?" Jerry asked. "Chaplain Kelley's already gone home. He left a couple of hours ago."

"Then I guess he came back because he's there now, and he sent for you," the guard said.

Even then Jerry didn't think about anything being wrong. Not really wrong. A little finger of worry poked at him, but he pushed it away. Br. Ben probably just had some news about a church that wanted their drama. The chaplain didn't come in at night often, but he had done it a few times when he needed to catch up on some work.

As soon as he went in the chaplain's office and saw Br. Ben's face, the finger of worry turned into a fist that grabbed hold of his heart and squeezed. "What's wrong?" Jerry asked.

"Sit down, Jerry," Br. Ben said gently.

"I don't want to sit down. Tell me what's wrong." Jerry could barely keep from shouting the words. "Just tell me."

But the chaplain came over, put his arm around Jerry's shoulders, and guided him to a chair. "It's bad news, Jerry." Br. Ben had tears in his eyes.

Jerry let the chaplain push him down in the chair. He couldn't say anything else. He just had to wait.

Br. Ben sat in a chair right in front of Jerry and kept his hands on Jerry's shoulders. "It's your mother. Hazel."

"Mom? What about her?"

"I'm sorry, son, but she's dead."

"Dead? What do you mean dead? She can't be dead." He couldn't let the words settle in his brain. He must have heard wrong. His mother couldn't be dead. "She was fine when she was here last month."

"There was an accident. On the farm."

Jerry wanted to shove the chaplain away from him. He wanted to run away somewhere where he wouldn't have to listen to any more, to some place where his mother would still be breathing, still be waiting for him to get out of prison and come home. But he made himself sit still as his mouth formed the words, "What happened?"

"She was mowing a field with a rotary mower. She was by herself so nobody really knows what happened, but she must have fallen off the tractor for some reason." Br. Ben hesitated, then went on. "Your father said she went under the mower."

For a second everything around Jerry was frozen. He didn't breath. The tear on Br. Ben's eyelash hung suspended and didn't fall on the man's cheek. The clock on the wall stopped ticking. Jerry's hands, still smudged with black where he'd changed the typewriter's ribbon earlier, lay motionless in his lap. His mother had probably already been dead then.

Jerry groaned as if somebody had just knocked him to the ground and stomped on his chest.

"Take a couple of deep breaths," Br. Ben was saying.

Jerry did as he was told. Didn't he always try to do as he was told? And now this was how he was repaid. How could the Lord let something like that happen? He didn't think he asked the question out loud but maybe Br. Ben knew him well enough to read his thoughts.

"Accidents just happen," the chaplain said.

"But the Bible says the Lord has all power. He could stop them."

"He could."

"Then why did he let this happen?" Jerry wanted to hit something. Anything.

"That's something we can't know. At least not till we join your mother in heaven, and then we'll know all the answers."

"I don't want to know all the answers. I just want this not to have happened."

"I know, son. So do I," Br. Ben said. "So do I." His fingers tightened on Jerry's shoulder as if trying to transfer some of his own strength to Jerry. They sat like that for a long time until the phone on the desk began ringing. Br. Ben looked at it and said, "That will be your father. I told him to give me a little time to break the news to you."

Br. Ben picked up the phone. "Chaplain Kelley here. Yes, he's right here." He handed the receiver to Jerry.

"Jerry." His father's voice was trembling. "Are you okay, son?"

"I don't know," Jerry said. "How about you?"

"Things are bad. I don't think I can stand it. I know I have to, but I don't think I can. She meant everything to me." His dad started crying.

No answering tears came to Jerry's eyes. He waited until his father pulled himself together before he asked, "What happened?" Br. Ben had already told him, but he had to hear it again. In more detail.

"I don't know. She was down in that lower pasture. It's flat, no dips or holes, and not the least bit rough, and she was on the Massey Ferguson. The 135. She's driven it thousands of times. You know how she liked mowing the pastures. She liked the fields to look neat before winter. I mean we were getting ready to move, but she said that was more reason than ever to mow the field and leave the farm looking good."

Jerry didn't say anything. He just waited till his father went on. "So you know the field I'm talking about. The Robinsons live in front of that field and Mrs. Robinson went out on her porch and thought something sounded funny about the tractor. She went out in the back yard to look and said she couldn't see anybody on the tractor. That it was just sitting there running and not moving, so she called me. I'm glad she didn't go over to check on Hazel herself. It wasn't something a woman should see."

"So Mom was dead when you got down there?" Jerry's words sounded flat and strange as if somebody else was talking through his mouth.

"Oh, son, you don't understand. She went under the bushhog. She was cut all to pieces. It was like I was back in the war, only worse. This was my wife." He started crying again.

"Is somebody there with you, Dad?"

"Milton's here and the preacher and a bunch of others. I don't know who all. Everything's in a daze right now. But it's you I need here, son."

"I know, Dad. I'd be there if I could."

After he hung up, he could still hear his father's sobs. He'd never heard his father cry like that. His father was tough. He'd been through the war. He'd seen things he said nobody should ever have to see, and now he'd seen this.

Jerry's eyes stayed dry as he looked at Br. Ben and tried to comprehend what the man was saying. He saw concern in his friend's eyes. He saw the man's mouth moving, but Jerry's ears couldn't take in the words. He was down in the lower pasture hearing the bushhog tearing through the weeds. Tearing through his mother.

Finally some of the chaplain's words made it through to Jerry. "Is there anything I can do for you, Jerry? I mean I'm praying for you and your father right now and I'm going to keep praying for you."

"That's good," Jerry said. "I'm sure Dad needs prayer."

"As do we all. Especially at times like this," Br. Ben said.

Jerry looked at the chaplain. "I think I just need to be alone for a while."

Br. Ben gave Jerry a long, considering look before he finally stood up. "All right, son. But if you change your mind and need somebody to talk to, you call me no matter what time of the night it might be."

"Okay, but I don't really want to talk right now. Or go back to the dorm."

"I understand. I'll tell the guards to let you stay in here tonight since you won't be doing any sleeping anyhow."

"I want to go in the chapel," Jerry said.

"All right. You and the Lord can talk it over in there," Chaplain Kelley said.

After the chaplain left, Jerry went into the chapel, shut the door, and locked himself in. He wanted to be alone. He didn't want anybody sitting beside him trying to fill up the silence with words that didn't mean anything. He walked down the aisle to the front. His eyes were still dry. He was too angry to cry.

The Lord shouldn't have let this happen. It wasn't right. He and his mother had just begun to connect, to be able to understand one another. He sat down on the front pew and stared at the wall behind the pulpit while the anger went from a hard knot inside him to a raging storm that engulfed him.

He looked up at the ceiling and started yelling. "Why did you let this happen? Mom and I were finally coming together. We loved each other." He jumped to his feet and curled his hands into fists, but there was no one there to punch. "We loved each other."

For a minute he felt near tears, but then the anger washed over him again like a tidal wave. "How could you take her from me? It's just not right. It's not fair." He thought of Dave's little boy, Davey. That hadn't been fair either. Or right. Or loving. One of the first Bible verses Jerry learned as a little boy in Sunday school popped into his head. *God is love.*

"How can you claim to be a loving God when you take something this precious away from me? After all Mom and I have gone through, what we've been through together, this should not have happened. No way. I was going to get out. We were going to start over. We were going to be okay."

Jerry stopped and let the words echo around him. And then there was silence. Intensely empty silence. God wasn't speaking to him in the silence. God didn't care about Jerry. God didn't care about his mother. Jerry banged his right hand down on the top of the pew. Pain shot up his arm. That was good. He wanted it to hurt.

And still the anger grew. God could stop the anger it he wanted to. God could do anything. Jerry had always been told that. He believed that. That was why he was so angry. God could have stopped what happened to his mother. God could have made it different.

Jerry walked up and down between the rows of pews, first muttering under his breath and then shouting. He hardly knew what he was saying as the anger kept spewing out of him like water spurting out of a broken pipe. It didn't matter what he said. God wasn't listening. God didn't care. God had severed the pipeline between them when he let Jerry's mother fall off that tractor. Jerry didn't want to have anything more to do with a god who would let that happen. Jerry stopped in front of a picture of Jesus knocking on a door.

"You can just go knock on somebody else's door. I quit!"

Somewhere in the deep of the night when he had no voice left to shout, when his hands were too tired to make fists, when he had no energy left to push it away, his mother's memory tiptoed back into his thoughts. He felt her work worn hands on his cheeks the last time she came to visit him. He saw the love in her eyes, and her words echoed in his head. *Jerry, if it took my life to get you out of prison, it would be worth it.*

"It should have been me, Lord," Jerry whispered. "If somebody had to die, it should have been me."

CHAPTER 41

He didn't want to go to the funeral. He wanted to remember his mother alive, not lying cold and still in a casket with all her lifeblood drained away. If he stayed there at the prison, he could still imagine her in the kitchen stirring up some brownies. He could see her on her knees weeding her flower bed and chasing him away since he couldn't tell a flower shoot from a weed when it first poked its head through the dirt. He could hear her banging out her favorite hymns on their old piano. He could see her at the kitchen table with her checkbook and the bills spread out around her. He could see her standing at the back door staring out the window toward the road where someday she was going to see her son coming home. If he went to her funeral, she'd just be dead.

But Br. Ben told him he didn't have a choice. "You have to go to your mother's funeral. Your father needs you there. You need to be there."

"I don't have to go anywhere," Jerry said. "I'm in prison. I can't go anywhere."

"You can go. Prisoners attend family funerals all the time."

"It's out of state. They won't pay a guard to go with me all the way back to Kentucky. I'd have to fly."

"I know. I've already booked you a ticket," Br. Ben said. "Just one ticket. The warden is giving you special permission to go on your own."

"Without a guard? They're going to let me out of here without a guard?"

"You don't need a guard." Br. Ben's eyes burned into Jerry's. "We trust you to honor the terms of your leave and be back on the day after your mother's funeral."

Jerry didn't feel trustworthy. He didn't feel anything. He'd come out of the chapel at daylight and gone back to his duties, but he felt as if his very soul had been sucked out of him and absorbed into the darkness of the night. His heart had shriveled down to the size of an acorn and he didn't care.

He didn't care about anything. He didn't care that his father was crying. He didn't care that Br. Ben couldn't stop frowning when he looked at him. He didn't care that he couldn't sing. He didn't care that he couldn't pray. He didn't care about anything. The Lord had deserted him, and Jerry had no plans to go looking for him. He was just going to breath in and out, push food into his mouth and chew, and do what he had to do. Br. Ben said the first thing he had to do was go to his mother's funeral.

The chaplain drove Jerry to the Atlanta airport and stayed with him until he had his ticket and had found the right gate to catch his flight. "I'll be back to pick you up on the sixteenth. Your flight leaves out of Louisville early early. Make sure you don't miss it."

"I won't," Jerry said automatically.

"I know you won't," Br. Ben said, his voice softening. "I wish I could go with you. To be there for you and your father. Your mother was a wonderful woman and she loved you very much."

"I know," Jerry said.

"Your uncle will be at the airport in Louisville to pick you up." Br. Ben peered at Jerry's face. "You will be all right, won't you, son?"

"I'll be all right," Jerry said.

Br. Ben looked as if he wanted to say more, but instead he mashed his lips together, put his hand on Jerry's shoulder for a brief moment and then turned and left Jerry alone in the airport.

Jerry sat there in a plastic covered chair and waited for them to call his flight. Other flights were called. To Dallas. To New York. To Philadelphia. He rubbed his fingers up and down the edge of his ticket and thought about going back to the counter and exchanging it for one that went somewhere else. Anywhere else.

He was alone. No one was guarding him. He could do it. He could just climb on some other airplane and disappear. Forever. He wouldn't have to go back to prison. He was smarter now than when he'd been caught when he was nineteen. He could figure out a way to stay free. He didn't mind working hard. He could get a job picking oranges or harvesting lettuce out in California or maybe sign on with a shrimp boat trawling the oceans around Florida. He liked Florida.

The announcement for the flight to Louisville came over the speakers. He stood up and moved toward the gate to go into the airplane as if his shoes had lead soles. He had just handed over his ticket to the perky lady at the entrance to the airplane when he heard the speakers. "Flight 223 to Miami now boarding at Gate 10."

He stood still and wondered how he could get to that other gate, but the woman was already holding his ticket. The man behind him was pushing forward impatiently, bumping Jerry with his carry-on bag. The pretty woman was still smiling as she said, "You are in seat 14A. There will be someone inside the plane to assist you if you need help."

Jerry walked through the tunnel to the door of plane. He found his seat and sat down. He'd missed his chance. His Uncle Milton would be watching for him at the other end of his flight. So he'd go to the funeral, and after it was over, he could decide what to do then. There would be another ticket back, another chance in Atlanta to get on another airplane and go wherever it flew.

The casket was open. Everybody who came in to view his mother's body seemed surprised by that. They'd heard the stories about how the mower had cut her body up and thrown pieces of it all over the field. They'd heard the stories about how the men had found his father cradling his mother's torso and how they'd had to pry his arms away from her. They told Jerry the stories, but he didn't ask his father if they were true.

He just looked at his mother's face in the casket and wanted her to open her eyes and sit up to tell him what had happened. How had she fallen off? Did she hit a groundhog hole that nobody could find now? Had she had a leg cramp? Had she passed out for some unknown reason? But she didn't open her eyes. She just lay there looking too still and quiet while the bruises kept darkening and showing up under the makeup the undertaker had caked on her face.

She didn't look like his mother. He sat back in one of the folding chairs and studied her profile in the casket while he tried to figure out why. It was his mother. Everybody else kept saying the undertaker had done a wonderful job. That she looked so natural.

It took Jerry a while, but he finally figured it out. It was her mouth. The determination that had always made his mother look ready to bite nails when she was trying to move heaven and earth to get things done the way she thought they should be done was gone. That didn't just make Jerry sad. It scared him, because deep inside where he hardly ever even dared look, he had believed she'd be able to make the authorities listen to her and get Jerry released from prison. It didn't matter that she hadn't been able to do it in four years. He'd always known that sooner or later she would find a way to bring him home.

And in one way, he supposed she had. He was home with no guard at his elbow, but he'd have to go back or never have a chance of coming home again. *Flight 223 to Miami is now loading.* The blare of the announcement he'd heard at the airport kept sneaking back into his head. But he couldn't think about that now. Not with his Aunt Violet telling him how good it was to see him and how bad it was that it had to be under such unhappy circumstances.

He had to be introduced to some of his cousins. He hadn't seen them for almost five years. Everybody had changed, maybe Jerry himself most of all, but of course everybody knew him. He felt every eye in the place fasten on him like rubber suction cupped arrows each time he entered the chapel where his mother was laid out. There would be a momentary hush and then a rush of whispers. He could imagine the words.

There's the son. You know the one who's serving time in Georgia. Poor Hazel. She never gave up on him, and he wasn't even really her child. He was Dewey's son by his first wife. You knew Dewey was married before, didn't you? Joletta was her name. I hear she was something else. More than old Dewey could handle anyway.

He didn't hear any of that, just imagined it. And the fact was everybody treated him great. They acted genuinely glad to see him, didn't look down their noses at him, or act as if they were afraid they might catch something if they shook his hand. They just stood with him and cried for him since he still hadn't been able to shed the first tear himself. They smiled and hugged him and didn't ask when he was going to get out of prison. They acted as if they thought he already had or maybe that he'd never been to prison, but had just been away working somewhere.

A lot of his buddies from both Shelby County High and Oldham County High came by to show their respects. It touched Jerry that so many people cared enough about his mother to stop whatever they were doing, put on their good clothes and stand in line to shake Jerry's hand and tell him and his father how sorry they were.

At the first kind word from anybody, Jerry's father broke down. He kept telling Jerry and everybody else how safe the Massey Ferguson tractor was and how he'd have never let Hazel go mow that pasture if he'd thought there was the least bit of danger of anything happening to her. He wanted to move the clock back and start all over. Jerry had to almost pull his father away from the casket after his final goodbye so the undertaker could close the casket and the pallbearers could carry his mother's body out to the hearse for the ride to the cemetery.

As Jerry walked out with his dad to the car waiting to carry them to the grave-yard behind the hearse, Jerry turned off his brain. He felt the sunshine heating up his black suit jacket. He felt the sweat forming in his hair as they gathered around the open grave and heard the preacher say "dust to dust" and talk about Hazel's new body in heaven. Back at the house, he opened his mouth and ate the food somebody piled on his plate. The day passed. He lay down on his old bed and slept. It felt too soft after all the prison bunks.

Uncle Milton and Aunt Adele spent the night at the house. Uncle Milton woke Jerry hours before dawn the next morning to make sure he didn't miss his plane. Aunt Adele fixed them breakfast. Jerry sat at the table and dutifully ate her sausage and pancakes even though he wasn't the least bit hungry. It was still dark when they left for the airport. Some men from the church had been doing the milking, so his father climbed in the back seat and rode along with them to the airport. His father and his uncle both felt honor bound to get Jerry back to Georgia. They had no way of knowing how *Flight 223 to Miami* kept playing through Jerry's head.

Or maybe they did. They waited with him till his flight was called, and they stood and watched him get on the airplane. Jerry imagined them rushing to a window to be sure he didn't step back out the plane's door, climb out on the wing, and slide to the ground before the plane got off the ground.

Jerry settled in the seat next to the window and looked out. The sky was just beginning to lighten in the east as the plane lifted off the ground, shot up into the sky, and then leveled off for the flight to Atlanta. The seat next to Jerry was empty, but the man in the seat across the aisle put his head back and began snoring. Jerry hardly noticed as he kept staring out the window at the clouds turning pink as the morning shook off the shackles of the night.

Far below in the gray dawn, trees were bushy toothpicks and farm ponds puddles. Specks of bobbing light wound along roads that looked like bits of string somebody had dropped willy-nilly. A few puffy clouds floated under the plane, and Jerry thought he surely must be closer to heaven than he'd ever been. All at once the rim of the sun broke up over the horizon and touched everything with a dazzling, golden light.

Plenty of times back on the farm, Jerry had stopped in his tracks on the way to the barn or to catch the school bus and admired the sky as the sun came up, but he'd never seen a sunrise like this. It was as if the Lord had just been waiting to get his attention, and now that he had it, he'd escorted Jerry to heaven's front porch, pushed him down in a chair, and told him to watch this. The sun seemed to almost leap over the horizon, shooting out rays that bounced off the airplane and through the window to touch Jerry.

The sunlight didn't just touch him on the outside. It reached in and warmed his heart. The Lord was wrapping his arms around Jerry, holding him, loving him. Tears slipped out of Jerry's eyes. "Forgive me, Lord," he whispered. "Forgive me for the way I acted in the chapel. Forgive me for blaming you for what happened to Mom. I know it's not your fault." Jerry paused a moment before he went on. "I'm ready to accept that Mom's gone now and to bear it with your help."

Jerry didn't shut his eyes while he prayed. He wanted to see every second of this sunrise. He wanted to feel every bit of love the Lord was sending him. Jerry knew now the Lord had never deserted him. The Lord had always been there, lifting him up, carrying him along, helping him through.

Again Jerry began whispering a prayer. "Forgive me for all the times I've failed you and for not trusting you to be right there beside me the whole way. Thank you for staying with me, for not giving up on me even when I was acting like an idiot. I know I don't deserve it, but please give me another chance. I want to be your faithful servant and continue serving you in every way I can. Just help me get through this one day at a time and help me find a way to help my dad. Let me lean on thy strength and thy power."

The sun was fully up now and practically pulsing with radiant light. Jerry put both his hands flat against the window. "Here am I. Use me. I'm ready."

CHAPTER 42

He got lost in the Atlanta airport. Jerry couldn't remember exactly where Br. Ben had said he and his wife would be waiting for him. *Flight 223 to Miami* wasn't playing through Jerry's head anymore. The sunrise had taken care of that. He felt renewed, burned clean of all doubts, and ready to do whatever he needed to do to stay the course with the Lord.

The first thing he had to do was not let Br. Ben down. The chaplain believed in Jerry and trusted him enough to get him the freedom to attend his mother's funeral. If Jerry didn't show up in a timely manner, Br. Ben might think Jerry had betrayed that trust. He might even call security. So Jerry had to find him and soon, but the Atlanta airport was huge. Maybe there was more than one main entrance or maybe he just hadn't found the main entrance yet or maybe that wasn't where he was supposed to meet the chaplain.

He was walking fast without the first idea of whether it was in the right direction or not when he heard his own name playing on the intercom instead of flight 223 to Miami. "Will the party of Ben and Jacqueline Kelley, Jerry Shepherd, proceed to Gate 5." Jerry had just passed gate eight so gate five had to be close. He picked up his pace.

Br. Ben and his wife were standing at the edge of the waiting area seats peering anxiously at the passing people. Br. Ben was standing a little up on his toes, a worried frown pushing any hint of a smile off his face. He looked as if he needed a whole pot of coffee. Mrs. Kelley caught sight of Jerry first and grabbed Br. Ben's arm to point Jerry out. Relief bloomed in both their faces.

"I'm back," Jerry said when he got close enough. "Sorry, I'm late. I got a little lost."

"Praise the Lord. I didn't know whether you were lost or we were," Br. Ben said. "But either way, you're a sight for sore eyes."

Back at the prison, some of the inmates looked surprised to see Jerry that night in the dorm. "Man, we never thought we'd see you again. We tried to get up some bets about whether you'd be back, but we couldn't find any takers," Jason, the inmate who bunked next to Jerry, told him.

"Which way?" Jerry asked him.

"Which way do you think! Nobody believed you'd come back. I mean you were out there free as a bird. If you'd had any sense, you'd have flown away."

"Don't think I didn't think about it, Jas, but I just didn't know what you old boys down here would do without me to sing you a goodnight lullaby every night."

"You're crazy, man." William chimed in from across the room.

"But you love me anyway, don't you, Willie?"

"Like I said, you're crazy," William said.

"Crazy for the Lord," Jerry said.

"Oh no," somebody groaned. "He's gonna start preaching."

The very next night, Jerry did go out to a church to give his testimony. He knew his mother would have wanted him to keep going. She would have told him to use what had happened to her as a way to reach even more people. She would have told him to make her death mean something. And getting up in front of the church and talking about his mother and how she'd never given up on him seemed to somehow honor her memory. At the end of the service, he sang "Just a Closer Walk with Thee" more for his mother than anybody in the church. It had always been one of her favorite songs plus this night it seemed to be an added testimony for both of them—for her because she was in heaven starting an eternal closer walk with the Lord and for him because he was praying for a closer walk here.

And so things settled back into a routine. He typed Chaplain Kelley's letters. He kept up with the AA correspondence. He went out to schools with Mr. Cleveland to do Operation Get Smart. He began a new set of college courses. Everything was the same and yet at the same time, totally different. Just knowing his mother wasn't there praying for him made it different, but Br. Ben said Hazel probably hadn't quit praying for him, that no doubt she was up there in heaven standing on the Lord's doorstep demanding he take some action to help Jerry.

After that, every time that nasty sad feeling started welling up inside Jerry, he'd think about what the chaplain had said and imagine his mom buttonholing everybody she met on heaven's streets of gold to enlist them in her campaign to get Jerry out of prison, and he had to smile.

Down here this side of eternity, Jerry tried to keep her campaign going by writing to Judge Rutherford to tell him why he wouldn't be getting any more letters from Jerry's mother. It just seemed to be the thing to do. She'd kept the judge up to date on Jerry's progress in prison as though Judge Rutherford was more a concerned uncle than the man who had sentenced Jerry to life in prison. And Judge Rutherford had always responded as if he did sincerely care what happened to Jerry. When Jerry had gone to the judge's church when he was part of the drama, *The Challenge of the Cross,* at Richmond, Judge Rutherford had told Jerry how much he admired his parents and especially his mother, Hazel.

Jerry even called Joletta to tell her. He wasn't sure why. He just thought she should know. She had moved back to Tennessee from California and had been promising to come for a visit.

Still, in spite of all the condolence cards he was getting from churches all over and having to tell people about his mother's death, prison life, in some ways, insulated Jerry from the grief of losing his mother. He knew she was gone, but at the same time he didn't have to go into the empty kitchen at the farm. He didn't have to go to church and see the empty pew three rows back on the left where his mother sat every Sunday. He didn't have to see her old black purse still sitting on the table by the door so she could just grab it up whenever she needed to run to town.

His father did. He seemed to be totally adrift without Jerry's mother, and Jerry didn't know how to help him. When his father called the chaplain's office, Jerry listened and tried to say something comforting. He prayed for his father every day and talked to Br. Ben about what he could do to help. But what his father needed most, he couldn't do. He couldn't be there to put his arms around him and support him through these hard days. He couldn't be there to help him pack up and get ready for the move to the new farm in McAfee, Jerry's mother's dream farm. He couldn't help him decide what to keep and what to give away. He couldn't be there to help him do the milking morning and night. He couldn't be there to help his father find a way to keep living without his wife and help-mate.

And then his father found his own way. In November, his father called Br. Ben with news he feared might upset Jerry. Not bad news. Actually good news, Jerry's dad told the chaplain, but he wasn't sure Jerry would understand that.

Jerry didn't. Br. Ben tried to break the news as kindly as he could, but there was no way to make it sound right to Jerry. His father had met another woman. They'd been dating. His father said he and Margaret had already talked about getting married.

"Getting married?" Jerry could hardly believe his ears.

"Now listen, Jerry." Br. Ben started talking fast. "I know it may seem a bit soon and it is a bit soon, but everybody handles things like this in different ways. You know yourself what a mess your father has been the last few weeks. He just can't make it on his own. He says he didn't plan on meeting somebody this soon, but he says since he did that he doesn't see any reason he has to keep suffering alone. He says Margaret understands about how he felt about your mother since Margaret lost her husband in sort of the same way as he lost his wife. Her husband was killed in a car crash a few years ago, and of course, she loved her first husband very much. That doesn't mean she doesn't have any love left for now."

"I think the operative words here are a few years ago. It hasn't been three months since we buried Mom."

"I know." Br. Ben fell silent as if he'd run out of words.

Jerry massaged his forehead with his fingers. After a minute, he looked up at the chaplain and asked, "Do you think Mom's death has affected Dad's mind?" That was all Jerry could think of that might explain how his father was acting. "Do you think he needs to be committed or something?"

"Now, son, let's slow down and think this thing through," Br. Ben said. "Your daddy's only fifty. That's not all that old, even though it may sound ancient to you. And you know yourself, your father has been totally lost without your mother. While it may not have seemed like very long to you since she died, it has probably seemed like an eternity to him back there getting up alone every morning, not having anybody to talk to."

"But it's a matter of respect."

"He knows how he respected your mother through their years together. He was a good husband, but his wife died. He grieved for her. You surely know how much from the calls he made down here hoping to get some kind of comfort. But now he's moved to a new farm, a new house, and he's left the old farm and his old life with your mother behind. I think he feels like he's turned the page. He's ready to start a new life."

"I just can't accept it. Not yet," Jerry said.

Br. Ben sat back in his chair and took a long drink of coffee. He slowly sat the cup down before he said, "You'll have to call him. I told him you would after we talked."

"I can't call him and talk about him being with another woman when Mom's not even cold in the grave."

"Yes, you can," Br. Ben said. "And you can try to understand, and if you can't understand, then you can still listen to what he has to say with the respectful attitude of a son to a man who has been a good father to him."

So Jerry called his father and listened to him talk about this Margaret. She was pretty. She was kind. She was lonely the same as he was. She was just what he needed to get on with his life. "You'll see when you meet her, son. She's a fine woman. Kind. Gentle."

"I'm not saying she isn't, Dad, but don't you think you should wait a while? Mom just died in September."

"I know. I never intended to go out and meet someone as nice as Margaret so soon, but I was going crazy at home by myself every day and every night. You just can't understand."

"But you can't be thinking about marrying somebody already. I mean it's bad enough you're dating, but you're even talking about getting married already."

"Well, not till the first of the year."

"But Mom's not even cold in the grave." He'd told himself he wasn't going to say that, but it just kept coming back at him how short a time it had been since his mother had died. His father shouldn't have even wanted to go on a date yet, much less think about getting married again.

"Well, I knew this might upset you, son, but a man's got to do what a man's got to do," his father said.

Jerry wanted to reach through the telephone wire and grab his father and shake him. He wanted to make him see how crazy this was, but instead he took a deep breath as the silence hummed between them. Finally he said, "Well, Dad, I don't think it's right, but I can't do anything about it. I'm down here locked up. You can do whatever you want to do. You're going to anyway."

"Yes, but I want you to try to understand. Just tell me you'll try. Maybe not today or tomorrow but in a couple of weeks when you get used to the idea."

Again Jerry let the silence hum between them for a minute before he said, "Okay, Dad. I'll try."

"Good. That's all I'm asking."

"Maybe we can talk it out some more when you come down to visit."

"That's another thing. I'm not going to be able to come for a while. I want to. You know I want to, but I haven't found anybody up here in McAfee that will do the milking for me. You know how me and your mother always took turn about. But we'll still get to talk. I'll call every week just like before."

"Okay, Dad."

"Things are going all right for you down there, aren't they? Chaplain Kelley says you're still giving your testimony real regular. That would have made your mother proud."

"I know."

"And I got a letter from Judge Rutherford. A real nice letter. He said he hoped he could help us. I think he's going to write another letter to the Parole Board."

"They didn't pay much attention to the last letter he wrote," Jerry said.

"You don't know that," his dad said. "Somehow I think your mother's death is going to make them take a new look. You know the Lord can make good come from the worst things that happen."

"I didn't want Mom to have to die to get me out of prison."

"Nobody says you did, son, but if she'd thought that would have turned the trick, she'd have given up her life gladly and willingly."

"I know. She told me that the last time I saw her."

"And she meant it. She used to tell me the same thing. So you just remember that the way I feel about Margaret doesn't have any reflection on the years I spent with your mother. But life goes on. We have to go on, too."

Jerry hung up the phone on Br. Ben's desk. His legs were weak and his chest hurt as if he'd just trudged a few miles through heavy mud. He leaned against the chaplain's desk. He was alone. The chaplain had left the room to give Jerry privacy while he was talking to his father. He'd said they could talk about it all again the next day after Jerry had gotten used to the idea.

Jerry looked down and saw the small cross fashioned out of three nails that Br. Ben sometimes held while he was counseling inmates. Jerry picked it up. There was love in those nails. His Lord had let them nail him to a cross. He'd given his life willingly to save Jerry from his sins. With love.

The metal of the nails warmed in Jerry's fingers. He'd never fully understood the love shown by the cross, but now he was getting a glimpse of the kind of love it had taken for Jesus to let them drive nails through his hands and feet. Jerry's mother had had that same kind of love for him.

CHAPTER 43

Christmas was never a good time in prison. No matter how much tinsel the prison officials let them string down the hall or how many trees were lit up in the rotunda area, it wasn't Christmas with their families. This Christmas was particularly hard for Jerry. He still got care packages, but each one just seemed to emphasize the care package he wasn't getting from his mother.

Even worse he couldn't talk to his father about how he missed his mother. All his father wanted to talk about was Margaret. Jerry couldn't even get him to talk about the new farm or how much milk the cows were giving. It was all Margaret, Margaret, Margaret. He was spending Christmas day with Margaret and her daughter and three grandchildren. He had a new instant family. And he was deliriously happy. Delirious at any rate.

Jerry couldn't shake the feeling that it was all too soon after his mother's death, but at the same time, he didn't really begrudge his father this new family. Back in high school, Jerry used to tell his friends how someday he wanted an instant family. Maybe it was because of the sister and brother his parents had given a home for a while and considered adopting when Jerry was a kid, but for whatever reason Jerry had a tender spot in his heart for children who needed a father. So he'd always thought about marrying somebody who already had children, and now his father was planning to do that very thing.

His father and Margaret set a date in January to get married, but then put the wedding off as rumors began to pop up that Jerry was going to be given an early hearing by the Parole Board. And then it was more than rumors. Mr. Cleveland said the Parole Board had agreed to a special hearing in April regarding Jerry's early release. Jerry was almost afraid to believe it. He wasn't due for parole consideration until April 1976, still two years away.

He tried not to let it affect his life as he went about his usual routine in the prison. If it happened, it happened. If it didn't, he had survived five years. He could survive two more. But his father was sure enough of it happening to put off getting married so that maybe Jerry could be at the wedding.

As the date for the hearing drew closer, Jerry began to think about what it would be like to step back out into the free world and not just for a visit the way he did now when he went out for Operation Get Smart or to sing at one of the churches. He'd be part of the free world. He'd be responsible for his own life.

He wanted that more than anything in the world, but at the same time, he was terrified at the idea. What if he couldn't handle it? What if he made the same mistakes all over again? While it was true he wasn't the same mixed up kid who had come into the prison system, who knew what might happen to him when he was released? Would he get crazy and mixed up again when he went back out into the free world?

Being in prison was like being in a separate world. He read the newspapers and heard the news on the radio and television, but it really didn't mean that much to him and the other men inside. They had their own world. Somebody told them when to get up in the morning. Somebody told them what to do all day. Somebody dished food out on their plates. Somebody told them lights out at night.

The inmates knew that other world was out there, but they weren't part of it. They didn't exist in that world. They had their own private world contained inside the confines of the prison.

Br. Ben kept telling Jerry he could make it. "This is what we've been pushing for, Jerry. You need to be out of here, home with your family, and building a new life with the solid foundation of your faith in the Lord. You can do it, because the Lord will help you do it."

"But it's been five years. I was eighteen when I came in. I'm not even the same person I was then."

"Praise the Lord. You don't want to be that person any more just as I don't want to be the person I was five years ago. I mean my knees might not pop and groan so much if I was, but even though this old body gets a little more worn out with each passing year, at the same time I'm closer to being the man the Lord wants me to be. We live and we learn and we begin to see that the Lord's way is not just the best way. It's the only way. We aren't perfect. We never get to perfect this side of heaven, but we strive toward perfection in Christ Jesus for that's the only way to live for Him. And when we fail—and we all fail—we ask for forgiveness."

"I know I'm forgiven, Br. Ben. I've prayed for forgiveness, and I've felt that forgiveness."

"And once you've genuinely prayed that prayer, the Lord not only forgives, he forgets. *As far as the east is from the west, so far has he removed our transgressions from us.*"

"But will the people out there forget?"

"Maybe not, Jerry. That's something you have to live with, part of the cost of what you did. But you said your family accepted you, loved you when you went back for your mother's funeral. They'll accept you and support you when you go out of here. You've paid your debt to society. You've looked deep inside yourself and wrested out the bad, and now you've set your feet on the right path. As long as you stay on that path with the Lord, you will be all right. Even better than all right. You'll do wondrous things for the Lord."

"I want to believe that," Jerry said.

"And you can believe it. Just think about all the decisions that have been made for Christ because of your willingness to give your testimony in the churches and schools. That doesn't have to stop when you get out. You can still stand up and tell what the Lord has done for you." Br. Ben put his hand on Jerry's shoulder. "Not only can you still do it, you must keep doing it as long as the Lord says do it."

"Everything's going to be different." Jerry leaned forward with his elbows on his knees and stared at the floor. "Everything. Mom's gone. Dad's getting married to somebody I don't even know. The farm's gone."

"But there's another farm. A better farm from what your father tells me. And you know you have a place there. Your father not only wants you to help him on the farm, he needs your help."

"But eventually I'll have to go out on my own. I can't live with my father the rest of my life."

"That's true. You can't," Br. Ben said.

Jerry looked up. "I'm afraid."

Br. Ben's face softened. "I know you are. But you are going to make it, Jerry."

"Will you pray for me?"

"I already do, son. You're always in my heart and my prayers."

Jerry hesitated a moment before he said, "You'll probably think this is half crazy, but did you ever feel like the Lord placed angels along the road to help you do the right thing? To point you in the right direction?"

"The Lord guides us in whatever way He chooses." Br. Ben looked at Jerry for a long moment before he asked, "Why? Have you been seeing angels?"

"I have," Jerry said. "In the crossroads of my life, there have been angels. Some of them I surely missed, but others I've recognized and heeded their directions."

"Then tell me what an angel looks like." Br. Ben smiled a little.

"They come in all shapes and sizes. One was a grandmother type in New Jersey. One was a drawn up old black man at Reidsville." Jerry looked straight at the chaplain. "One looks just like you."

The chaplain blinked back tears. "Son, you have no idea how much I'm going to miss you. I want you free. I want you out there being the man the Lord wants you to be. Maybe a husband and a father. But at the same time, when the Parole Board finally does see that you're ready to go out into the free world, your leaving is going to tear a mighty big hole in my heart."

The hearing didn't happen in April. The Parole Board had some kind of backlog. They delayed the meeting. "Governmental red tape, that's all," Br. Ben told him. "They'll reschedule it in a month or two and then you'll be out. I know you will." Br. Ben picked up his cup and finished off his coffee.

"You want me to make you a fresh pot?" Jerry asked.

"In a minute. First we've got something else to talk about. I got some other news. Good news, but sad too."

"You got your promotion." Jerry tried to make his voice sound glad, but the promotion meant Br. Ben would be moving to Atlanta where he would be over all the chaplains in the state's prison system.

"That's right. It looks like I'm going to be moving out of here ahead of you."

"That's fantastic. They couldn't have gotten a better guy." Jerry was having a hard time holding on to his smile. "But you won't mind if I cry a little."

"I'd be disappointed it you didn't. Especially since we'll most likely be crying together. You've been like a son to me, Jerry. I wish I could take you along."

"Me too," Jerry said. "But I don't think my trusty status includes free access to the state capital buildings."

"No, but you won't be here much longer. You'll be free to go home to Kentucky in no time at all."

"But I don't know whether I can make it without you here to help me."

Br. Ben smiled but his eyes looked ready to run over. "You'll do fine, son. Just take it one day at a time and keep your prayer line open to the Lord."

"You'll keep praying for me, too, won't you? I mean even after you move up there with the bigwigs."

"You know I will." Br. Ben stood up and threw his arm around Jerry's shoulder. "Every day, and I'll be calling to check up on you. I won't forget the number here."

"What if I mess up after you leave?"

"You won't. You'll do fine. Mr. Cleveland will still be here to keep you straight. He's going to be filling in for my job till they hire somebody," the chaplain said. "So stop worrying about yourself and worry about me. I'm the one with problems. I have to go up to the big city where I'll have to try to find somebody who can make coffee just the way I like it."

"Anybody can make coffee," Jerry said.

"Maybe so, but can't just anybody type out a letter the way I want it to be no matter what I actually said."

"You can teach them."

"With enough time, I guess, but what about finding somebody who can sing whatever song I start humming?"

"Two out of three's not bad," Jerry said with a little shrug. "I wouldn't want you to forget me all that easy anyhow."

"Don't worry, son. There's no way I could ever forget you. Not after some of the things you've done." Br. Ben laughed, but then he got serious again. "But I will miss seeing you and talking to you every day. You're a big part of the reason I got the promotion. Because of all the programs you've helped us get started here at the prison. The Lord has his hand on you, Jerry. Let him keep blessing you and others through you."

It was hard seeing Br. Ben leave. It seemed Jerry was always losing people, but as Br. Ben reminded him before he left, the one most important person in Jerry's life would never go away or change. The Lord would always be there right beside him helping him, showing him the way, putting angels into his path. Jerry set his Bible on the right corner of his desk in the chaplain's office so he wouldn't forget that. He put the cross made out of three nails Br. Ben had given him on top the Bible. And then he learned to make coffee the way Mr. Cleveland liked it as he settled back in to wait to see what the Parole Board was going to do.

Back in Kentucky, his father couldn't wait any longer, and he married Margaret in May. So Jerry had a new stepmother he'd never met. He'd said hello to her on the phone a few times, but neither of them had known much to say. He couldn't imagine what she must be thinking about taking on a convict for a stepson.

Then one morning Mr. Cleveland told Jerry that Judge Rutherford was working to get Jerry's life sentence commuted to fifteen years. If that happened, Jerry could be paroled at any time.

The letter came the middle of July. There was no hearing. He didn't have to appear before the Board. He was going to be released.

Mr. Gerald Warren Shepherd, D-1902

After careful investigation and deliberation, the Parole Board has decided to release you under parole supervision. This means you will be allowed to serve the rest of your sentence, minus credited good time, outside of prison where you may earn your own living and lead a normal life.

There were a couple of paragraphs about the conditions of parole and how he was the only one who could send himself back to prison by not abiding by the conditions of his parole and how his parole officer would be a friend and an advisor.

You have our best wishes in your efforts to begin a new life. You went to prison because you failed to abide by society's rules. We think you are ready to abide by those rules and be an asset to your community instead of a liability. This is why we grant you parole.

Finally they got to the vital information.

You are scheduled for release on parole on July 24, 1974. We wish you success and happiness.

July 24th. Less than two weeks away. He let out a shout and hugged Mr. Cleveland before he did a little jig in the middle of the floor. And then he prayed for courage. And more angels. Lots more angels.

CHAPTER 44

It felt funny walking out of the prison in his free world clothes and knowing that this time he wasn't going to have to go back inside that night. He'd taken off his prison uniform for the last time. He'd told everybody goodbye. The guards had good-naturedly threatened him with bodily harm if they ever saw him inside again. The men in the dorm had punched his arm and grinned while they asked how much they should wager on his return.

"Better hang onto your cigarettes and not be betting on that," he'd said. "As much as I like you old boys, you can be sure I won't be coming back to see you."

Before he left, he went down to the chaplain's office for one last time. He stood in the middle of the floor and let the voices of his past circle around him. Governor Carter and his wife asking him about *The Challenge of the Cross*. All the letters he'd answered from AA groups all over the United States. His mother and father calling him on Br. Ben's phone to hear his voice and know he was all right. The fury of the storm when his mother died. And Br. Ben. Most of all Br. Ben. All their talks over morning coffee. All the advice. All the prayers.

Even though Br. Ben had been gone for several weeks, the office was still his, would always be his in Jerry's mind. His laugh echoed off the walls. Jerry could see Br. Ben holding up his coffee cup for a refill. He could feel Br. Ben's hand resting on his shoulder as they prayed together. He could hear Br. Ben telling him he could make it as long as he kept his eyes fixed on the Lord.

Mr. Cleveland came in the office and caught Jerry standing there. "Telling the place goodbye?"

"Yeah. I spent a lot of hours in here."

"You did, but now you're ready to start the next chapter of your life. A better chapter."

"I hope I'm ready," Jerry said.

"You're ready." Mr. Cleveland stepped closer to him and smiled. "I remember the first time I saw you at Reidsville. I wasn't sure you'd survive prison."

"I might not have if it hadn't been for you helping me get involved in AA and Rinc."

"Well, I had to. Your mother insisted. We either had to send you home for her to take care of you or take care of you ourselves."

Jerry smiled. "Mom was good at insisting."

"That she was," Mr. Cleveland agreed. "Come on. I'll walk out with you to meet your dad. He wants to introduce me to Margaret."

"He'll have to introduce me, too," Jerry said.

"You'll like her," Mr. Cleveland said.

"How do you know?"

"A little bird named Br. Ben told me when I talked to him yesterday. He said to tell you not to worry about anything and especially not your new stepmother because no doubt she would turn out to be one of those angels you told him about."

"Well, Dad thinks so anyway, but it's not her I'm worried about. It's me. It's been five years."

"You'll be fine," Mr. Cleveland said. "Just remember the Lord is right beside you all the way and that nothing can ever separate you from his love. Not tribulation, or distress, or persecution, or famine, or nakedness, or peril, or sword. Nothing. Not even our own fears."

"That's in Romans, isn't it?" Jerry asked.

"Well, not the last part about our fears, but the rest of it is. And the important thing is do you believe it?"

"I believe it."

"Then rest on that belief and trust the Lord. He's taken care of you in here. He can take care of you out in the world."

Jerry's father was smiling all over when Jerry came out to the release point. An attractive dark haired woman stood beside him. Her smile looked a bit tentative, but her eyes were kind as they touched Jerry's face when his father pulled her forward to introduce her. "This is Margaret. Didn't I tell you how pretty she was?" his dad said.

She blushed but her smile grew surer. "I'm glad to finally meet you, Jerry." She turned to Mr. Cleveland. "And you too, Mr. Cleveland."

And that's all she said. Jerry didn't know whether it was because she didn't know what to say to an ex-convict, especially one going home with her, or whether it was because his dad kept chattering on about first one thing and then another and didn't leave anybody else room to get a word in edgewise.

Jerry had never heard his father talk so much. He kept talking about the surprise he had waiting for Jerry back at the farm. He kept talking about how wonderful it was going to be to have Jerry helping him with the cows and the hay. He kept talking about how they'd fixed up a room in the new house with all Jerry's old furniture. But it was what they didn't talk about that kept the awkwardness in the air. Nobody mentioned Jerry's mother and what this day would have surely meant to her.

The surprise, sitting in the driveway beside the house at the farm in McAfee, was a brand new two tone blue 1974 F-100 Ford pickup truck. His dad looked almost ready to explode with happiness when he handed Jerry the keys. "This is yours."

"Dad, you shouldn't have spent that kind of money on me," Jerry said even as he was yanking open the door to breath in the heady new truck smell. He slid in behind the wheel to let the smell soak into his skin. He checked out the dials on the dash, hit the turn signal, flashed the lights on and off before he jumped out to pop the hood so he could admire the engine. "Man, this is great."

"You'll need wheels," his dad said.

"I don't even have a driver's license anymore." Jerry ran his hand along the fender. His own truck. He wanted to climb back in it and just drive until his foot got too tired to push the gas pedal.

"You'll get one. You can go apply for a permit tomorrow."

"I'll look cute taking the permit test with all those high school kids."

"You'll just do what you have to do, Jerry."

That's what he would have to do about everything. He would have to get used to having a stepmother. Although he hadn't met his stepmother's daughter yet, he would have to get used to having a stepsister and two nieces and a nephew. He'd have to learn to operate the milkers. He'd have to learn to sleep in a quiet room in a soft bed again.

That first night as he was getting ready for bed, Margaret came to the door of his room to make sure he had everything he needed. When he said he did, she hesitated a moment before she said, "I'm glad you're home."

She turned away without waiting for him to say anything. As he watched her disappear down the hall back into the kitchen, he knew she meant it. She might not be a person who talked much, but there was a gentleness about her. And a peacefulness.

As Jerry lay in his bed and stared at the window open to the night air, he felt that same peacefulness in the very air of the house. There would be no yelling in this house. He wouldn't have to be perfect for this woman. She knew he wasn't perfect. She knew what he'd done. She knew he'd been in prison, and she still wanted him there. Jerry had felt the honesty of her words. No wonder his father had wanted to marry her and share that peace and love.

Jerry didn't want to shut his eyes and go to sleep. He wanted to let the sound of the katydids and crickets outside penetrate his very being. A whippoorwill called in the distance and then he heard a screech owl. A car passed by out on the highway. He had forgotten how good those things sounded. He didn't have to listen to the sound of a hundred men settling down to sleep. He was never going to be awakened by a guard running a billy bat along the wall of the dorm again. He had his life back.

In the morning, he could get up and pull on blue jeans and go to the barn. He could sit in his new truck, turn the key, and listen to the engine purr. He could throw a stick for Hugo to fetch. He could tell Margaret he wanted three eggs sunny-side up for breakfast instead of whatever size glob of scrambled eggs some inmate worker plopped on his plate. He could start working on the farm to pay his father back for all the years he'd stood by Jerry.

On Sunday, Jerry and his dad got up early so they could get the milking done in time to go to church. His father and Margaret were still driving back to Mitchellsburg Baptist where Margaret was a member. She'd been going to the church there for years and it wasn't all that far to drive.

"You'll get to meet your new sister this morning," Jerry's dad said as they parked in front of the church. "She lives just around the corner from here in Margaret's old house. Connie is just as sweet as her mama, so you won't be able to help liking her."

"I always wanted a sister," Jerry said.

"Well, now you have one. And she comes with three of the cutest kids you ever saw. Right, Margaret?"

"I think so, but then they are my grandbabies," Margaret said.

"What are their names again?" Jerry asked. He wished he had a pen so he could write cheat notes on his hand.

"Tab's the baby. He's three. Then there's Christy. She's four and as friendly as a little puppy. She made up with Dewey right away. Shayne's seven and it may take you a little longer to win her over," Margaret said.

"How about your son-in-law? Will he be there?"

For a minute Jerry didn't think Margaret was going to answer him, but then she said, "No. Robert doesn't usually go to church."

"Robert's a whole other story," Jerry's dad started.

Margaret stopped him with a hand on his arm. She said softly, "A story we can tell another day. Not on Jerry's first Sunday home."

Jerry was curious, but he didn't ask any questions. He'd already found out in the few days he'd been home that he couldn't find out everything about everybody in his new life here overnight. He had to take it one thing at a time.

Sunday school hadn't let out when they went inside and found an empty pew. A few of the people already in the sanctuary came over to shake hands with Jerry and welcome him to the church. They were so friendly that Jerry wondered if anybody had told them where he'd been. He didn't feel as if anybody should have to tell them. The prison air was surely still clinging to him and giving him a stinking odor that would take months, maybe years to shake off.

A bell to signal the end of Sunday school sounded back in the Sunday school rooms and people began streaming out into the church. Jerry was watching the church members coming through the door and wondering if he'd recognize his new stepsister from the photo Margaret had shown him when a young woman with dark brown hair curled around her face herded three kids into the sanctuary.

Bells started going off, but not back in the Sunday school rooms or even in the church bell tower if the church had one. These bells were clanging wildly in Jerry's head as the woman moved toward him. She was the most beautiful woman he'd ever seen, and she was smiling straight at him. His heart started pounding, and his knees went weak.

He'd heard people talk about this kind of thing happening, but Jerry had never really believed them. Not at first sight. Not before you even knew a girl's name. But it was happening to him. Not only happening, it was engulfing him. He wanted to reach out and take her hand and ask her to marry him on the spot.

And it wasn't just because he'd been in prison. Plenty of pretty girls had made eyes at him when he was playing in the band at Reidsville and there were always some unattached girls at the churches where he'd gone to give his testimony. He'd flirted with those girls. He'd dreamed about some of them, but he'd never seen one who knocked him off his feet the way this girl was doing.

He could hardly breath by the time she got to the pew where they were standing up to greet her. The little boy had run straight to Margaret. The oldest girl was hanging back behind her mother and the other little girl was looking at them with big, round beautiful brown eyes. Eyes almost as beautiful as her mother's. Jerry took a deep breath to try to slow down his racing heart. He sucked in the smell of her perfume and felt so dizzy he had to grab hold of the back of the pew in front of him.

He didn't want Margaret to tell him who she was. He didn't want to hear that this woman he'd fallen instantaneously in love with was his sister. Not only his sister. His married sister.

He gripped the back of the pew and tried to look calm as Margaret said, "This is Connie, Jerry."

Connie reached out and took his hand. "Welcome home, brother." Her smile was warm. "I've always wanted a brother."

Jerry took her hand and managed to stammer, "Yeah, me too. I mean I've always wanted a sister."

She laughed and the bells rang louder in Jerry's head. "How about one with three kids?"

"The more the merrier." Jerry tore his eyes off her face and looked at the children. "I like kids."

Connie put her arm around the oldest girl and pulled her up beside her. "This is Shayne. That's Christy, and Mama has Tab. All right, guys, say hello to your Uncle Jerry."

An obedient chorus of hello, Uncle Jerry followed. The organist started playing and they sat down. Shayne stayed close to her mother, but Christy climbed straight into Jerry's lap and settled in as if she'd known him all her life.

Jerry hardly heard a word of the sermon. His ears were still ringing with the echo of the bells that had gone off at first sight of the woman sitting beside him. His stepsister. His married stepsister. His married stepsister with three children. Not exactly the best person to fall for head over heels.

He told himself he just hadn't been getting enough sleep. He told himself that freedom had gone to his head. He told himself that he was crazy. Still every time her arm brushed against his, the bells started going off in his head all over again.

He'd prayed for angels to be in his path before he'd left prison, but he hadn't expected to fall in love with the first one he saw.

CHAPTER 45

After church, they went home with Connie and the kids for lunch. Jerry's dad said it would be a good chance for them all to get better acquainted.

"Is Robert there?" Margaret asked Connie as they headed for the parking lot.

It seemed a casual enough question, but it made Connie miss a step. For just a second her smile disappeared, but then it came back so bright it was almost brittle as she said, "He was there when we left for church this morning. You know Robert. He keeps his own schedule."

Now Margaret sounded worried. "Are you sure it will be okay for us to come over for lunch?"

"Of course," Connie said. "I put a roast and some potatoes in the oven this morning. There'll be plenty for everybody. And the kids need to get to know their new uncle." Connie smiled over at Jerry.

Jerry smiled back and managed to keep walking. He was going to have to get a hold on his emotions. This was his sister. His married sister. He needed to keep shouting that word over and over in his head. Married.

He didn't like Robert at first sight. Jerry smiled when they were introduced and said he was glad to meet him, but there wasn't a smidgen of gladness in his heart. Robert smelled of alcohol and didn't look as if he'd shaved for a couple of days. The man didn't show the first hint of any gladness at seeing any of them either. He was barely civil to Jerry's father or Margaret. He was lying back in his easy chair watching a baseball game on television. He didn't stand up to greet them, wave them toward a chair, or even make the first move to turn down the sound on the television to talk to them.

"Big game today?" Jerry's father asked.

"Yeah, the Reds and the Dodgers." Robert kept his eyes on the screen. Then without looking around at Connie, he asked, "How long's it going to be before we eat?"

"It'll be ready in a few minutes." Connie hurried toward the kitchen. The oldest girl, Shayne, was still right beside her, a shadow almost. She hadn't even looked at her father. Without a word, Margaret grabbed the other two kids and headed toward their bedroom to help them change out of their Sunday clothes.

241

That left Jerry and his father alone with Robert. An awkward moment passed before his father said, "Come on, Jerry. I'll take you next door to show you the store Margaret used to run with her first husband. They had a pretty good business going here."

"Still would be bringing in money if Connie hadn't let her mother practically give it away to that low life who runs it now," Robert muttered. He picked up an empty glass off the table by his chair and yelled toward the kitchen. "You got anything in there to drink, Connie?"

Jerry's hands curled into fists, but his dad took hold of his arm and pulled him toward the front door. "Come on, Jerry. We'll walk around outside. We wouldn't want to disturb a man's ballgame."

When they were outside with the door shut behind them, Jerry said, "He always that sweet or was he just putting on a show for us?"

Jerry's dad just shook his head. "I'm not going to talk about a man in his own yard on a Sunday afternoon." He looked back toward the door and his eyes narrowed. "But I could."

The conversation at the dinner table was strained. Margaret and Connie talked about the people they'd seen at church and tried to get Tab to eat his green beans. Shayne kept her eyes on her plate while she ate, stealing first glances at her father and then Jerry. Jerry watched for her eyes so that he could smile or make a silly face when she looked at him. Before dinner was over, he was rewarded with a shy smile. Christy was the only one who seemed totally unaffected by the tension between the adults around the table. She kept stabbing her potatoes with her fork and giggling when the potato chunks shot away from her fork and landed on the table.

They left right after Margaret helped Connie get the dishes cleared away and the leftovers put up. Connie told them not to rush off. She was still smiling, trying to make Jerry feel like one of the family, but at the same time she kept looking at Robert as if afraid she might be saying the wrong thing.

On the way home, Jerry told Margaret what a nice daughter she had. "And the kids are even cuter than you said they were."

"Connie is an angel," Margaret said, but her words sounded almost sad.

The word angel tickled Jerry's brain. Connie was an angel, but somebody else's angel. The thought pierced his heart, but he kept smiling as he said, "She did look like an angel. Beautiful like you."

"Listen to you." Margaret smiled back at him, but then her smile disappeared as she asked Jerry's dad, "Do you think he was drinking?"

"He's always drinking," Jerry's father said.

"I should have asked her to come home with us," Margaret said.

"She wouldn't have come."

"I know," Margaret said.

Jerry's father reached over to put his hand over Margaret's hands in her lap. "We've done what we can. We've told her we'll get her out of there. We've already got an option on that house over on Green Wilson. It's empty. We could move her into it tomorrow, but she has to take that next step. She has to say she's ready for us to help her."

"It's not a good marriage?" Jerry was a little ashamed of the spark of happiness that thought ignited inside him.

"No, I'm afraid not," Margaret said. "But they have three children, and Connie says she made a vow for better or worse."

"There's worse and then there's way past worse to unbearable," Jerry's father said.

"She's coming around to believing that," Margaret said. "She told me she had filed for divorce."

"Well, what's he doing there then?" Jerry's father asked.

"He doesn't know it yet. She's afraid to tell him."

That night when Jerry and his father came in from milking, Margaret was sitting at the kitchen table staring at the telephone with tears running down her cheeks. She'd been talking to Shayne. Jerry's dad looked at Margaret and said, "He's been hitting her again."

Margaret nodded. "Poor little Shayne. The other kids were taking a nap, but Shayne heard it all. She had to talk to somebody about it."

"Connie know she called?"

"No, of course not. Connie doesn't want us to know how bad it is."

"As if we can't see the bruises," Jerry's father said.

Jerry stood there in the middle of the kitchen and felt sick. He'd seen a lot of mean things while he was in prison, but he could hardly stand the thought of anybody hitting the beautiful woman he'd just met that morning. "Maybe you should go get them," Jerry said.

"I can't. I promised Shayne I wouldn't tell her mother she called me, and they're probably okay now. Shayne said Robert had left," Margaret said.

"Call Connie and make sure she's all right," Jerry's father said. "You won't have to tell her you talked to Shayne. Just tell her you thought she looked a little blue today and that the offer still holds about getting her out of there. Tell her about the house over on Green Wilson again. We can make sure she and the children are safe."

Margaret looked up at Jerry. "I'm sorry you had to come home to this, Jerry. But I can't help it. I'm worried sick about her. When Robert's drinking, he, well, he gets mean sometimes."

"It's okay, Margaret," Jerry said. "She's my sister. I'll help anyway I can."

"As long as you keep a cool head," Jerry's dad said. "You can't afford any trouble."

"I won't make trouble, Dad. I'm not that stupid."

"You can't even respond to trouble, son. You have to stay calm and stay free."

They sat around the table and prayed for Connie and the children. Jerry's dad even managed to say a prayer for Robert, but Jerry found it hard to echo the prayer in his heart. What kind of man would hit a beautiful angel like Connie?

The next morning their prayers were answered. Before she went to work at the clothing factory, Connie called her mother to say she'd stayed up all night packing. She'd put the baby pictures of the kids and her photo albums in the trunk of her car. Before the kids had gone to bed she'd made a game of them putting their favorite toys in pillowcases. She told her mother she was praying for forgiveness for breaking up her marriage, but she'd looked into Shayne's eyes the night before and knew she couldn't raise children in a house like this. She knew how a home was supposed to be. She told her mother how happy she'd been when she was growing up and how she wanted that kind of love and peace for her own children.

By then, Margaret couldn't answer her. She was crying too much. She handed the phone to Jerry's dad. "It's okay, Connie," he said. "We'll take care of everything. You go on to work the same as any other Monday. That way if Robert comes around he won't know anything's going on until it's too late to do anything about it. Margaret will go get the kids at the sitter's, and Jerry and I will take the truck to get your stuff."

So they drove to the house and loaded up the big truck. They didn't feel bad taking the furniture since most of it belonged to Margaret from the time when the house had been a happy home. Margaret had picked up the kids and was following the truck out when Robert sped past them and veered toward Margaret's car. She swerved away from him off the road into a ditch.

"This isn't good," Jerry's dad said as he pulled the truck over.

"What's he trying to do?"

"Who knows." Jerry's dad opened his door. "You stay put and let me handle this, Jerry." As he climbed down out of the truck to go confront Robert, he said, almost as a prayer, "Keep the kids in the car, Margaret."

In the side mirror, Jerry watched Robert jump out of his car and head toward Jerry's dad. Jerry's heart sank when he spotted the bulge in Robert's back pocket. The man had a gun. Jerry quietly opened the truck door and climbed out. Robert didn't see him. He was totally focused on Jerry's father who was beside Margaret's car making sure none of them were hurt. Robert jumped in front of Jerry's father. That put his back to Jerry. When Robert reached toward the gun in his back pocket, Jerry picked up the cattle prod his dad carried in the truck.

Jerry had been out of prison for a week, not nearly long enough. He took in a lung full of free air as he whispered, "Lord, I guess this is the last of my free time." But he couldn't just stand there and let this man shoot his father. Not even if it meant he'd have to go back inside for the rest of his life.

CHAPTER 46

Jerry raised the cattle prod. He couldn't let Robert pull the gun out of his pocket.

Jerry's dad looked over Robert's shoulder at Jerry and shook his head the tiniest bit. The gun was still in Robert's pocket, so Jerry lowered the stick to his side and said in a loud voice, "What do you think you're doing, Robert?"

Robert jumped and whirled around to face Jerry. He hadn't expected Jerry to be there, and when he saw him, it was as if he was remembering where Jerry had been for the last five years. And why. Jerry kept his eyes tight on Robert. He knew how to stare down bullies. He'd had plenty of practice in prison, and if the stare didn't work, he still had the stick. He swung it back and forth a couple of times to make sure Robert knew he'd use it if he had to.

"You can't take my kids," Robert said, but the man's courage was running out. His hands were shaking as he held them out in front of him as if to ward off Jerry. He made no move to reach for the gun.

"The kids belong with their mother," Jerry said. Behind Robert, Jerry could hear the children crying. He wanted to look over at them, give them a smile, and let them know he was going to make everything okay, but instead he kept his eyes on Robert.

"What's it to you?" Robert said. "You just got out of the pen."

"That's right, but Connie's my sister now. It's a brother's duty to protect and take care of his sister." Jerry kept his voice calm, almost pleasant, but there wasn't anything even remotely pleasant in the look he gave Robert. "And I plan to do whatever I have to do to protect mine."

Jerry's dad stepped forward a little. "Now, Robert, we don't want any trouble. And you know the kids need to be with their mother."

Robert pulled his eyes away from Jerry's face to look at Jerry's dad. He seemed to regain a little courage. "They're my kids, too. I'm their father."

"More reason than ever for you to just get in your car and leave, Robert. You do that we won't call the police and tell them how you tried to ram the car your children were riding in," Jerry's father said. "Somebody could have gotten hurt. One of your kids could have gotten hurt."

"I wasn't going to hit the car. I was just making her stop," Robert said, but all the fight had gone out of his voice.

"Just leave, Robert," Jerry said. "Smile and wave goodbye to the kids and leave."

Robert looked back at Jerry. "She can't do this to me."

Jerry stood still and stared back at him. "It was what you can't do that you did to her that caused this."

"She didn't tell you that I hit her, did she? She's always telling lies about me," Robert said. "It's not my fault that she's so clumsy and always bumping into things. And if she told you I shot at her, that's just another lie. The gun went off by accident."

Jerry's grip tightened on the cattle prod as he said, "Leave."

Robert must have heard something in Jerry's voice that made him stop talking and turn toward his car. He didn't even look toward Margaret's car where his son was screaming and his two daughters had their faces up against the window glass watching him with wide, frightened eyes.

They waited until Robert's truck went out of sight over the next hill before they helped Margaret get her car back on the road. Once they had the car out of the ditch, Jerry leaned down to the window and grinned at the children. "Everything's going to be okay, guys. Your Uncle Jerry will see to it."

They all three looked at him as if they weren't sure they could believe him. Then Shayne smiled a little. She'd been the last one he'd expected to smile, but he felt sort of the way he imagined a new father must feel when a tiny baby reaches up and grabs hold of his father's finger. This little girl had grabbed hold of his heart with her smile.

"Let's go see what your new house looks like," he said.

They had the truck unloaded by the time Connie showed up at the house. Two of her friends from work had escorted her to the new house, one driving in front of her and the other driving behind her to protect her. That afternoon after they'd convinced Robert to leave the children alone, he'd shown up at the factory where Connie worked and called her outside. He'd let her know that he had a gun. He'd told her she couldn't just leave him without giving him a chance to talk things out with her. She'd told him she couldn't talk to him right then because she had to go back to work. Then to get him to leave, she'd promised to meet him after work even though she had no intention of meeting him anywhere ever again. She didn't like lying, but she was scared.

Once Connie and the children were settled into the new house, Jerry took on the task of making sure they were safe. At night after he got through with the milking, he'd drive over to Green Wilson Street and make circles around the block to be sure Robert wasn't around. When Jerry passed Connie's house at night, the drapes would be pulled tight and everything about the house would look closed and locked away. She was still scared Robert would find her even though she hadn't heard the first word from him since that day at the factory.

Jerry started stopping by after he'd made his rounds of the neighborhood. She and the children were always glad to see him. The kids kept calling him uncle and she kept telling him how much fun it was having a brother. He pretended he felt the same about her as a sister, but what he felt every time he looked at her didn't have the first thing to do with sisterly love.

Still if she wanted to think of him as a brother, he'd act like a brother. He didn't want to do anything that would make her stop smiling a big welcome every time he showed up at the door which started being every night. They watched television together, and often as not, he ended up dozing off on whatever program was on because he had to get up so early to milk the cows. When it was her bedtime, she'd turn off all the lights except the one in the kitchen and leave him sleeping on the couch.

Whenever he woke up, Jerry let himself out the back door and headed home. The times he slept till the wee hours of the morning, he'd creep out to his truck and open the door inch by inch to keep from making any noise to wake the neighbors and maybe make some of them, especially the retired minister who lived right next door, think less of Connie for letting Jerry stay so late. Then he'd shift the truck out of gear and let it coast down to the end of the driveway before he shut the door and started the engine.

When the opportunities to give his testimony started coming in as Br. Ben and Mr. Cleveland had assured Jerry they would, he invited Connie and the kids along just so they'd have somewhere to go. At least that's what he told them and his father. The truth was he wanted to be with Connie as much as possible. Every minute of every day wouldn't have been too much time together for him. And the kids already seemed almost like his own. They ran to meet him whenever he showed up and pulled on his hands to come look at this or that.

Still she thought he was her brother. And his father thought Jerry had embraced Connie as his sister the way he now accepted Margaret as his stepmother, and that's why he was being so extra nice to Connie and the kids. His father had no idea Jerry felt like a giddy teenager every time he looked at Connie. His father thought Jerry was in love with a girl back in Oldham County who'd been a good friend through school and had tried to keep the friendship going while he was in prison with a letter now and again. When Jerry drove to Oldham

County one Saturday to see Carrie and some of his other old friends, that seemed to settle things in his father's mind. Jerry overheard him telling Margaret that Carrie would make the perfect wife for Jerry.

But things were far from settled. Carrie was a dear old friend, but his heart still skipped a beat every time Connie smiled at him. He just didn't know how to tell her. He asked the Lord for guidance, but Connie kept treating him like a brother and he kept acting as if he was her brother. He made himself at home on her couch, raided her refrigerator without asking, and teased her about her new hair-style. But what he wanted to do was put his arm around her while they were watching television. He wanted to run his fingers through her hair. He wanted to feel her head resting on his shoulder.

So he waited for an opportunity to let her know how he really felt, but when she did open the door for him to tell her the truth by asking him about his visit with Carrie or what kind of girls he thought were cute, he always let the chance slip by. Then he would berate himself as a coward all the way back to his house and pray for more courage the next time he got a chance. The Lord finally took pity on him and threw open the door for him.

Connie and the kids had gone with him to a church over in Indiana. Jerry didn't know how the church got his name. He just knew if they invited him, the Lord must have a reason for him to go there. That's the way it had been at all the churches he'd gone to since he'd been home from prison. He'd give his testimony and people would respond. Jerry didn't really think it had all that much to do with him. He was just the mouth the Lord was using. Jerry told his story and tried not to get in the way of the message, but on this day, the Lord had a message for Jerry. Or maybe for Connie.

After the service, one of the deacons came over to thank Jerry for coming. "That was great, Brother," the man said. He looked to be in his seventies and had told Jerry he'd been a member of that church all his life. He shook Jerry's hand and then smiled at Connie and the kids who were helping Jerry pack up his equipment. "And we're so glad you brought your family along. You have three beautiful children and it's always wonderful to see such a loving family. Me and my wife, we got married here in this church forty-five years ago. Some people don't believe it, but we're just as happy now as we were then. And I can see the two of you feel the same way about each other. I can see it in your faces how much you and your lovely wife are still in love with one another."

Jerry looked at Connie and grinned. Color was blooming in her cheeks, but she didn't jump in to tell the man Jerry was her brother. So Jerry just said, "Well, thank you, sir." It seemed too much hassle to go into the family story. It was already almost one o'clock and the kids were hungry. Besides he was tired of telling people Connie was his sister. He was ready for people to think they were a beautiful family. He was ready for them to be a beautiful family.

Neither of them said anything about what the man said until they were in the car driving away from the church. Then Connie said, "It was funny what that man said about us. I guess we should have told him it wasn't true, but it's sort of a complicated relationship."

"You can say that again," Jerry said.

"And the kids are hungry."

"I could go for one of those pimento cheese sandwiches you packed up for our lunch myself," Jerry said.

She pulled sandwiches out of the sack between them on the front seat and handed one to Jerry and some to the kids in the back seat. They always drove Connie's car to the churches. Her arm brushed against him when she reached over the seat to help Tab with his sandwich. An electric jolt went through Jerry. He tried to make his mouth open to say he thought the old deacon had seen things pretty straight, but instead he stuck the sandwich in his mouth and took a bite. He didn't particularly like pimento cheese, but he'd never told Connie that.

"Do you want a soft drink?" Connie asked. "The ice in the cooler has melted, but they're still a little cold."

"Sure," Jerry said.

She handed him a drink. "That boy who came up to talk to you after the service? Were you able to help him? He looked really upset."

"I think so," Jerry said. "He's sort of got off track and has been running around with the wrong crowd and stuff, but he wants to do what the Lord wants him to do."

"I guess sometimes it's hard to know what that is."

"Yeah," Jerry said. But he knew what the Lord was trying to help him do right then. He could almost hear the Lord whispering in the back of his head, go ahead and tell her for Pete's sake.

He opened his mouth. "You know," he started, but just then Tab spilled his drink in the back seat and Shayne screamed when the soft drink soaked her Sunday dress. Jerry had to pull over to let Connie clean up the mess, and somehow when they were back on the road again, the moment had passed.

But as he kept driving, he vowed that before he left Connie that day, he would somehow let her know he had something besides brotherly feelings for her. All afternoon he kept trying to pull the perfect moment back up, but something kept happening. The kids got into fights. Connie dozed off in her chair. He couldn't decide the best words to say. At suppertime he had to go home to help his father do the milking.

He started not to go back to Connie's. He'd been there all day, but the Lord nudged him, made him remember his vow. The day wasn't over. He drove back over to watch television with her. This night he didn't doze off on the couch. He had too many nervous little ants crawling around inside his clothes. Connie put the kids to bed and he still didn't know what words to say. He thought how Br. Ben would have never believed Jerry could be so at a loss for words. Words were usually spilling out of him, and actually he was talking practically non-stop, but he wasn't saying what he wanted to say.

Finally he got up to go home. "We both have to get up early," he said.

She walked him to the door the way she did every night when he didn't fall asleep on the couch. "Thanks for taking me and the kids with you this morning," she said.

"It's me that needs to thank you. We go in your car. You fix us a lunch. You help pack the equipment in and out."

"It's no trouble. We like helping you." She smiled at him.

All the nervous ants started biting him to make him do something. He put his hands on her cheeks, leaned over, and kissed her forehead. Sparks flew. He didn't see them, but he felt them. He didn't stick around to see if he was the only one feeling sparks. He took off around the corner of the house toward his truck. Once out of sight of the door, he jumped up in the air and clicked his heels together.

"Yes, yes, yes!" he shouted in a whisper. He hadn't forgotten the preacher asleep in the house right next door. He didn't know when he'd ever felt so good. He wasn't sure he ever had. He had no idea what Connie might be thinking inside the house. He would worry about that tomorrow. Tonight he was just going to enjoy the feeling.

The next morning after he and his dad had turned the cows out to pasture and were walking back to the house where Margaret would have breakfast waiting, Jerry looked over at his father and asked, "Can you marry your sister?"

CHAPTER 47

"Marry your sister? What are you talking about? Can who marry whose sister?" his father said. Then it slowly dawned on him what Jerry meant. "You mean you and Connie? But what about Carrie?"

"Carrie was your idea, Dad. Connie's mine. I love her."

His father had stopped walking and was staring at him. "But what about the children?"

"What about them?" Jerry said. "I love them, too."

His father looked down at the dried cow manure on his boots and then to the east where the sun was rising up above a bank of rose colored clouds. Finally his eyes came back to Jerry's face. "You haven't known her but a few weeks."

"How long did you know Margaret?"

"Long enough," his father said.

"That's how long I've known Connie."

"What's she say about getting married?"

"I haven't told her yet."

His father looked at him for another long moment. "Then maybe you should," he finally said before he started on toward the house.

Jerry followed him. "What do you think Margaret will think?"

"I don't know. I guess you'd better ask her yourself, but you might do better to worry about what Connie thinks."

Margaret didn't look as surprised as his father. She hardly paused in stirring sugar into her coffee after Jerry blurted out the same question to her at the breakfast table that he had to his father. "Can you marry your sister?"

She took a sip of the hot coffee and sat her cup back down before she looked straight at Jerry. "If you're talking about Connie, technically she's not really your sister. You aren't related at all except by marriage."

"So you think it would be okay?" Jerry hadn't eaten the first bite of the eggs and bacon on his plate. He wasn't a bit concerned about food this morning.

Margaret smiled a little. "I don't think it matters what I think. What does Connie think? That's what matters."

"I haven't asked her yet."

Margaret's smile got wider. "Well, don't tell the whole world before you tell her."

"No ma'am," Jerry said. "She's next on my list."

"It could be she should have been first on your list," Margaret said. "But you have time. You can't get married until her divorce is finalized anyway."

"When's that?" Jerry asked.

"I think around the middle of November," Margaret said. "A couple of months from now."

"A good month for a wedding," Jerry said.

"You Shepherd men don't believe in long engagements, do you?" Margaret said with a smile over at Jerry's father.

Jerry's father grinned back at her. "We see something good, we go for it."

"Like father, like son," Margaret said as she looked back at Jerry. "But at least your dad didn't keep it a secret from me."

"I'll tell her," Jerry said.

"Maybe you should consider asking rather than telling," Margaret suggested. "Now eat your breakfast before I have to warm it back up in the oven."

He did intend to ask, but once he had talked it over with his father and Margaret, it seemed as if it had already been decided. It was as if he'd already asked and she'd already said yes. It was as if all they needed to do was to decide when and where. And he was more than willing to let Connie do that.

That's what he told her the next time he went to her house. He waited until she put the kids to bed and then when she came back into the living room, he patted the couch beside him. She didn't hesitate. She came right over and sat down beside him. It seemed as natural as morning following night to put his arm around her. She leaned against him as if she'd wanted to do that very thing forever.

"We're getting married," he told her. He brushed the top of her hair with his lips.

"Oh?" She sounded a little breathless as if she'd just chased Tab down the hall to make him put on his pajamas.

"Yes," he said as he tightened his arm around her.

"Okay," she said.

"You pick the time and place," Jerry told her.

"My divorce won't be final until November."

"I know. Margaret told me."

"They know?"

"Yes. I asked them if a person could marry his sister?"

"I'm not really your sister."

"But you always wanted a brother."

"Well, yes, that's true, but I guess the Lord decided to answer my other prayer first."

"Which prayer is that?" Jerry asked.

"The one where I've been asking him to send somebody to help me raise my children. After I got married and Robert was the way he was, I prayed that he would change. I don't know whether Mama told you or not, but I divorced him once before, but he said he'd changed. I thought maybe the Lord had helped him change and he was going to be a good husband to me and a father to his children, but once we got married again, he went back to being the way he always was. I tried hard to be the wife he wanted me to be, but he was always so angry. So unhappy. He always wanted somebody else besides me. Other women." Tears were running down Connie's cheeks. "I know what the Bible says about marriage. I wanted to be married that way. I always intended to be married that way."

Jerry tipped her face up toward him and brushed away the tears on her cheeks. "None of what happened was your fault, Connie. He's the one who broke your marriage vows, not you," Jerry said softly.

"But the Bible says you shouldn't be married but once."

"Maybe so, but what about you saying you prayed for a good father for your children, and now here I am? Who are we to fight against what the Lord wants for us?" He kissed the last of the tears off her cheek. "I vow to be the best father Shayne and Christy and Tab could ever have. And that's not all. I vow to be the best husband you could ever have." At last he touched her lips with his.

They talked to the preacher at Connie's church in Mitchellsburg first, but though Br. Brown had been begging Connie to leave Robert for several years and had actually said a Praise the Lord when she told him she had filed for the divorce last May, he said he couldn't marry them. He was afraid he'd lose his position as preacher if he performed the wedding ceremony.

When they both changed their membership to the Harrodsburg Baptist Church, a church closer to where they lived, Br. Williams, the pastor there told them the same thing. He wanted to marry them, but he wasn't ready to risk losing his pastorate if the powers that be weren't understanding about him performing a marriage where one of the parties was divorced.

Jerry wanted to tell Br. Williams that the real power that be, the Lord, had been more than understanding. The Lord had brought them together. He'd put the love in their hearts. The Lord wanted them to be married. Jerry had never been as sure of anything in his life.

As November got closer, Jerry suggested they be married at the courthouse by the judge. Nobody was in favor of that. Not Connie. Not Margaret or his father.

Connie looked ready to cry as she said, "I always thought you needed a preacher to marry you. I wouldn't feel like the marriage was blessed if a preacher didn't perform the ceremony."

"But the preachers aren't cooperating," Jerry said. "Maybe we could go to Georgia and get Br. Ben to do it."

"I can't go to Georgia. Shayne's in school," Connie said.

"And we want to be there, too," Margaret said. "And you know we can't leave the cows without anybody to milk them."

Jerry's dad spoke up. "What about if we just have the wedding here at the house? Church can be anywhere believers are gathered. Where two or more are gathered in his name."

"Sounds good to me," Jerry said.

"But we still don't have a preacher," Connie said.

"Just leave that up to me. I'll find a preacher." So Jerry's father made it happen the same as he'd always done. The same as Jerry's mother would have done if she'd still been living. He found a preacher.

Jerry and Connie didn't ask him if the preacher knew she was divorced. The preacher didn't ask Connie or Jerry about their marital status. Maybe he knew. Maybe he didn't. Either way he promised to come to the farm on November the twentieth to perform the ceremony.

A few aunts and uncles came to witness the event including Jerry's Uncle Milton and Aunt Adele who had been right beside his mother and father all the time Jerry had been in prison. Aunt Adele could hardly look at Jerry and Connie without tearing up. "I'm just so happy for you both, and I know your mother would have been, too. I know she's looking down on you proud as punch."

It was good to have somebody actually mention his mother. Jerry loved Margaret, had even started calling her Mom, but he hadn't forgotten the debt he owed his mother for the love and faithfulness she'd shown him while he was in prison. "I always wanted to make her proud."

Aunt Adele dabbed her eyes with a tissue. "And you did. Believe me. I was as close to Hazel as I ever was to any of my sisters. She didn't do everything right. She was the first to admit that, but she couldn't have loved you any more if you'd been her own child."

"I was her child."

Aunt Adele smiled at him through her tears and nodded. "You were."

It was a beautiful day. Cool but with the sun streaming down out of a clear blue sky. The children were practically spinning in place they were so happy. While Jerry and his father milked the cows a little early that afternoon, Connie and her mother dressed the kids in their Sunday best. The girls wore matching dark pink dresses and Tab had on a white shirt with a little blue bow tie that kept sliding sideways. Connie kept straightening it until finally Jerry told her it looked cuter crooked.

The preacher knocked on the door a few minutes before seven. Jerry's father introduced him all around. Br. Marksbury opened his Bible and stood up in front of Connie and Jerry and spoke the words they were so ready to hear. "Do you take this woman to be your lawfully wedded wife? Do you take this man to be your lawfully wedded husband?"

They gave all the right answers, and at last Br. Marksbury smiled at them both and said, "I now pronounce you man and wife. You may kiss the bride."

And so Jerry did. Aunt Adele and Margaret cried. Jerry's dad clapped his hands together, and the children squealed.

They were still standing in front of the minister, still both smiling, when Tab pulled on the bottom of Jerry's suit coat. "Uncle Jerry, Uncle Jerry, can we call you daddy now?"

The preacher looked a little taken aback. That must have been something else Jerry's father hadn't exactly explained to him. Jerry just grinned at the preacher and shrugged a little before he leaned down to pick up Tab. "You sure can, son. I'm your daddy now and I love you."

Things went a little crazier after that with Shayne and Christy jumping up and down shouting daddy. Everybody started laughing, and the preacher joined in even though he didn't look as if he was sure he should be laughing. Christy and Shayne began pulling Jerry toward the table with the cake and punch. They were ready to finally get to eat some of those little pink and white mints Aunt Adele had brought.

Jerry kept his eyes wide open because he didn't want to miss a second of the best day of his life, but he sent up a prayer from his heart to the Lord. *Thank you, Lord, for not giving up on me. Thank you for all the angels at the crossroads and for the times you opened my eyes so I could see them. Thank you for life. Thank you for my beautiful angel, Connie, and for this wonderful family you've blessed me with.*

He could have gone on forever, and in fact, the praises did keep singing in his heart as laughter rang off the walls while they went through the rituals of feeding each other cake and trying to take sips of punch with arms intertwined.

Later when everybody was busy talking and he thought nobody would miss him, Jerry slipped out onto the porch to get a breath of fresh air. He still felt like doing a little dance of joy each time he opened a door and stepped outside into the air. No guards. No checkpoints. No fences. Just free air. And stars up in the sky. At the prison there were always too many lights to see the stars. He took a deep breath and let the night air wrap around him as he stared up at the sky.

Behind him, the door opened, and Connie came out on the porch. "Oh, here you are. I was wondering where you'd got to," she said as she stepped up beside him. "What are you looking at?" She peered up at the sky.

"The stars." He put his arm around her and drew her close to his side.

"The stars in the heavens," Connie said.

"My mom's up there watching us."

"And my dad," Connie said. "Do you think they're happy for us?"

"I think they're laughing and dancing with the angels." Jerry held out his hand. "Feel the angel dust they're knocking down on us?"

Connie laughed and put her hand out beside his. "Angel dust." Then she looked at Jerry. "We're going to be happy, aren't we?"

"Yes, we are, Mrs. Shepherd. Yes, we are."

AUTHOR'S AFTERWORD

In early 2004 as the Patriot Quartet was returning to Kentucky from a Gospel Singing Cruise with the Eddie Crook Company, the Lord nudged the idea of writing down Jerry Shepherd's remarkable story into my head. My husband sings bass for the group and at that time Jerry was singing tenor with them. While they are extreme opposites in singing ranges and in life experiences as well, both of them have a solid unshakable faith and a sure knowledge of the Lord's will for their lives at this place and time.

The group had been singing together for about three years, but had just gotten a bus to travel in the year before. Gospel quartets become small families as they travel around singing on the weekends even without traveling together on a bus. But once "the bus" enters the picture and allows the group to travel together in the same vehicle, the family feeling grows stronger. Spending hours bouncing along on an old bus to whatever church has opened its doors for the group, eating together, trying to sleep sitting up on the all night rides to the next singing or home, having intense "road discussions" on where to stop to eat or how often to stop for relief tests the mettle of the fellowship of the quartet members and their wives. And you get to know one another pretty well. Along with the harmonizing, the singing family shares laughter, sorrows, stupid moments, joys, favorite songs, testimonies, and their pasts.

Years before the Patriot Quartet was even a dream, I'd heard Jerry give his testimony while singing with another quartet at a church in Burgin, Kentucky. My husband, who has been singing gospel music for over thirty years, was in a different group that sang at the same church that night. When Jerry said he'd killed a man and been sentenced to life in prison for murder, it was as if the man in front of me had turned inside out.

I'd started watching him singing tenor in the group with one impression and ended, after his testimony, seeing a whole different man. A man who said he had taken another man's life. A man who thought he would be in jail most of his life. A man who said he was only standing there in the front of that church due to the grace of God and the love of his parents who never gave up on him.

God had a purpose for Jerry's life, and no matter what Jerry did against that purpose, God didn't give up on him. The Lord kept guiding Jerry by sending angels to help him at the crossroads of his life. The Lord stayed by Jerry's side even when Jerry chose the wrong forks in the roads. The Lord kept loving him even when Jerry believed he was beyond help. The Lord was there reaching for him, wanting him to step into the purpose he had for his life instead of running along on his own.

It was many years before I met Jerry again, now as part of the same quartet my husband was in. I remembered his testimony, and as we traveled to singings together, he shared more about his past in bits and pieces. Those bits and pieces were enough to make me wonder if the Lord had brought us together with a new purpose in mind. I've been writing for many years and had recently had an inspirational novel accepted for publication, but I'd never even considered writing another person's story. I wrote about characters I made up, characters who only found life and breath on the pages of my books.

Then while we were in Florida after the cruise, Jerry told a few stories about his time in prison and I knew I'd have to try to get his story on paper. The more I learned about his life, the more amazing it was to see how God's hand had guided Jerry and was always there to pick up the pieces when Jerry stepped out from under the protection of that hand. It was inspiring to see the way the Lord sent people to help Jerry, and to hear how Jerry had blossomed under the constant, never ending, never changing love of our Lord.

I owe a great deal of credit for this story to Jerry's mother, Hazel, who kept every letter Jerry wrote home and made copies of many of the letters she and Dewey wrote on Jerry's behalf while he was in the service and then in prison. The letters quoted in the book are unchanged and word for word just as Jerry wrote them or received them while he was in prison with the exceptions of the letter from Joletta (not her real name) and the one Hazel wrote from the prison parking lot after she read Joletta's letter. Both of those letters were lost in prison transfers.

The story is Jerry's. Although I invented many minor characters to interact with Jerry and came up with my own vision of the actual people who played a part in Jerry's life and then put words in their mouths and in Jerry's, each event is true to either what Jerry told me or what his letters revealed to me. The names of the people he met along the way, including the many angels at his crossroads, have been changed to protect their privacy. Surely they will recognize themselves if they should come across this story of hope and redemption and pardon and feel joy to have been a part of this man's journey.

And Jerry's journey's not over. He's still following the Lord. Over the years since he was released from prison, he has been involved with music as a soloist and speaker telling his story of dealing with drugs, alcohol and prison life. He has been the Youth and/or Music Minister at several different churches. For a few years he traveled around the United States doing Home Mission work for the Southern Baptist Convention. He has sung tenor for two Southern Gospel Quartets, The Joymakers and The Patriot Quartet. He was an Over the Road Company truck driver as well as an owner operator driving long hauls for many years.

Now he and Connie live on a farm in Burgin, Kentucky where he raises alfalfa hay. He works as a safety director for a trucking company and still sings and tells his story. Shayne, Christy, and Tab have all grown up, and are happily married. They've blessed Jerry and Connie with six beautiful grandchildren who love their Daddy J.

978-0-595-38707-6
0-595-38707-1